CURRENT ISSUES IN ECONOMIC INTEGRATION

Current Issues in Economic Integration

Can Asia Inspire the "West"?

Edited by

BERNADETTE ANDREOSSO-O'CALLAGHAN
University of Limerick, Ireland

and

M. BRUNA ZOLIN
University of Ca' Foscari, Venice, Italy

ASHGATE

Published by
Ashgate Publishing Limited
Wey Court East
Union Road
Farnham
Surrey, GU9 7PT
England

Ashgate Publishing Company
Suite 420
101 Cherry Street
Burlington
VT 05401-4405
USA

www.ashgate.com

British Library Cataloguing in Publication Data
Current issues in economic integration : can Asia inspire
the "West"?.
1. Economic history--21st century. 2. International
economic relations. 3. Asia--Foreign economic relations.
4. Asia--Economic conditions--21st century.
I. Andreosso-O'Callaghan, Bernadette, 1959- II. Zolin, M.
Bruna.
337-dc22

Library of Congress Cataloging-in-Publication Data
Current issues in economic integration : can Asia inspire the "West"? / [edited] by Bernadette Andreosso-O'Callaghan and M. Bruna Zolin.
p. cm.
Includes bibliographical references and index.
ISBN 978-0-7546-7956-1 (hardback) -- ISBN 978-0-7546-9896-8 (ebook) 1. Asia--Economic integration. 2. International economic integration. 3. Financial crises. I. Andreosso-O'Callaghan, Bernadette, 1959- II. Zolin, M. Bruna.
HC412.C877 2010
337.1--dc22

2009052508

ISBN 978-0-7546-7956-1 (hbk)
ISBN 978-0-7546-9896-8 (ebk)

Mixed Sources
Product group from well-managed forests and other controlled sources
www.fsc.org Cert no. SGS-COC-2482
© 1996 Forest Stewardship Council
FSC

Printed and bound in Great Britain by
TJ International Ltd, Padstow, Cornwall

Contents

List of Figures

List of Tables

List of Abbreviations

ABF1	Asian Bond Fund 1
ABMI	Asian Bond Markets Initiative
ACU	Asian Currency Unit
ADBI	Asian Development Bank Institute
AMF	Asian Monetary Fund
ANDA	Abbreviated New Drug Application
ASEAN	Association of South East-Asian Nations
BIS	Bank of International Settlements
BPO	Business Process Outsourcing
BRIC	Brazil, Russia, India, China
BSA	Bilateral Swap Arrangement
CAP	Common Agricultural Policy
CBD	Central Business District
CEC	Commission of the European Communities
CGIM	Credit Guarantee and Investment Mechanism
CMI	Chiang-Mai Initiative
CMIM	Chiang-Mai Initiative Multilateralization
CPI	Consumer Price Index
CRT	Credit Risk Transfer
DG	Directorate General
DTC	Double Taxation Convention
EC	Emerging Country
ECB	European Central Bank
ECSC	European Coal and Steel Community
ECU	European Currency Unit
EMEAP	Executives' Meeting of East-Asia Pacific
EMS	European Monetary System
EP	European Parliament
EPA	Economic Partnership Agreement
ESRB	European Systemic Research Board
FAO	Food Agriculture Organization
FDI	Foreign Direct Investment
FIE	Foreign Invested Enterprise
FTA	Free Trade Area
GATT	General Agreement on Tariffs and Trade
GDP	Gross Domestic Product
GL	Grubel and Lloyd

GMO	Genetically Modified Organism
HSIP	Hsinchu Science-based Industrial Park
HSR	High-Speed Rail
ICT	Information and Communication Technologies
IIT	Intra-Industry Trade
IMF	International Monetary Fund
IMPACT	International Model for Policy Analysis of Agricultural Commodities
IPR	Intellectual Property Right
IT	Information Technology
JV	Joint Venture
LDC	Less Developed Country
LLL	Linkage, Leverage, Learning
LNG	Liquefied Natural Gas
M&A	Mergers and Acquisitions
MFA	Multi-Fiber Agreement
MNC	Multi-National Corporation
NAFTA	North American Free Trade Area
NIE	Newly Industrialized Economy
NIPAs	National Income and Product Accounts
NTB	Non-Tariff Barrier
NT$	New Taiwanese dollar
OECD	Organization for Economic Cooperation and Development
OLI	Ownership Location Internalization
OTC	Over the Counter
PBC	People's Bank of China
PRC	People's Republic of China
RCU	Regional Currency Unit
R&D	Research and Development
SDR	Special Drawing Rights
SOE	State-Owned Enterprise
SME	Small and Medium-Sized Enterprise
TFP	Total Factor Productivity
TNC	Trans-National Corporation
TVE	Township and Village Enterprise
UNCTAD	United Nations Conference on Trade and Development
VSTFF	Very Short Term Financing Facility
WOS	Wholly Owned Subsidiary
WTO	World Trade Organization

List of Contributors

David E. Andersson, Assistant Professor, Institute of Public Affairs Management, National Sun Yat-sen University, Kaohsiung Taiwan.

Bernadette Andreosso-O'Callaghan, Jean Monnet Chair of Economics and Director, Euro-Asia Centre, Kemmy Business School, University of Limerick, Ireland.

Giovanni Balcet, Professor of International Economics and International Business, Department of Economics, University of Turin, Italy.

Silvia Bruschieri, Economist, Italian Institute for Foreign Trade (IIFT) and Department of Economics, University of Turin, Italy.

Reinhard Drifte, Emeritus Professor of Japanese Politics, Newcastle University, United Kingdom and Associate Researcher, Centre de Recherche et d'Etudes en Gestion (CREG), Pau University (France).

Guilhem Fabre, Professor of Economics and Chinese studies, Université du Havre, France, and Institut Universitaire de France.

Esmeralda Gassie, PhD Candidate, Euro-Asia Centre, Kemmy Business School, University of Limerick, Ireland.

Ju Hu, Lecturer in Economics, Department of Business Administration, Henan University of Urban Construction, Henan, People's Republic of China.

Jacques Jaussaud, Professor of Management, University of Pau, France.

Dino Martellato, Professor of Economics, Ca' Foscari University, Venice, Italy.

Woosik Moon, Professor of Economics, Graduate School of International Studies, Seoul National University, Korea.

Françoise Nicolas, Associate Professor of Economics, Paris-Est University (Marne-la-Vallée), and Senior Researcher, Institut Français des Relations Internationales (IFRI), Paris, France.

Hwanhee Oh PhD Candidate, Graduate School of International Studies, Seoul National University.

Tomoko Oikawa, Researcher, Euro-Asia Centre, Kemmy Business School, University of Limerick, Ireland.

Oliver F. Shyr, Assistant Professor, Department of Urban Planning, National Cheng-kung University Tainan, Taiwan.

Michael von Wuntsch, Professor of Taxation and Multinational Financial Management, HTWB, University of Applied Sciences, Berlin, Germany.

Xiaojun Wei, Chair, Asia Pacific Management and Institute of Asia Pacific Studies, School of Business, Grant MacEwan University, Edmonton, Alberta, Canada.

M. Bruna Zolin, Professor of Economics, Ca' Foscari University, Venice, Italy.

Acknowledgements

Without the support of Ca' Foscari University of Venice and the unbounded commitment of the contributing authors, to whom we are immensely grateful, this publication would not have been possible. Special thanks go to Professor Guido Cazzavillan, Head of the Department of Economics of Ca' Foscari University for his continuous support throughout the entire research project.

We are highly indebted to Frank O'Callaghan for his precious work on the proofreading stage of the manuscript, and to Gianna Marella and Matilde Cassin for their invaluable help at the various stages of the editing process.

Introduction

Bernadette Andreosso-O'Callaghan and M. Bruna Zolin

The financial crisis starting in the Autumn 2008, which manifested itself first on the US financial markets and which subsequently spread to other world financial markets and to the sphere of the real economy in the USA and elsewhere, seems to have a dual impact at a world level. First, it reshuffles the world's economy by unquestionably shifting the economic center of gravity away from Western countries, and in particular away from the USA. Second, it demonstrates clearly that an economic system based on unrestrained capital movements is bound to eventually become unsustainable.[1]

To many observers, the 1997 Asian crisis had shown the limits of the 'Asian model', at a time when the US economy was indisputably seen by many as *the* world example of a successful economy, where seemingly unshakable banks and information technology-based corporations had flourished thanks to the implementation of ultra-liberal policies. This dynamism and outstanding performance were to be seen in contrast to the many inefficiencies characterizing the Asian banks and capital markets at the time, as well as to a hesitant European Union where the nascent euro was just worth 0.9 USD. In the Autumn of 2008 – as in the Asian case of the late 1990s – the instability in US (and to some extent European) bonds, stocks, derivatives and currency markets coupled with insufficient supervision and regulation of world financial markets, were the familiar symptoms of a need for an inevitable major readjustment. The fact that many of the cumulated disequilibria (such as the current account deficit) involved primarily the USA, and that these disequilibria could be transmitted with ease elsewhere, led to a financial/economic global crisis.

As some of the chapters in this book will show, many of the Asian countries did learn some fruitful lessons from their past mistakes. In the aftermath of the 1997 Asian crisis, many Asian countries successfully reformed their financial systems allowing them to shield away from financial shocks, and in particular from the adverse effects of the current global crisis (ADB 2009). A higher degree of financial independence has nevertheless been achieved at the expense of greater unbalanced trade openness, for the Asian region is judged too dependent on external demand emanating from outside the region. As a result, the Asian Development Bank advocates a number of policies in response to the current crisis, such as

1 This view very much echoes the teachings of the French regulationist school (the interested reader can refer to Aglietta (1976)).

the strengthening of intra-regional trade by boosting domestic demand, and an effective management of financial globalization, which entails in particular the establishment of regional financial markets aimed at the efficient use of regional savings (ADB 2009).

At a more general level, and in the sphere of the real economy, this crisis manifests itself in the sudden change in a number of indicators: production capacity is under-used everywhere; retail sales are at an all-time low; trade flows have declined sharply with, for example, charter rates for container ships decreasing by more than 15 percent at world level between mid-2008 and mid-2009; during 2009, the rate of bankruptcies has accelerated in both the USA and European Union (EU) countries, such as Spain[2]; finally, unemployment rates have reached their highest levels in modern history (the rate increased for example to 5.7 percent in July 2009 in Japan).

With regard to the financial and monetary sphere, many countries' budget deficits and public debts have reached unprecedented proportions. Many already debt-stricken Western economies (USA, France…) have amplified these types of disequilibria by engaging on the path of stimulus packages, and of ailing banks' rescues. In the case of the USA, the budget deficit climbed from US$ 459 billion in October 2008 to US$ 1.4 trillion in October 2009, or nearly 10 percent of GDP (Congressional Budget Office, 2009). According to the Congressional Budget Office (2009), this formidable increase is explained largely by the US government's $ 787bn economic stimulus, by the 'Troubled Asset Relief Program' in favor of financial firms, and by the rescue of large mortgage firms such as Fannie Mae and Freddie Mac. The real economy disequilibria mentioned above, coupled with the accelerating pace of the weakening US dollar have led the Obama administration during the Summer of 2009 to increase the US debt ceiling which is soon to reach US$ 12 trillion, a figure that represents more than 85 percent of the 2009 US GDP.[3] This instability stimulates capital outflows from the USA which, in turn, have a detrimental impact on the value of the US dollar.[4]

These various stimulus packages have nevertheless led to a slowdown in the speed of contraction of the global economy, and they explain much of the small improvement visible in the growth rates of several countries – including that of the USA – since the Summer of 2009. These rebounds do not seem to prevent the accelerating of an inexorable trend: the decoupling from the dollar zone by

2 Between June 2009 and September 2009, there have been more bankruptcies in the USA than during the whole of 2008.

3 See *Wall Street Journal*, 12th September 2009.

4 The measurement of 'distressed' or 'toxic' assets held by US banks differs according to the source; the IMF (2009) puts the figure at US$ 2 trillion for the USA, but it forecasts that asset depreciation linked to 'distressed' loans could reach US$ 3 to 4 trillion by end of 2009, in the USA alone. For an insight into the general problem of statistical discrepancies, inconsistencies and omissions, see for example the case of France as analyzed by Lorraine Data (2009).

countries in Asia, South America, Middle East as well as in Europe. This trend jeopardizes the central role that the American economy has assumed over the past decades. The crisis is gradually giving way to a new growth model, that of 'decoupled growth'. Many of the Asian countries (China, India, South Korea and the Association for South East Asian Nations) are determined to embark upon a path of 'endogenous' growth. It seems therefore that these countries, as well as some of those of the euro area,[5] are in a better situation than the USA to face the current crisis.

Indeed, the current economic crisis gives the EU-27, the largest and richest economic and trade bloc of the world at the time of writing, an unprecedented opportunity to respond adequately to two main challenges of today's global economic system, namely:

i. Addressing the problem of a failing monetary system based on the US dollar. Judged as being a safe-haven currency, the euro could see its exchange rate revalue *vis-à-vis* the US dollar to the point where the euro area would eventually run the risk of being suffocated by too strong a currency.
ii. Exerting pressures on the USA, the International Monetary Fund (IMF) and the Bank for International Settlements (BIS) in the area of banking and financial regulation. The role of the EU is fundamental in shaping a new financial architecture with clear and fair rules, such as, for example, the reintroduction of strict underwriting guidelines for taking a company public[6]. Also, the EU's role is essential in dealing with the ultra-speculative strategies in the physical-commodities market (such as corn, wheat and oil). It needs to push for the reintroduction of the 1936 law empowering the US Commodity Futures Trading Commission to place limits on speculative trades in commodities.[7]

It is cleat that, by asserting itself in these crucial areas, the EU would show the way in reconciling the general interest with 'particular wills' (in the sense of Jean-Jacques Rousseau); the EU would thus appear as a key player in recasting tomorrow's world. However, whether the EU – and its constituent member states

5 At the time of writing, the euro area comprises the EU-15 minus the UK, Denmark and Sweden, plus Slovenia, Slovakia, Cyprus and Malta.

6 In the case of the USA, the company in question had to be in business for a minimum of five years, and it had to show profitability for three consecutive years; conceived and implemented after the Great Depression, these guidelines were designed to guarantee a certain level of quality in the companies traded in Wall Street. Ultra liberal thinking led to the abolishment of these guidelines.

7 This law was abolished in 1991, when the CFTC issued Goldman & Sachs bank a free pass (a '*Bona Fide* Hedging' exemption), allowing the bank's subsidiary to exceed the limits placed on speculators. Other exemptions were issued to another 14 companies in the ensuing years.

– is up to this task is profoundly debatable. The lack of political drive with regard to the EU agenda existing in some of the main EU countries as well as weak leadership at the core of the EU executive process have already been highlighted (Thinking Enlarged Group 2002). At EU level, the crisis has demonstrated the need for an immediate and coordinated crisis management response. Yet, in spite of the mid-June 2009 Council Decision to implement the proposals of the de Larosière Committee on a European financial supervisory architecture, with, for example, the setting up of a European Systemic Risk Board (ESRB), current circumstances in the EU, such as the preparation for a new European Parliament, new Commissioners, and implementation of the Lisbon Treaty by the end of 2009 are far from being favorable conditions for the swift implementation of the de Larosière proposals (Lannoo 2009). Immediate post-crisis decisions needed to be made at EU level, but, more than 20 months after the demise of the UK bank Northern Rock – a rather clear signal that a sub-prime caused financial crisis was on the way in one of the major EU banking systems – the lengthy EU legislative process had still not provided a swift and cohesive response to the crisis. In light of this slow response, it is doubtful whether the EU can be seen, in other regions of the world, as a key player in the near future; the attention might therefore be refocused in favor of the fastest growing region of the world, Asia, which, after all, may well end up 'inspiring the West'.

It is along this line of thinking that this book has been conceived. This volume brings a novel dimension to the study of EU-Asia relations – a study that has traditionally focused to a large extent on the applicability of the EU as a model for Asia – by both refocusing the discourse on Asia, and by placing the EU in the context of the group of 'western' economies. In a purely economic sense, 'the West' is understood here to encapsulate the EU-27 and the USA, whose many differences are smoothened by an inescapable common thread: neo-classical thinking is the dominant economic paradigm of reference in terms of economic policy making in both regions. This is in contrast to many Asian economies that can be broadly characterized as being 'developmental states' (Low 2004).

The main objective of the book is therefore to ultimately question the pertinence and the exportability of the EU model of economic integration to Asia. The book aims at analyzing whether, given its rising geo-economic role and its relative resilience to the crisis, Asia can suggest a number of avenues for the many distressed economic actors in both the USA and European countries. By looking at the regional responses to the financial crisis, the book will also discuss the way the current crisis impacts economic integration at both monetary and trade levels in the Asian region.

Arising from a research seminar held at Ca' Foscari University of Venice in January 2009, the book is divided into two distinct parts. Each part encompasses a number of chapters dealing with a range of issues relating to economic integration at both the macro- and meso/micro-economic level respectively.

The first part sets the scene by providing a number of chapters dealing with the financial/monetary sphere and other macroeconomic issues. The first chapter examines the likely future direction of real interest rates across the Atlantic and in Asia after their prolonged descent, and the impact of their possible rise on economic growth. With due reference to a number of economic theories, the chapter discusses China's recent proposal to replace the US dollar as the international reserve currency with a truly international reserve currency formed by a basket of national currencies. Using a systemic approach, the second chapter analyzes the issue of inter-linkages and dependency between the EU-15, China and the USA. It introduces the concept of 'economic vulnerability', and proposes a vulnerability indicator by applying it to the new triad (China, EU-15 and USA) over the period 1995–2005. The indicator combines a number of economic variables drawn from the real as well as the monetary economy. The findings show that the USA was the most vulnerable economy over the period up to the crisis, with the EU being the least vulnerable of the three. The specific issue of the relationship between the USA and China is explored in the third chapter on 'Chimerica'. This chapter shows how the financial crisis is gradually leading to a marked shift in the geo-economic balance in favor of China, whilst China decouples away from the USA. Looking at a broader group of Asian countries, Chapter 4 connects the monetary and the real economies by analyzing how and why intra-regional trade patterns impact exchange rate policy decisions in East Asia and whether and how the recent global financial crisis may change the current state of play. Whereas in the case of the EU, *de jure* (government-led) trade integration was instrumental in paving the way for monetary integration, *de facto* trade integration has been more prominent in East Asia and has had an impact on exchange rate policy decisions in the region. The chapter argues that conditions for institutional cooperation are bound to improve in East Asia, and that the emergence of East Asia as a better structured economic bloc will challenge mainstream economic thinking in 'the West'. Improved cooperation is also an issue taken up in the fifth chapter, which takes stock of the aftermath of the Asian crisis by delving into the timely topic of economic and financial integration in East-Asia. The chapter shows that, in spite of traditionally poor institutionalization, weak regional identity and insufficient political leadership, East Asian countries have demonstrated a certain degree of pragmatism by developing crucial initiatives such as the Chang Mai Initiative (CMI) and the 2009 Chiang Mai Initiative Multilateralization (CMIM) which, according to the authors, augurs well with respect to the emergence of common institutions in East-Asia. Finally, Chapter 6 concludes this first part of the book with a note of caution. Although slow growth and a temporary neglect of primary commodity and agricultural markets on the part of institutional investors shift attention away from the problems of food sufficiency and energy sufficiency onto financial considerations, the chapter warns against a generalized risk of complacency. As argued in this chapter with reference to yet another 'impossible trinity theorem', the global economic crisis is temporarily making the global rise in energy and food prices a latent phenomenon, and appropriate policies need to be devised and implemented so as to avoid major disequilibria in these markets whenever growth will resume on a global scale.

Part II of the book provides some empirical knowledge on new developments at firm and industry level in Asia and in relation to Western economies. Chapter 7 analyzes the emerging phenomenon of Chinese business in Japan, using a methodology based on press releases, interviews conducted in Japan and Toyko Keizai data. This study shows that this phenomenon exists across various industries, that Chinese firms succeed in keeping control over their subsidiaries and joint ventures, and that the current economic crisis does not dampen Chinese vistas in expanding into Japan. Chapter 8 on Indian multinational enterprises also deals with the new phenomenon of investment from emerging economies. Based on a critical analysis of traditional foreign direct investment (FDI) theories and on a rich set of empirical data, this chapter provides elements of a ground-breaking theory that would better be suited to the analysis of FDI from emerging countries. It underlines that emerging countries (such as China and India) can exploit their skilled and unskilled labor cost advantages in tandem with investments and production abroad, in contrast with the conventional wisdom and the theoretical stream that focus on exports. Chapter 9 analyzes the fiscal challenges resulting from the growing influence of value added concepts and shareholder value orientation in Europe and East Asia. This discussion is applied to the case of cross-border R&D investments and R&D policy in China. It shows how the transnational corporations (TNCs) take advantage of their conglomerate structure by shifting profits to low tax areas, and how these TNCs tend to offshore their research and development. The case of Chinese R&D investment and policy allows a review of the fiscal instruments related to R&D activities (and their impact) in China; the Chapter concludes by arguing that China's modernization strategy based on science and technology allows the country to make the transition from sustained to sustainable growth. Starting with the 'equipment hypothesis', Chapter 10 examines the interconnection existing between skills, technology and cyclical economic growth (as epitomized by Kondratiev's business cycles) in one specific industry. The chapter explores and compares the die and mould-making industry in Japan and Ireland over the pre-current global crisis period. With the help of company interviews held in both countries, the study finds an equal importance of skills to equipment investment for successful performance in the two countries. Chapter 11 takes a comparative angle and deals with policy support for small and medium-sized enterprises (SMEs) in China and the EU. In both countries, SMEs are seen as the backbone of business and economic development and as a way out of an era of stagnant or slow growth. By comparing and contrasting Chinese and EU SMEs, the Chapter finds a number of similarities such as policy design, and differences such as the level of centralization. The chapter highlights the need to take account of social networks and of cultural characteristics of private small and medium-sized firms when dealing with SME policy, particularly in the context of an economic crisis. Finally, Chapter 12, on Taiwan's high-speed rail, brings a focused perspective on how these new transport systems impact the use and the price of land in two medium-sized Taiwanese regions (Hsinchu and

Tainan). This is of particular relevance since the development of infrastructure places yet another burden on land prices, and since these prices are normally an adjustment variable during times of economic crises. Using hedonic pricing, the chapter finds a much greater land price effect in Hsinchu and it concludes by suggesting policies favoring the connection of urban centers and knowledge nodes that are not too distant from each other. Taking one step further, it is argued that the findings pertaining to the case of Taiwan can eventually be used and applied to a number of emerging EU economies with high population densities, and might therefore question the pertinence of EU policy in terms of trans-European networks.

References

ADB 2009. *The Asian Development Outlook – 2009 Update*. Manilla: Asian Development Bank.

Aglietta, M. 1976. *Régulation et crises du capitalisme*. Paris: Calmann-Lévy (translated and published in English as: *A Theory of Capitalist Regulation – The US Experience*. London and New York: Verso Classics 1979).

Congressional Budget Office 2009. *The Budget and Economic Outlook: An Update* (August). Washington: Congress of the United States.

IMF 2009. *Global Financial Stability Report Market Update*. Washington: International Monetary Fund, Monetary and Capital Market Department.

Lannoo, K. 2009. *The Road after De Larosière*. Centre for European Policy Studies, No. 195/7, August. London: CEPS Policy Briefs.

Lorraine Data 2009. *Le grand truquage: Comment le gouvernement manipule les statistiques*. Paris: Collection La Découverte, Cahiers libres, mai.

Low, L. (ed.) 2004. *Developmental States – Relevancy, Redundancy or Reconfiguration?* New York: Nova Science Publishers, Inc.

Thinking Enlarged Group 2002. *Bridging the Leadership Gap – A Strategy for Improving Political Leadership in the EU*. Bertelsmann Foundation and Center for Applied Policy Research (eds). Munich: Bertelsmann Foundation Publishers.

PART I
Current Macroeconomic Issues

Chapter 1
Real Interest Rates and the Crisis: Where are the Rates Heading?

Dino Martellato

Introduction

A large part of the strongly expansive fiscal and monetary policies implemented during 2008 and 2009 (in the USA, China and Japan) or merely called for (as was the case of the European Economic Recovery Plan) was based on the idea that the world real economy was experiencing a correction in the trend of sustained growth of the past two decades. If this were really so, the unprecedented stimulation would make the correction brief and growth return to the pre-crisis trend. The price to be paid for reducing the impact of the disaster created by the excessive growth of private debt is the rise in public debt, but it is hoped that a return to the high growth regime of old will pay for it. Yet the odds of a quick return to high growth with low inflation – the 'goldilocks scenario' – that the world economy experienced before the crisis are, at best, uncertain as the past experience was characterized by the increase of large imbalances between advanced and emerging economies and sectors. All these imbalances are going to change since the rate of savings is increasing in the private sector in advanced countries, but decreasing in the public sector almost everywhere. A debate is also in progress about the likelihood of deflation and inflation. One possibility is deflation; some countries – such as Germany – while still stuck in recession, are already experiencing a fall in prices. The other is inflation – not a remote possibility since central banks have delivered a global and unprecedented monetary expansion which may lead to an inflation surge even though employment is far from being full. Commodity prices, the cost of credit and other costs can increase on their own even if central banks start absorbing the existing excess liquidity. There are obvious big differences among the different scenarios envisaged so far. The great moderation, or 'goldilocks economy' scenario requires low real interest rates,[1] but this condition can hardly be considered as certain. In increasingly indebted economies, deflation would be extremely negative for everybody. In the inflation scenario, only some economic

1 The most important concept in the explanation of macroeconomic phenomena according to Kennedy (2000).

agents would pay for it, and exchange rates would be unstable.[2] Central banks are trying to inflate out of the current crisis assuming they will be able to stem inflation in due course. This poses the obvious problem of the banks' credibility. Will they have the necessary credibility when required? If not, they must regain it and, thus, they will be forced to raise real interest rates significantly and possibly for a long time. What if real interest rates surge? After the long descent that took place after the inflation of the 1970s and 1980s, we should not be surprised to see inflation return in an environment characterized by rising real interest rates. Deflation would lift real interest rates and deflate all asset values, i.e. collaterals. This would prolong and certainly worsen the problems in the housing market and the banking sector. At first sight, the odds of a surge in real interest rates are thus quite high. Indeed, if debt is poised to rise everywhere, savings must do the same. Should not the savings rate and the real interest rate increase as well? If so, the chances of a quick return to a high growth regime depend on a turnaround in the housing market. This requires an end to the fall in real estate prices, sufficient availability of credit, low interest rates, and the will of consumers to use that credit to buy new homes. It seems, therefore, quite interesting to consider real interest rates since the possibilities of a sustainable recovery critically depend on the level of perceived real interest rates. Without a resurgence in the internal markets and particularly in the housing market, growth in exports would not be sufficient to avoid the economies of the world limping along for years. Japan, for instance, was not able to compensate the stagnation in its internal demand with the growth in its foreign exports. Section 1 of the chapter focuses on real interest rates in the USA, Europe and Asia, whereas Section 2 considers the prediction that can be obtained from economic theory by focusing on real factors (Section 2.1), monetary factors (Section 2.2) and business cycle aspects (Section 2.3). In Section 3, the peculiarities of the Chinese interest rate and the connections between the Chinese and the US interest rates are considered. Finally, Section 4 provides some conclusions.

2. Real Interest Rates in the USA, Europe and Asia

Real interest rates – defined as the difference between the benchmark 10-year Treasury bond yield and the US Consumer Price Index (CPI) inflation rate – fluctuated throughout the period January 1983–January 2009, which suggested a prolonged downward trend (Figure 1.1). The same is true for all European countries and notably for the 10-y German bund, i.e. the benchmark rate in the euro area. Figure 1.2 displays the average yield of the 10-year European government benchmark bonds computed by the European Central Bank (ECB) with a changing composition. In the case of the USA, the whole period can be divided into three separate sub-periods. During the first, a descending trend can easily be detected

2 With a possible huge depreciation of the US dollar and other deficit countries' currencies.

from July 1984, when the rate was close to 10 percent, to December 1990, when it was almost 2 percent (average 5.6 percent). The second sub-period was one of stability with an average rate of 3.7 percent with dampened short-run oscillations. During the third sub-period the benchmark interest rate headed down again and on average was 1.8 percent. The average for the whole period was 3.6 percent, but on the basis of the averages of the 10-year benchmark interest rate in three separate sub-periods the USA had a blissful 24-year period as the government and an increasing number of debtors paid less and less in real terms for the use of the savings of others.

As for the Euro area, Figure 1.2 shows high volatility in the years that followed German reunification and the crisis in the European Monetary System (EMS), but after the start of the first phase of the euro, real yields across Europe started a clear downward trend. The trend ended with a double dip in January 2006 and in July 2008. The final jump clearly resembles that in the USA. Indeed, the euro area and the USA share the double dip and final jump. This is not the only similarity since the average real interest rate computed in the euro area over the period 1991–2009 is 3.6 percent and coincides with that found in the USA in the 1963–2009 period, although not with that in the 1991–2009 period (2.7 percent in the USA).

One strand of thought claims that aggregate demand and supply are brought into balance by the interest rate. The other strand of thought was started by Keynes, who observed that periods of prosperity and periods of recession (and even depression) alternate and who built a theory according to which it is the level of economic activity

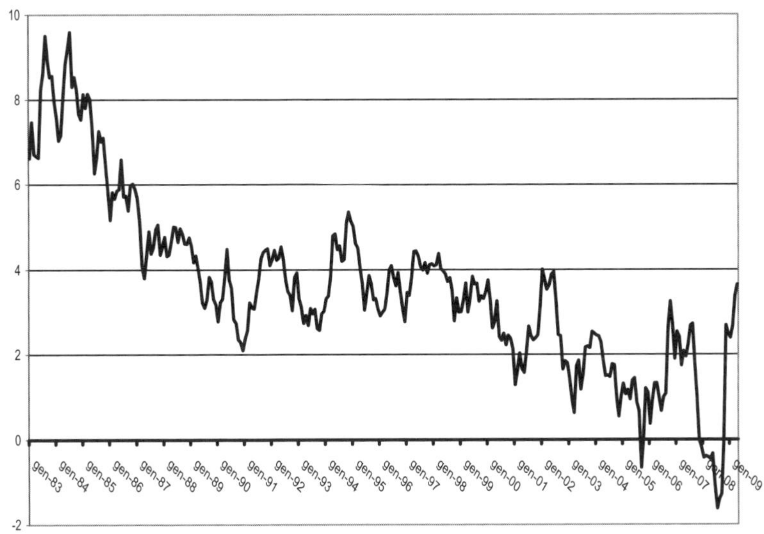

Figure 1.1 Real interest rates US 1983–2009
10-year US Treasury bond yield CPI-deflated
Source: Federal Reserve Bank.

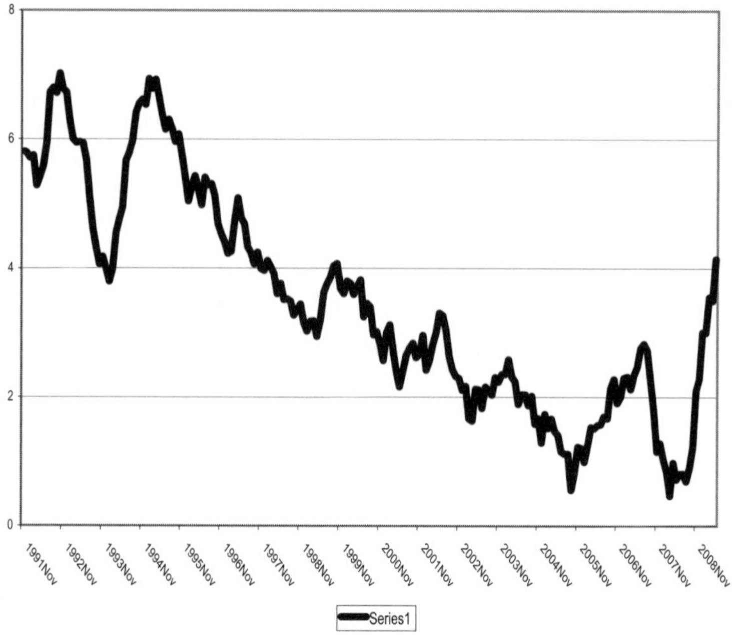

Figure 1.2 Real interest rates Euro area 1991–2009
10-year Government benchmark bond (changing composition) yield HICP-deflated

Source: European Central Bank.

that keeps in balance the flows of savings and investment. According to Keynes, the rate of interest is the return that individuals get by holding their wealth in the form of bonds instead of liquidity. The progressive reduction in the average real interest rate both in the USA and the EU can therefore be explained in two different ways, which, as we shall see below, are only partially different from that warranted in China. On the one hand, it may be argued that people were keen to hold bonds – particularly 10-y government securities – at an increasingly lower price, or that the current 10-y real interest rate followed a declining normal real interest rate. Earnings yields, i.e. the returns observed in the stock market, have been consistently higher than bond returns, thus implying a premium of stocks over bonds. On the other hand, savings were surging worldwide because of sustained global income growth and this allowed mainstream economists to argue that the equilibrium in the loanable funds market was reached at an increasingly lower natural interest rate. In both cases, therefore, a reduction has taken place in the equilibrium level of the real interest rate, i.e. the rate that has played a key role in contemporary monetary policy ever since the adoption of inflation targeting. This policy is based in one way or another on some interest-rule and some idea of the equilibrium or neutral real interest rate. The equilibrium rate can be conceived as the rate compatible with macroeconomic equilibrium in the sense that if the economy settled at it for some time, output would constantly match the potential, and inflation would be low and stable. Central banks, therefore, have merely managed short-term rates to follow a supposedly declining equilibrium level. The equilibrium level is not directly observable and can only be estimated and central banks perhaps discover this step by step in doing their job. Recent research on the joint estimation of the level of the natural real rate of interest[3] and the level of the output gap for the USA (Lauback-Williams 2003) and for the Euro area (Garnier-Wilhelmsen 2005) point to the common conclusion that the natural rate has declined gradually over the past forty years. In the case of the euro area, the decline was from 4 percent to 2 percent. One hypothesis is that the large availability of savings, particularly in the emerging economies, was the enhancing factor behind the rate fall.

Another possibility is that of a deviation from the equilibrium rate of interest (i.e. the rate at which some form of macroeconomic equilibrium is assured) and of a slow reversion pace. The downward trend of interest rates over the last twenty years could accordingly indicate that the economy has taken a detour from the equilibrium rate and that it is poised to revert to it sooner or later. Following Wicksellian monetary theory, one could argue that banks and capital markets (i.e. global finance) were able to make the volume of bank loans independent from the flow of national savings thus accommodating the increasing demand for loans at ever lower rates. If rates had increased, rather than decreased, particularly in deficit countries, the gap between market rates and the equilibrium real rate of interest would have reverted to the equilibrium level. Yet this hypothesis is not convincing since inflation was subdued everywhere until the surge in commodity prices started to fuel the rise in consumer prices in 2006.[4]

The benchmark real interest rate fell below zero in July 2006 and then returned to a regime of high volatility just before the onset of the crisis in 2007. The crisis represented a break in the old trend and should give an indication of its future direction. Figure 1.3 shows that the US real interest rate plunged below zero in 2005. Then it rose again, only to fall below zero just two years later, and then dipped even lower just before the worst weeks of the crisis. After November 2008, the rate rocketed up again. Figure 1.4 highlights a similar story for Germany's 10-y bund real yield. The only difference is the much smaller range of variance. While in the US case the yield basically goes from -1 to 3 percent, in the case of Germany the yield hovers in the 1 percent–3 percent interval. The profile, however, is rather similar. The yield increased slowly from October 2005 to June 2007, i.e. until the outbreak of the crisis. The crisis brought about a sharp fall in the real

3 Originally, i.e. in Wicksell (1898, 1935), the natural rate of interest is the rate determined by the real factors such as the marginal product of capital. To pursue price stability, the monetary authority must change the money rate of interest to make it adhere to the time-varying, natural rate of interest.

4 Wicksellian theory predicts inflation when the market rate is lower than the equilibrium rate.

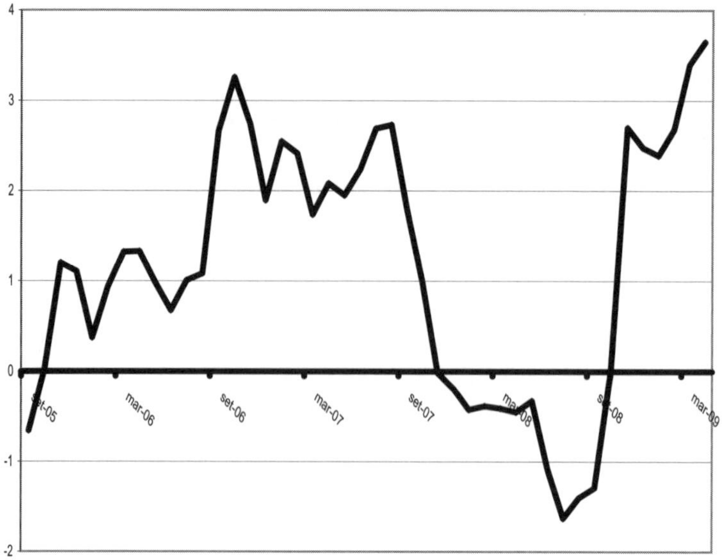

Figure 1.3 Real interest rates in US 2005(IX)–2009(IV)
10-year US Treasury bond yield CPI-deflated

Source: Federal Reserve.

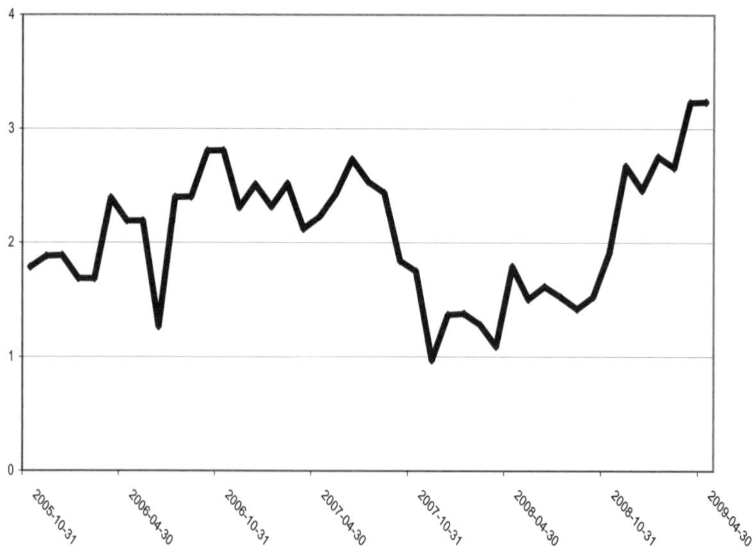

Figure 1.4 Real interest rate Germany 2005(X)–2009 (IV)
10-year bund yield CPI-deflated

Sources: Bundesbank and Statistiches Bundesamt.

interest rate to 1 percent and then a slow recovery until November 2008 and then a steady increase just above the 3 percent line.

Both cases show that the crisis, in particular from the turning-point in September 2008, marked a change of direction in interest rates. Will the surge continue in the future? What can we predict about real interest rates on the basis of theory? What will be the impact of the surge? Before addressing the theory, let's briefly consider what happened in China, which is obviously an important reference for what pertains to emerging Asian economies. Available data offer a short track because the People's Bank of China (PBC) was the only bank in charge and the money and bond markets were non-existent until recently (Fan and Johansson 2009). Since there is constant excess demand for bills and bonds, one could argue that yields are low also because of this. The government does not need to finance its expenses, but the PBC needs to sterilize the liquidity created by the commercial surplus. Official interest rates, and particularly the 1-year rate, seem to be the most important benchmark instruments in the hands of the PBC for controlling yields in the bond market (Fan and Johansson 2009). A distinct feature of the Chinese experience is the short track. The PBC is in charge of managing the renminbi, in order to favor growth and control inflation. This difficult task is achieved with a parsimonious use of the official rates. After the Asian crisis in 1998, the PBC lowered the official rates quite sharply from around 6 percent in 1998 to about 2 percent in 2004. Then it returned to higher rates and then to lower rates for a short while before starting to hike rates again in 2006. The profile of bond rates resembles that of official rates and that of the USA and the Euro area.

To look at Asia during 2009 is useful. Asia showed quite a large dispersion in nominal interest rates in April (Figure 1.5). Indeed, while India and Indonesia have traditionally had relatively high nominal rates (above 7 percent in 2009), Japan, Taiwan, Malaysia, Singapore and Hong Kong were around 2 percent. China, South Korea, Thailand and the Philippines lay between 4 and 6 percent. Differences in inflation explain such differences only up to a point. In April 2009 real interest rates were around 4 percent in Indonesia, India and South Korea, while they were lower than 2 percent in Japan, Singapore and Taiwan. Real interest rates, however, were much more aligned in August. During the months to August, real interest rates declined somewhat, which could go some way towards explaining why emerging Asian countries posted the rebound that in the second half of the year made the whole global economy hopeful that it would recover from the downturn. Differences also narrowed in Asia as variance more than halved (Figure 1.5).

Figure 1.6 shows, however, that real interest rates increased slightly in the USA and the euro area, on average. Thus, one basic feature of the macroeconomic scenario that has characterized the last twenty years – namely a long-term real interest rate higher than the rate of potential growth in the Western economies, but definitely lower in the emerging economies of Asia – was left unchanged by the crisis, at least during 2009. Were this condition to prolong or even worsen, this would be no minor problem for the Western economies. The worsening in public finances that financial stimuli are producing there might have the effect of widening the gap between the

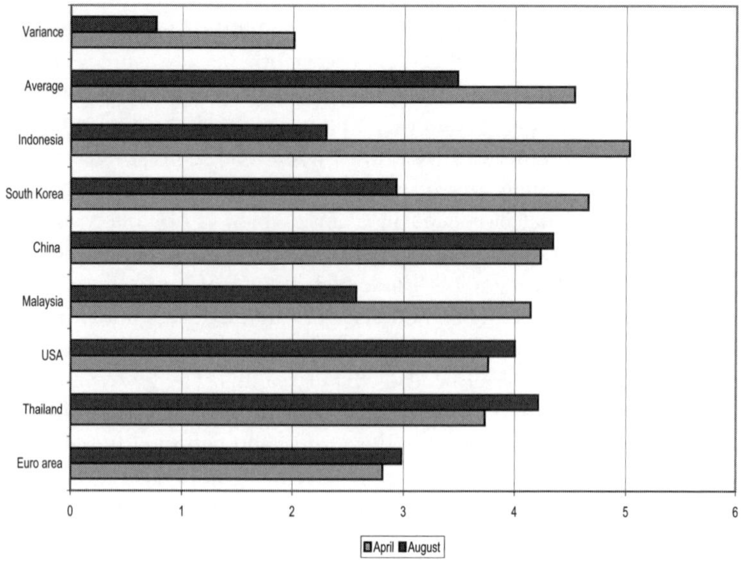

Figure 1.5 Real interest rates in selected Asian countries, USA and Euro area 2009 (IV)–2009(VIII)
10-year Government bond yield CPI-deflated
Source of data: *The Economist* (various issues).

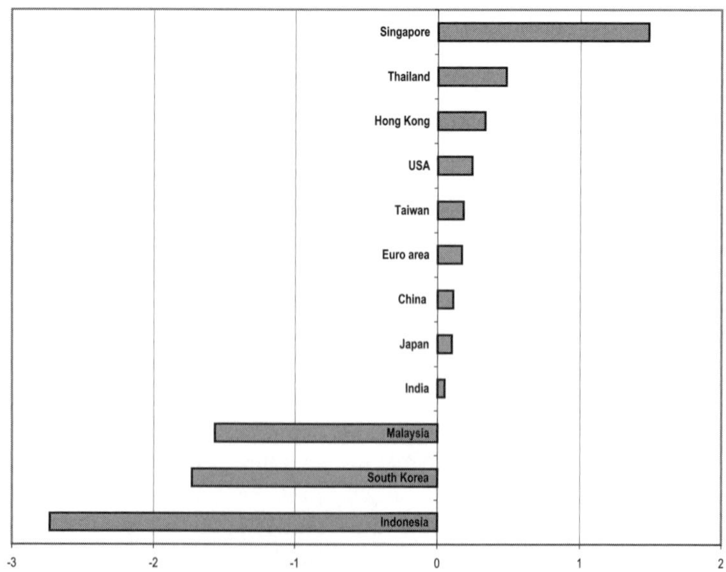

Figure 1.6 Changes in real interest rates in selected Asian countries, US and Euro area 2009 (IV)–2009(VIII)
10-year Government bond yield CPI-deflated
Source of data: *The Economist* (various issues).

real interest rate and the rate of potential growth. This makes possible the prospect of the Western economies stalling or growing only a little for years, not unlike the case of Japan. During the 1990s, indeed, Japan experienced a long period of stagnation, even though it always had low long-term real interest rates. The Western economies, however, could find themselves trapped in a worse condition, in which high debt acts negatively on real growth through high average long-term real interest rates and weak real growth feeds back negatively on the mountain of debt. This is not the case in Asia (Japan excluded) since the Asian economies face the downturn without the constraints of excessive public debt.

2.1 Real growth and real interest rates

There are at least four different models that are worth considering in order to get an idea of what determines the real yield on productive, i.e. physical, capital. In the Solow (1956) and the Ramsey (1928) growth models the rate of profit and the equilibrium real rate of interest are closely linked as they reflect the quantity of capital in the economy.[5] In Diamond's model the real interest rate depends on the government budget. In the Pasinetti model of growth and structural change (Pasinetti 1981) the real interest rate is actually in relation to income distribution rather than to capital and to its real yield as Pasinetti even denies that capital can be conceived as a productive factor of production with a decreasing marginal productivity. Pasinetti asserts that the real rate of interest, therefore, is not a rate return, but rather something inversely related to the real wage, i.e. to income distribution. In this perspective it should be equal to the rate of increase in the productivity of the total amount of labor required to produce the final output,[6] and income distribution would be constant. Indeed, with a constant rate of profit, real wages would grow at a rate equal to total factor productivity (TFP). In the Pasinetti model, therefore, monetary policy is not a neutral instrument of regulation, but rather something that – instead of technology and thrift – drives the real interest rate. From this premise, it is suggested that the rate of increase in TFP should be used as a rule for fixing equilibrium in distributive income shares rather than in the hypothetical market for loanable funds.

Aggregate growth theory disregards short-term fluctuations in business activity and assumes that the real interest rate is always at its equilibrium level. This would be possible only if investments in productive capital yielded a return comparable to that on financial assets and if arbitrage were enough to exhaust all available opportunities. In the Solow and Ramsey models, the equilibrium real rate is determined only by real factors with no relation to nominal variables, but the mechanism that lies behind it varies according to the model adopted, but, nevertheless, always reflects the quantity of physical capital in the economy.

5 It is understood that when capital rises, the real interest rate and the rate of profit fall.

6 I.e. total factor productivity.

In the Solow model, the real interest rate basically depends on the marginal return of capital which depends on the capital stock relative to the labor input. Given the depreciation rate, the rate of interest is: $r = f'(k) - \delta$. In the long run, the capital stock adjusts to a pair of exogenous factors which are the labor force and technical progress $K(t) = [sY(t) - \dot{K}(t)] / \delta$.

On the basis of this equation it can be argued that an increase in the propensity to save s increases the stock of capital, but reduces the marginal return of capital and thus the real interest rate. A similar argument leads to the conclusion that an increase in the rate of technical progress has an opposite effect on the real interest rate. In conclusion, an acceleration in the rate of technical progress implies an increase in the demand for savings and thus the interest rate, while an increase in the supply of savings yields a reduction in the interest rate.

In the Ramsey growth model, households optimize consumption over time on the basis of their time preference rate ρ , which is exogenous. According to optimum conditions, the marginal utility of consumption in two different periods $u'(C_t)$ and $u'(C_{t+1})$ obeys the following rule: $u'(C_t) = u'(C_{t+1})(1+r)/(1+\rho)$. If the rate ρ is high relative to the real interest rate r , consumers are impatient since they weigh present consumption more than future consumption, and *vice versa*. Future consumption increases if current consumption is reduced; and delayed consumption yields a return which is the real rate of interest. By assuming that utility[7] is: $u(C_t) = C(t)^{1-\theta} / (1-\theta)$, the optimal condition above reads: $1 + r = (1+\rho)(1+g)^{\theta}$ or, more simply: $r \approx \rho + \theta g$. This is a positive relationship between the growth rate of consumption (in the steady state it would be $r = \rho$) and the real interest rate. This equation offers a prescription for the real interest rate: the rate of interest should be positive when the economy expands, but negative when it contracts (as is currently the case). By using the optimal condition as a predictive tool for consumption: $g = (r - \rho) / \theta$, we could argue that consumers will postpone consumption only when there are favorable conditions for investment and only when the marginal utility of consumption does not decrease too much when consumption increases. If consumers were more interested in keeping the current consumption level constant rather than in increasing future consumption, savings would be pointless. Only if the real rate of interest is greater than the time preference rate are consumers willing to postpone consumption. The Ramsey model holds that the real interest rate is a function of the time preference rate (instead of the savings rate as in the Solow model). Thus if consumers become more impatient, i.e. if they increase the rate of time preference, they save less and the real interest rate rises, and vice-versa. A rise in the rate of growth of technical progress and population has also a positive effect on the interest rate, as in the Solow model.

7 In the function $C(t)^{1-\theta}/(1-\theta)$ the utility of consumption decreases with $\theta > 1$, but the marginal utility $u'(C_t) = C_t^{-\theta}$ is positive irrespective of the value of θ. The parameter determines the degree by which the marginal utility diminishes when consumption increases, i.e. the willingness of households to shift consumption between periods.

The prediction of the effect on the real interest rate of government purchases in this model is very clear. If the change in government purchases is expected to be permanent, the real interest rate is unaffected; but if it is expected to be transitory, the interest rate will change.

In Diamond's (1965) overlapping generations model, the real rate of interest very much depends on government policy. It turns out that without government purchases a clear verdict on the level of the real interest rate is possible only if $\theta = 1$. In the general case where $\theta \neq 1$, there are multiple solutions, i.e. multiple stable levels of the unit capital stock and of the corresponding real interest rate. By considering government purchases, however, the same model gives predictions which are at odds with those of the Ramsey model. If the increase in the government purchases is expected to be permanent, the real interest rate will permanently increase. In the case of a temporary increase in purchases, the real interest rate also increases, but only temporarily. This is a conclusion which says much about the future level of real interest rates.

To sum up, the existing most well-known growth models give quite disparate predictions about the level of the real interest rate in a growing economy, but, at least in the writings that belong to mainstream economics, the absolutely prevailing wisdom (e.g. ECB 2004) is that an increasing demand for capital produced by an increase in the labor force or by capital intensive technology or by a decrease in thrift has an unambiguous positive effect on the real rate of interest.

2.2 Monetary theories of the real interest rate

Economists have developed theories trying to assess whether the current level of the real interest rate is in line with some reference value. Such a value is reckoned to be able to guarantee some kind of desirable equilibrium: price stability in the case of Wicksell; full employment in the case of Keynes; stability in income distribution in that of Pasinetti. Such theories describe what happens when the actual rate is out of line with the reference value and the mechanism of adjustment. The most notable example of such an idea is Wicksell's (1935) theory of the natural interest rate. According to that theory, the coincidence between the natural and the actual real interest rates makes current and potential levels of output coincide, thus making the level of prices stable. A difference between the actual and the natural interest rate – instead of that between the supply and demand of money – signals a potentially inflationary or deflationary environment and the resulting adjustment in prices makes the interest rate revert to its natural level. The practical use of the theory is in the possibility of using the deviation from the natural level as an indicator of monetary policy stance and of using the natural rate as a benchmark for guiding the official rate and, possibly, market short-term interest rates. Woodford (2003) reformulated Wicksell's theory in order to precisely investigate the effects of interest rate rules. As contemporary monetary policy, at least until the current crisis, is largely based on the control of interest rates, it can be argued that inflation and deflation risks can be ascribed to wrong interest rates rather than to the quantity of money. On this premise, Woodford builds various models in the spirit of Wicksell showing the relationship between the long-run inflation rate and the long-run average of the equilibrium real rates of interest and the long-run average of short-term or policy nominal interest rates. According to one of Woodford's simplest models (2003: 51), if exogenous real factors induce changes in the equilibrium real rate of interest which are not matched by the corresponding adjustment in the central bank's reaction, there will be a change in the equilibrium price level. The Wicksellian rule for the rate of interest is $i_t = \overline{i}_t + \phi \cdot p_t$, where p_t is the equilibrium level of the log-price level and $\overline{i}_t$ is a time-varying intercept. The equilibrium price level fluctuates around the long-run average value of the log-price level $\overline{p}$ in an interval bounded by the long-run average of the equilibrium real rate of interest which reflects real factors ($\overline{r}$) and the average of the short-run interest rate which reflects the monetary policy ($\overline{i}$). The long-run average value of the log-price level, therefore, reflects both long-run real and short-run monetary factors as shown by the formula $\overline{p} = \phi^{-1}(\overline{r} - \overline{i})$.

According to this approach, in the economies where the interest rate gap (i.e. the difference between the actual and the equilibrium real interest rates) is negative, the output gap (i.e. the difference between the actual and the potential levels of GDP) is positive and inflation risks are lower. The policy prescription which follows from the theory is different not only from the traditional quantitative rule for the quantity of money, but also from interest rate rules, such as the Taylor rule, which links the official interest rate to the inflation rate and to the output gap.[8] What emerges from the Wicksell and Woodford approach is that the central bank should be focused on the level of the natural rate of interest and on its changes and be quick in targeting the actual interest rate to that level. In the current situation, where most central banks (and notably the Fed) have enormously expanded the scale of their balance sheets, their primary goal should be to keep the market interest rate in line with the new equilibrium level, rather than to try to reduce securities and liquidity as soon as the economy recovers.

In contemporary dynamic stochastic general equilibrium models, private agents are forward-looking, which means that the current levels of the inflation rate and the output gap depend *inter alia* on their expected levels. In forming their expectations, forward-looking agents are assumed to share the predictions formed on the basis of the model. One of the most well known of such models (e.g. Galì 2008) is a blend of Keynesan, Wicksellian, Lucasian and Taylorian elements. The interest rate gap, i.e. the difference between the current and the natural real rate of interest, plays a key role in the determination of the current level of the output gap g_t. The corresponding equation reads: $g_t = -\frac{1}{\sigma}\left[i_t - E(\pi_{t+1}) - r_t^n\right] + E(g_{t+1})$, where the equilibrium level of the real interest rate depends on the expected future level of the natural level of output y_{t+1}^n, given the inter-temporal discount factor ρ: $r_t^n = \rho + \sigma E(\Delta y_{t+1}^n)$. In the remaining two equations of the model, the output

8 Unlike Woodford, who sees inflation as a consequence of wrong interest rates, Taylor makes interest rates the tool for rebalancing the economy.

gap directly feeds up on the inflation rate, while the current nominal interest rate i_t follows a policy rule *à la* Taylor. In such a model, fiscal policy is virtually absent and output is basically driven by the interest gap. If the central bank adopts an accommodative stance, the hike in the natural real rate of interest increases the output gap and thus the inflation rate.

Monetary policies inspired by more articulated theory are based on the idea that the market interest rates reflect the balance between demand and supply in the corresponding market. The bond market and the stock market have their own rates of return and it is well known that the bond yield and the earning yield usually differ by a quantity which is higher than that justified by the risk premium on equities. The key element in the money market is money demand or liquidity preference. Keynes departed from the traditional theory by claiming that the interest rate has the capacity to balance the demand for and the supply of money rather than savings and investment. Interest rates, therefore, are determined by the liquidity preference, which depends on the current and the normal level of interest rate. The latter is not determined in the model, but can be defined in various ways. It can be defined as the rate of interest at which full employment investment is balanced by available savings. The chances of full employment, therefore, critically depend on the relationship between the normal interest rate and the minimum interest rate, i.e. the rate at which people prefer to hold their wealth in liquid form. Lack of confidence, which is a distinct feature of recessions and depressions, increases the minimum to above the normal level. The actual real interest rate cannot stay below the minimum and thus cannot decrease sufficiently to promote full employment investment. Keynes argued that a reduction in wage bills and excessive increase in the money supply – which are often claimed to be necessary to solve recessions – could actually worsen slumps because they have negative effects on market confidence.

One big difference that exists between the Keynesian model and the other models is that while in the Wicksellian and Wicksell-inspired models the current real interest rate is attracted by the natural real rate, in the Keynesian model the current real rate is not necessarily bound to converge to it quickly. Liquidity preference and what lies behind it are much more important than the unknown natural or normal real rate of interest. Arguments more focused on the business cycle, rather than on a hypothetical and unknown natural or equilibrium interest rate, therefore, could offer useful perspectives.

2.3 The business cycle and real interest rates

During the current crisis asset prices and credit mutually reinforced each other, taking asset prices and credit volumes to historical heights. A central role in the circular process has been played by interest rates, which per se represent the price needed to induce individuals to hold their wealth in the form of bonds, rather than in other assets or in liquid form. Indeed, if interest rates had not decreased so much during the 1990s and beyond, the process of credit creation and asset appreciation would have been dampened down. Real interest rates could move pro-cyclically, i.e. decrease too much during expansions and increase too much in recessions. If this were true, they could rise now and hinder recovery.

The long decline in real interest rates that ended in 2008 reflects various factors. The reduction in actual inflation is the first. By declining from above 10 percent to around 2 percent, and almost to zero during the crisis, actual inflation dragged down real interest rates. This took place both directly by reducing inflation expectations and indirectly by inducing central banks to keep short-term real interest rates low. The second factor was the reduction in the risk premium, i.e. the compensation that risk-averse lenders require for longer maturities in relation to higher default risks and lower liquidity. A convenient way of representing the decomposition of the annual nominal interest rate $n-$year or long-term bonds is the following: $i_{nt} \approx r_{nt} + \pi^e_{nt} + p_{nt}$, where: $r_{nt} \approx (r_{1t} + r^e_{1t+1} + r^e_{1t+2} + ... + r^e_{1n})/n$ is the long-term annual real interest rate, i.e. the average of the current and the expected annual short-term real interest rates. π^e_{nt} is the average expected inflation rate over the n-year period and p_{nt} is a risk premium for the same period. For the annual nominal interest rate of risk-free three-month Treasury bills, the decomposition would be: $i_{1t} \approx r_{1t} + \pi^e_{1t}$. Observe that while r_{it} is the current short-term real interest rate such as the 3-month bills rate – an interest rate which is normally under the indirect control of the central bank – the other short-term interest rates r^e_{1t+k}'s are expectations as to the future level of the same rate. It is well known that during deflation, the central bank actually loses its power on r_{it}. The link between the official rate and the short end of the yield curve in real terms breaks down when the official interest rate hits the zero percent floor, deflationary expectations ($\pi^e_{nt} < 0$) make short-term r_{1t} and r^e_{1t+k}'s and long-term real interest rates $i_{nt} - \pi^e_{nt} = 0 - \pi^e_{nt} + p_{nt}$ actually increase.

The point about the reduction in long term nominal interest rates made above was in regard to all components included in the right-hand side of the equation $i_{nt} \approx r_{nt} + \pi^e_{nt} + p_{nt}$. If the central bank predicts a low average inflation rate because people expect low inflation (π^e_{nt} low), it will keep the short-term real interest rate low over the period concerned and consequently expected future short-term real interest rates (r^e_{1t+1}........r^e_{1n}) will be low. Since individuals expect that the central bank will be able to deliver a stable inflation rate and thus an easily predictable one, they will also bear a proportionally low risk of being wrong. By the same token, if they feel that future inflation becomes difficult to predict, they would be less sure about the correctness of their predictions and would feel they are bearing an inflation risk. This feeling would make them ask for a higher compensation p_{nt}. The point above neglects other influences on risk-aversion. Indeed it is well known that financial innovation and, particularly, the process of securitization that took place in the late 1990s and beyond have induced a massive under-valuation of risks, thus yielding a sharp reduction in default and liquidity premiums, i.e. two components of p_{nt} which added to the contraction in real interest rates. Summing up, it can be argued that the various risks (e.g. inflation risks, default risks and liquidity risks) subsumed in the premium p_{nt} have decreased during the last ten years, as was the case of r_{nt} and π^e_{nt} thus implying that lenders have asked for increasingly lower compensation in nominal terms.

Various factors are at work in shaping the level of interest rates: monetary policy, business cycle and debt issuance. Monetary policy aimed at price stability rather than at keeping short term interest rates i_{1t} at a low level, contributes to the reduction of nominal interest rate i_{nt} because it helps to reduce the expected inflation rate π^e_{nt}, but also the risk premium p_{nt}. In other words, to deliver low nominal i_{nt} and real interest rates r_{nt} in the medium term, monetary policy has to raise i_{1t} and r_{1t} (and possibly i_{nt} and r_{nt}) in the short term. This seems counterintuitive, but there exist various examples of this mechanism, the most evident being Volcker's recession. Fiscal policies aimed at reducing the budget deficit and the government debt also have the effect of keeping real interest rates low. This interpretation proved to be correct particularly during the launch of the euro, when a well-known convergence process among European currencies was able to make long-term real interest rates converge to the low German benchmark. A credible plan of fiscal consolidation has had an effect on long-term real interest rates which was more than proportional to the actual reduction in public debt. By the same token, it makes people believe that by increasing government debt and the risk of inflation, the government raises the various components of long-term interest rates.

The bond market is key as yields act as a balancing mechanism. Normally bond yields rise when confidence takes hold because this diverts savings away from the bond market and into the stock market. At some point, the surge in real interest rates r_{nt} inevitably depresses business activity; this entails a loss in confidence which attracts funds back to the bond market and reduces yields. This is the basic direct connection between the business cycle and the bond market, and thus interest rates. While monetary policy is primarily focused on the left-hand of the yield curve, the mechanism described above moves the right side of the curve up or down. Other mechanisms are at work, however. The central banks' direct purchase of bills and bonds and the issuance by the Treasury have obvious effects on market prices. Rising issuance may imply rising yields if the market sees this as a sign of weakening in public finances. Government debt issuance does not need to be in conflict either with corporate issuance or with the credit market in order to see real yields rise. Indeed, even if the economy is not close to full employment, we can see real yields heading up when issuance increases. Increased issuance together with rising unemployment and weak real growth – as is currently the case – combine in creating the problem of debt sustainability and thus increase the risk premium. By bidding up bond prices through debt monetization, the central bank pushes nominal yields i_{nt} down. Only if current and expected inflation is stable and only if the positive effect of increased issuance by the Treasury just mentioned does not prevail, can the current real yield be dragged down for a long time by the central bank. In the current situation of extra strong monetary expansion, to keep π_{nt} really stable and deliver low real interest rates in the medium term, sooner or later central banks could be forced to raise the real rates r_{1t} to keep inflation expectations in check and thus r_{nt} low.

Bond yields i_{nt} could rise also in an entirely different situation, viz. in the case of a fall in confidence in the domestic currency. If investors sell the stocks and bonds they hold because they fear a currency depreciation, yields certainly go up. This applies to the countries that keep their currency floating, as is the case of the USA and the euro area as a whole. In the case of countries which keep their currency strictly pegged – as is particularly the case of the individual member countries of the euro area, or the case of the countries with a currency pegged to either the US dollar[9] or the euro[10] – the adjustment mechanism in the internal real exchange rate is the real wage rate. In that case, the required reduction in real wages needs an increase in unemployment and slow output growth, which is usually the result of a slow and painful process, particularly when inflation rates tend to be uniform, as they are in a monetary union. The case for a country inside the Euro area is particularly tough if the euro is appreciating since that country must adjust its real exchange rate both towards internal and external commercial partners. The alternative to the real exchange rate mechanism could be a rise in government expenditure and government debt for a protracted period of time. Since in both cases, yields will inevitably surge, the problem of debt sustainability will resurface.

In conclusion, the rise in nominal yields can be induced by any component in the definition $i_{nt} \approx r_{nt} + \pi^e_{nt} + p_{nt}$ and to assess the current prospects, one should focus on all of them. Alternatively, one could concentrate on one side only of the relationship $i_{nt} - \pi^e_{nt} \approx r_{nt} + p_{nt}$ and argue that a rise in the real interest rate indicates that confidence in the economy's prospects has returned, but also that confidence in the domestic currency is fading and fiscal sustainability is in doubt.

4. China's interest rate policy

In countries where financial markets, and particularly interest rates, are not completely liberalized, nominal yields do not correctly reveal components such as the expected inflation rate and the risk premium, but directly reflect the policy stance of the monetary authorities and their targets even more clearly than is the case of economies where markets are completely liberalized. In the latter case, indeed, monetary stimulus has an impact on the yield curve that is only indirect, while in China the impact is more direct. The most important example of a partially

9 Typically those Asian countries that have a structural surplus with the USA, the Gulf countries and other countries in South and Central America.

10 We allude not only to the EU members expected to converge to the euro by keeping their currency stable *vis-à-vis* the single currency, but also to the European countries which are preparing to enter the EU (e.g. Serbia and Iceland), as well as to the countries which are simply strongly tied with the EU (e.g. Switzerland) and the UK.

liberalized economy obviously is China. It started liberalizing interest rates only in the aftermath of the Asian crisis, although it had made some decisive steps already (Feyzioglu *et al.* 2009, Fan and Johansson 2009, Geretto and Pauluzzo 2009). In the late 1990s, the PBC set a floor and a ceiling to the lending rate for financial institutions, respectively i^{l}_{floor} and $i^{l}_{ceilingr}$, and a floor and a ceiling, respectively i^{d}_{floor} and $i^{d}_{ceilingr}$, on the deposit rate of same institutions.[11] In this way, the PBC is able to control the profitability of banks through these spreads ($i^{l}_{floor} - i^{d}_{ceilingr}$ is the minimum spread for a given maturity). These benchmark rates still seem to be more important than the interbank money market rates[12] and together with the reserve requirement ratio, the control over the supply of liquidity and the issuance of government securities, they allow the monetary authorities to keep under control even the long-term government bond yields. Figure 1.7 displays 10-year bond nominal yields from 2000 to 2009, showing that market yields change very infrequently as do the benchmark deposit rates as if the 10-year maturity were driven by the deposit rates. Also the yields on the maturities up to 5 years have been shown to be driven more by the monetary authorities than by market forces (Fan and Johansson 2009). During the period in question, the average yields on all maturities have been higher on the one-year deposit rate which seems to be the most important policy rate. The yields show, in particular, that the PBC kept the yield low after the slowdown that spread out after 2000 until 2006, but quickly drove it up when the economy started overheating in 2006. It obviously drove it down after the onset of current crisis in 2007. The profile of yields clearly resembles much more the peculiar profile of repos or official rates around the world rather than market yields. The explanation of this close and direct connection between official rates and long-term yields – something that central bankers in the West can only dream of – lies in the actual control of interest rates pursued by the PBC. The PBC started liberalizing $i^{l}_{ceilingr}$ and i^{d}_{floor} until it removed them altogether only in 2004. By doing so, the PBC not only keeps control over the other two benchmark rates, i.e. i^{l}_{floor} and $i^{d}_{ceilingr}$ and thus the profitability of banks, but it retains the capacity to drive long-term nominal and thus real interest rates which bear on real demand and inflation. Indeed it can be argued that the yield on bonds cannot go lower than $i^{d}_{ceilingr}$ since if $i_{nt} < i^{d}_{ceilingr}$, bonds became unprofitable *vis-à-vis* deposits, while if $i_{nt} > i^{l}_{floor}$, bonds would be more profitable than deposits and lending. Since the PBC pegs the renminbi, it must manage the massive commercial surplus, which means that it needs to sterilize it. This can be done by promoting domestic bills and bonds which for banks are an alternative to credit extension. Since demand for bonds seems to be larger than supply, the yield stay well tuned to $i^{d}_{ceilingr}$. Fan and Johansson (2009: 8) found that the central bank has in the 1-year deposit rate (as well in the other deposit rates) a tool to be used as an instrument to model bond yields.

11 The index of maturity is omitted.

12 Fan and Johansson (2009).

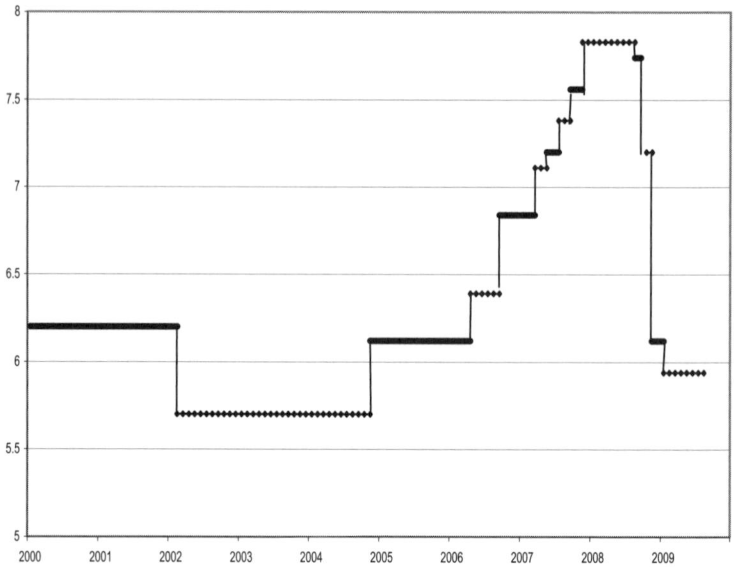

Figure 1.7 Nominal interest rate in China 2000–2009
10-year Government bond yield
Source: People's Bank of China.

Having briefly summarized how the PBC is good at driving domestic bond yields, it may be worthwhile to ask what this ability could mean for interest rates in the USA, if not for the whole global economy or, *vice versa*, to ask whether it is the policy decisions of the central banks in emerging Asia (the PBC included) that are dominated by the interest rate policies of the USA or the ECB. Almost all central banks, and notably those just mentioned, at least until 2008, used interest rates as their major policy instrument. There are at least two different answers to this question. According to the theory of currency blocs (Flatzacher 2002), deeper financial integration has made interest rate movements increasingly aligned. Obviously, all central banks are not equally credible and countries are not of equal size, thus, whatever the form of flexibility adopted in the exchange rate, monetary independence is not guaranteed to all members. The differences in the degree of autonomy, credibility and size leads to polarization and makes the relationships between interest rates asymmetrical, which means that the decisions of the leading central bank dominate the decisions of the others[13]. The advantage for the satellite countries is the imported credibility of the national central bank and less inflation. The dollar bloc, the euro bloc and the Yen bloc are examples witnessing this interpretation.

13 This holds *a fortiori* when a country adopts a currency board, dollarizes its economy or pegs its currency to that of the leader country.

There is currently no Renminbi bloc – although the PBC wants to make the renminbi gain more visibility in the international financial system. The PBC started pegging the renminbi to a basket of currencies and has recently advocated the establishment of a true international reserve currency formed by a basket of national currencies. Even if the PBC does not allow capital to move freely across its borders, it is not free to set its interest rates at levels entirely out of line with the chosen exchange rate target, that implies a misalignment of the US dollar. This is the essence of the so-called Bretton Woods II (Dooley et al. 2003, 2004), a regime that the authors think holds true for many emerging Asian economies. Basic macroeconomics suggests that huge and permanent external imbalances are not sustainable;[14] thus, the deterioration in the US external position requires an adjustment of the real dollar/renminbi exchange rate – a line of thought that the IMF has long put forward (e.g. IMF 2006). A second effect of the unbalance is the accumulation of foreign reserves, of which China has a mountain. About half of the approximately US$ 2,000 billion of its reserves are invested in US Treasury bills and bonds. China has also a lot of dollars. The accumulation of reserves can continue if it is sterilized by the PBC, but it decreases when the ensuing inflationary effect makes the real exchange rate adjust towards its equilibrium. China, however, necessarily wants to keep stable the value of its holdings of dollars and US debt. To do this, it is obliged to keep buying Treasuries and US dollars. If it were not to do that, markets would unavoidably interpret any cessation in buying US financial assets as a selling signal for their own dollars and Treasuries. Such a market reaction would make the US dollar and the US government debt crash. Yields on the US debt would then inevitably surge. The required adjustment in the real exchange rate, therefore, could come out both from relative prices[15] and from nominal exchange rate changes. Before this happens, Chinese savings, and particularly that part of it which is invested in dollar-denominated assets, will continue to exert a negative impact on the long-term interest rates both in the domestic and in the US markets. The scenario just envisaged equally holds for other Asian economies and it implies a stable downward pressure of Asian savings on the US interest rates. It is different from that based on the notion of a dollar bloc in which the US dollar reigns supreme and the Fed's interest rate policy sets the agenda for everybody else. Yet China is not dominated by the Fed policy since its huge reserves give it some power over the decisions taken in Washington and New York. The large trade surplus is the reward that China receives by adhering to the so-called Bretton Woods II, a regime that is a pillar of the current Chinese development strategy which delivers low inflation and rapid growth with the downward pressure on interest rates as a by-product. China would be keen to change such a successful strategy only in the case of inflation and lower growth.

14 Indeed, the original Bretton Woods system collapsed in 1971.

15 This is an inflationary scenario.

4. Conclusions

This chapter examined the likely future direction of real interest rates across the Atlantic and in Asia after their prolonged descent. The basic point is that the current crisis and the ensuing deep recession will change the previous trend. The financial crisis started in the housing market and soon hit the banking system, the money market, the stock market and the credit market i.e. the heart of the contemporary global finance in the US and EU economies. The landing after the expansion which followed the 2002 recession was quite hard indeed and it suddenly turned the business cycle in 2008 from one of increasing inflationary expectations into one of deflationary recession. The burden of the debt was, and still is, big in the private sector in some places (e.g. the USA and the UK) and in the public sector elsewhere (e.g. Japan and Italy). All this has made the crisis and the downturn extraordinary in many respects. Had monetary authorities and governments not intervened – sometimes even in a coordinated way – the 2007–8 crisis would have thrown some (perhaps all) economies into turmoil.

Government intervention was obviously necessary and virtually no one questioned it. Central banks were desperate to revive money markets and the whole monetary transmission mechanism using both conventional and unconventional measures. Households quickly turned to the virtuousness of thrift. We now live in an entirely new economic environment in which a complete U-turn has occurred in economic policy. Governments have abandoned the 1990s imperative of balancing the budget as they must now manage rising deficits and debts. Central banks have been obliged to forget their single-minded anti-inflation strategy and have been forced to redesign the range of their targets and instruments used. Economic consensus has changed completely after the crisis: government intervention and regulation look necessary again. However, governments and central banks must now find a way out of a budget regime and a monetary regime which were started because they were necessary, but which are abnormal and thus not sustainable indefinitely.

It is thus entirely unlikely that real rates of interest can prolong the old trend and the obvious key question is: after the long descent briefly documented in this chapter where are they heading? This is not mere academic curiosity, since if they were really heading up, the economy, the housing market and private and public finances would not be able to bear higher long-term interest rates as the only way to ban default is real growth. Higher real interest rates, therefore, could be very harmful to indebted governments, households and companies. By addressing economic theory, we have argued that highly respectable theories of real growth seem quite unable to offer practical guidance to predict the future direction of long-term real interest rates, at least in this instance. Monetary theories of real interest rates fare no better. Even though it is conceivable that current real rates must gravitate towards some reference value, some norm or average value, the value of that reference value looks like one of the many statistical chimeras that populate the landscape of economic theory. It seems much more practical to look day after day at the very basic elements into which economic theory believes a real interest rate can be decomposed: namely the risk-free cost of capital and the risk premium, or the nominal interest rate and the expected inflation rate; indeed, the two different key mechanisms that are constantly at work on the two sides. In the bond market situations happen quickly and if the inflation rate went out of the central banks' hands, savers would be quick to demand proportionally higher real interest rates no matter what the level of the nominal interest rate was. By the same token, if growth remained subdued, unemployment would rise too much and the government would be forced to excessively prolong its deficit spending, and savers would then ask for a higher risk premium. In both cases, interest rates are bound to rise and the only hope is that higher real interest rates will be able to temper the inflation surge. In conclusion, one should not count on stable real interest rates nor on easily predictable ones since nowadays interest rates are interdependent.

References

Diamond, P. 1965. National debt in a neoclassical growth model. *The American Economic Review*, 33(5), 1126–50.

Dooley, M., Folkerts-Landau, D. and Garber, P. 2003. *An Essay on the Revived Bretton Woods System*. NBER WP 9971.

Dooley, M., Folkerts-Landau, D. and Garber, P. 2004. *The Revived Bretton Woods System: The Effects of Periphery Intervention and Reserve Management on Interest Rates & Exchange Rates in Center Countries*. NBER WP 10332, March.

European Central Bank, 2004. *The Natural Real Interest Rate in the Euro Area, The Monthly Bulletin*. May, 57–69.

Fan, L. and Johansson, A.C. 2009. *China's Official Rates and Bond Yields*. Stockholm School of Economics, WP 3.

Feyzioglu, T., Porter, N., and Takáts, E. 2009. *Interest Rate Liberalization in China*. IMF Working Paper 171.

Flatzacher, M. 2002. *The Euro Bloc, the Dollar Bloc and the Yen Bloc: How Much Monetary Policy Independence can Exchange Rate Flexibility Buy in an Interdependent World*. ECB WP no. 154, June.

Galì, J. 2008. *Monetary Policy, Inflation and the Business Cycle: An Introduction to the New Keynesian Framework*. Princeton, NJ, Princeton University Press.

Garnier, J. and Wilhem Wilhelmsen, B.J. 2005. *The Natural Rate of Interest and the Output Gap in the Euro Area*. ECB Working paper Series No. 546, November.

Geretto, E. and Pauluzzo, R. 2009. The Chinese banking system; economic performance and prospects for future development. *Transition Studies Review*, 16(1), 92–113.

Kennedy, P.E. 2000. Eight reasons why real versus nominal interest rates is the most important concept in macroeconomics principles courses. *The American Economic Review*, 90(2), 81–4.

Laubach, L. and Williams, J.C. 2003. Measuring the natural rate of interest. *Review of Economics and Statistics*, 84(4), 1063–70.

Pasinetti, L. 1981. The rate of interest and the distribution of income in a pure labour economy. *Journal of Post Keynesian Economics*, 3(2), 170–82.

Ramsey, F.P. 1928. A mathematical theory of saving. *Economic Journal*, 38, 543–59.

Solow, R. 1956. A contribution to the theory of economic growth. *Quarterly Journal of Economics*, 70(1), 65–94.

Wicksell, K. 1935. *Interest and Prices*. New York, Kelley (first published in 1898).

Woodford, M. 2003. *Interest and Prices: Foundations of a Theory of Monetary Policy*. Princeton NJ, Princeton University Press.

Chapter 2
Economic Vulnerability: China, EU and USA

Bernadette Andreosso-O'Callaghan[1]

Introduction

The emergence of China (and India) as a new economic challenge, combined with monetary integration in Europe through the advent of the Euro, the dwindling role of the US dollar and globalization, have all created a multipolar and interdependent world. The modern wave of globalization is unprecedented, in that a larger proportion of goods, services and investment are involved in world exchanges than ever before, and that nearly all economies of the world take part in the process. With the increasing integration of China in the world economy, its dependency (assessed for example through trade linkages) upon the European Union (EU) and the USA has increased, and *vice versa*. However, when dependency is beyond the control of national economic policy, due to the very nature of linkages, vulnerability arises.[2] The opening up of economies weakens the impact of national economic policies, starting with monetary policy. This *état de fait* has widely been documented by economists and political scientists alike (Hettne et al. 1999; Cameron and Gross Stein 2000).

This chapter suggests to investigate the economic linkages (i.e. trade, investment and financial) existing between China, the EU and the USA, by analyzing them in the light of the concept of economic vulnerability. Its objective is to define and apply an index of vulnerability to the three economies, so as to analyze their relative exposure to economic shocks or imbalances. This stems from a core idea, which is that in the current era of globalization, all economies, even large and

---

1 A first version of this work was presented at the Institute for European Studies, Vrije Universteit Brussels, 21 June 2007. The author would like to thank the participants at this seminar, in particular Dr Xiaokun Song and Dr Willem Van der Geest for their useful comments and support.

2 At *prima facie*, one can say that the 'turbulences' observable in Asian currency markets in 1997 and the employment situation in the EU and US textile and clothing sectors after the Multi Fiber Agreement (MFA) expired reveal a degree of exposure, perhaps of vulnerability of these economies to exogenous factors. Monetary policy in the first case, and industrial policy in the second case, were clearly dictated by external factors.

dominant ones, are prone to the risk of being affected by exogenous factors. The risks in question are stunted economic growth, increasing unemployment, and, in the limit case, an economic crisis. Consequently, even the USA can be qualified as being a vulnerable economy, albeit, given its dominance and its engine role in the world, this is more due to endogenous rather than to exogenous factors. Therefore, to understand fully the concept of vulnerability, the analysis will start with the case of the US economy. The ultimate interest in the question of assessing the extent of economic vulnerability is to inform policy makers on the risks associated with too high a level of dependency; it is also to prevent contagion effects from the US economy, and therefore to take corrective action before a major downturn/crisis unfolds in its 'satellite' economies such as the EU and China.

Starting with some definitional issues, the ensuing section of this chapter will discuss the rationale for the study by analyzing briefly some endogenous issues in the USA. It will then provide a brief review of the pertinent literature. The third section will identify and develop the different components of the vulnerability index. A fourth section will apply this index to the three major economies of the world, namely the USA, China and the EU, and it will discuss the results, their analysis and their policy implications. Two time periods are selected for the analysis: 1995 and 2005, the latter being a year immediately preceding the major restructuring of the world financial system culminating with the current economic crisis. A final section will list a number of conclusions.

1. Global Integration and Vulnerability

1.1 Defining linkages, dependency and vulnerability

Linkages and dependency can easily be assessed with reference to the degree of openness of each economy. Born with the work of Alfred Hirschman (1958), the concept of linkages refers to simple economic connections between economic industrial structures. Taking the Hirschmanian definition one step further, and applying it in the framework of international economics, linkages can best be represented by inter- or intra-industry trade flows, by foreign direct investment (FDI) bilateral flows and by financial flows between countries. Dependency implies the disengagement by an economy from an entire economic activity (for example, a production activity), which is only of minor importance to this economy. The degree of 'importance of an economic activity' can be assessed and measured through input-output analysis (see for example Schultz 1977, and Sonis et al. 2000 for an elaboration of the notion of 'key industry'). As shown by Smarzynska Javorcik (2004), elements of input-output analysis are also useful for the determination of FDI linkages. An example of dependency is provided by US consumption, which during the 'knowledge economy era' has been fuelled by imports of consumer goods from China. Therefore, US consumption in the consumer goods category depends upon the Chinese economy. By extension, interdependency refers to a situation where dependency by country A on country B in a minor industry *i* exists in parallel with dependency of B on A in another (minor) industry *j*. Dependency *per se* does not, however, imply vulnerability. Indeed, vulnerability arises only when dependency is such that it weakens the impact of national economic policy; this is the case when it permeates industries or sectors of economic activity which are not minor, but which are 'key' sectors. Dependency on energy sources, combined with dependency on producer durables (the famous 'equipment hypothesis'),[3] on vital know-how and on financial investment (international savings) are the obvious ingredients of vulnerability. These areas point us in the direction of the relevant variables that ought to be selected for the construction of the vulnerability indicator. Because the three economies under review are not on an equal playing field, with the USA still being the engine of economic growth in the world, the concept of vulnerability needs to be qualified further. This implies taking a hierarchical view of the concept, by starting the analysis with the case of the USA. Indeed, as was seen in the very early 2000s, major economic imbalances in the USA translated into the diffusion of economic shocks elsewhere, whereas the reverse would not have happened with the same intensity.

1.2. Performance of the US economy

A brief account of the US economy is necessary given the leading role of the US economy during the time under review (1995–2005), and the signs of weaknesses that have been perceptible in this economy for quite some time – an issue to which we are turning now.

1.2.1. Endogenous issues in the USA Since the early 1990s, the USA has enjoyed the longest economic expansion in US economic history (Field 2007). This 'renaissance' is commonly explained by the emergence of the knowledge economy, and by the information technology (IT) 'revolution' as its major component. As documented by the OECD (2005), the IT revolution has been the source of sustained productivity increases and job creation over the 1990s. As a result of this sustained growth, the NASDAQ composite index peaked in March 2000 at 5,132, the highest value ever recorded in its history. Following the 'dot-com crash' in the early 2000s, its abrupt decline was the first obvious sign of weakening and/or deteriorating macroeconomic indicators. There are indeed a number of barometer

3 This hypothesis claims that there is a significant and positive relationship between the share of equipment goods in GDP and the rate of growth of output (see de Long and Summers 1991 and also Chapter 10 in this volume). Equipment goods generate spillover effects in using industries in the economy. When this equipment is 'controlled' by national entities, dependency and eventually vulnerability are less likely to materialize. This hypothesis found a renewed interest amongst economists in Europe in the 1980s and in the USA in the early 1990s.

macroeconomic variables that can inform on the likelihood of stunted economic growth in any country. These non-financial and financial variables are precursor signs or early symptoms of a serious economic downturn or of a crisis.

Among the non-financial variables, private consumption and household borrowing deserve particular mention. Private consumption has been responsible for driving recent economic growth, representing more than 70 percent of US GDP over the period (OECD 2006). Private consumption was greatly stimulated by an increase in borrowing and also, until recently, by relatively low energy prices. Financial innovation (i.e. easier and increased access to credit), the rise in households' financial wealth – due to appreciating values on the stock markets in the 1990s – the appreciation of housing prices, and the rise in labor productivity, all explain falling savings rates (FRBSF 2002). Beyond the controversies on the imperfect way the National Income and Product Accounts (NIPAs) calculate the savings rate in the USA (FRBSF 2002), it is undeniable that the household savings rate has reached an all time low, unseen since the 'great depression'.[4] It recorded a low average of 1 percent at the beginning of the 2000s and went into negative figures since 2005. At a macroeconomic level, a low personal savings rate is a matter of concern only in so far as it deprives domestic investors from readily available financing possibilities.[5] The current US account deficit, its composition, the decline in factory orders, and the housing slump reinforced by a business construction collapse, are all other relevant non financial barometer macroeconomic variables.

Given that recent financial crises have manifested themselves first in the financial sphere, financial indicators are even more useful than non financial indicators; they serve as early warnings of an unfolding economic recession or crisis. With regard to the present crisis, erratic and adverse movements on financial markets have included a depreciating dollar, the plunge of both the NASDAQ index to a value less than 1,500 in late 2002 (recovering to less than half its peak value, at 2,402 mid-March 2007) and of the Dow Jones Industrial Average receding to a value less than 9,500 in October 2008, compared with all time high values of more than 14,000 in October 2007.[6] Despite immediate remedies in the Autumn of 2008 (such as the rise in the cost of non performing loans by US banks and repeated

4 The savings rate is defined as the ratio of personal saving over disposable personal income.

5 Indeed, we leave aside here the implications of the life-cycle model of saving (according to which low savings in t might imply lower living standards in $t+1$), as well as the reasons for the low savings rate in the USA, for the attention is placed on the channeling of savings through the banking system.

6 Another policy element that created some havoc was the decision by the Federal Reserve to stop publishing figures on M3 in Spring 2006. Note that overseas investors own more than $4.4 trillion in US debt denominated in the form of bonds and securities. The Chinese threat of selling part of these assets has been looming for some time; as documented by the press (*Telegraph*, UK edition, August the 10th, 2007; *International Herald Tribune*, 9th March 2007), a large share of China's accumulated reserves have been invested in US

cuts of short-term lending rates by the US Federal Reserve), uncertainty on world financial markets did not lessen, for in late November 2007, panic withdrawals from money market funds and derivatives, judged as being too risky, occurred in China and South Korea. This led to slumps in the region's stock markets (including in Tokyo where the Nikkei reached its lowest level in more than a year) a first sign that the US credit crunch could not be ignored any more in Asia. This also showed clearly that the two economies (i.e. the USA and Asia – and in particular China) could not be seen as being 'decoupled'. This brief account shows how major imbalances on the financial markets of the leading economy spread to other regions. This is why the USA is the starting point of our analysis.

The question at this juncture is: given its excessive dependency on some areas (see below), how vulnerable is the US economy? Consequently, because of linkages effects, how vulnerable could the Chinese and EU economies become? All depends on the strengths of economic linkages (i.e. trade, direct investment and financial) existing between the three economies and on the degree of dependency. This leads us to the analysis of economic interdependency between the three economies.

1.2.2. Exogenous shocks on EU and China in an interdependent world The three economies and the connections between them can be best conceived as an open system, a concept borrowed from general systems' analysis developed by Bertalanfy (1968). In this large body of literature, a system is defined as a sub set of the real world, where time and space matter, and which is characterized by causal relationships between its different constituent parts. Interactions (or flows) between these different parts are crucial to the understanding of systems' analysis. They imply an exchange from an element of the system to the next, with as a consequence, a transformation of the latter. Feedback effects or retro-action imply that flows from the transformed part of the system affect eventually the other parts. The three economies under review, with the USA as being the core part of the system, represent an open system (as opposed to a closed system), for they have connections with the outside word. As shown in Table 2.1, the system envisaged here represented 42.1 and more than 60 percent of world merchandise trade and of inward FDI stock respectively just before the advent of the 2008 crisis. The system's viability is guaranteed as long as it operates in equilibrium. Whenever fundamental equilibria are violated over a certain period of time (for example the equilibrium holding between savings and investment), necessary adjustments take place; in the worse case scenario, this could take the form of an economic crisis.

As was again exemplified by the 1997 Asian crisis, imbalances tend to spread first through the stock exchange market. As argued by Yang (2005), an increased dependency of the Chinese economy on world markets since the economic reform, has meant that the Asian financial crisis had negative consequences on Chinese

Treasury Bonds and other Government securities. On the optimal debt level in the case of the US economy, see Stein (2006).

Table 2.1 EU-US-China share of world merchandise trade and FDI (2005)

Trade	**Imports**		**Exports**		**Total Trade (*)**	
	Billion €	%	Billion €	%	Billion €	%
USA	1,367.6	20.7	710.7	11.4	2,078.3	16.2
EU	1,176.1	17.8	1,061.8	17.1	2,237.9	17.5
China	472.7	7.2	602.7	9.7	1,075.4	8.4
World	6,593	100.0	6,214	100.0	12,807	100.0
	Inflows (#)		Outflows (#)		FDI balance (#)	Inward FDI stock
FDI	bn US$	%	bn US$	%	bn US$	bn US$
USA	95.9	14.8	229.3	31.4	+133.4	1,625.7
EU	216.4	33.4	279.8	38.3	+63.4	4,499.1
China	60.6	9.3	1.8	0.2	-58.8	317.9
World	648.1	100.0	730.3	100.0	-	10,129.7

(*) Intra-EU trade excluded. (#) Data for 2004.

Sources: EUROSTAT and IMF for trade figures; For investment flows: World Investment Report 2005, Transnational Corporations and Internationalization of R&D, UNCTAD: Geneva and New York, derived from p.2. For investment stocks: World Investment Report 2006, UNCTAD: Geneva and New York.

export-oriented firms. In more recent times, and shortly after the 2007 falls of both the Dow Jones Industrial Average and the NASDAQ, the Shanghai stock exchange fell by 9 percent (on the 27th of Feb. 2007). This is an example of a transmission mechanism between economies through the stock exchange; in this case, this mirrors the fact that China's (and Asia's) growth is explained substantially by its exports, primarily to the USA. Transmission mechanisms, linkages and dependency effects have been the centre of a abundant literature in economics. To this brief literature review we now turn.

1.3. Literature review

Although of relatively recent vintage, the concept of economic vulnerability is not new. It has however been confined to a small number of cases. First, to the case of developing and late industrializing countries, in order to assess their relative weaknesses and efforts in entering world markets (Guillamont 1999). Second, to small open economies that are notoriously dependent upon foreign markets (Demas 2002, Hogenbirk and Narula 2001). Third, to the area of financial markets (Goldfajn and Valdès 1997, Cartapanis et al. 1999). For example, Guillamont

(1999) investigates the idea of economic vulnerability and its measurement in the case of less developed countries. Demas (2002) describes the threats arising from globalization faced by small open economies in the Caribbean Islands, whereas Hogenbirk and Narula (1999) investigate the case of globalization in a developed economy, namely the Netherlands. What is notable is the paucity of studies in the area, as well as the very restrictive way in which the concept has been applied.

By contrast, the concepts of linkages, dependency and interdependency between economies have been widely analyzed and applied. In particular, there is a myriad of studies dealing with the case of interdependency (and contagion), albeit these studies have been mostly confined to the area of financial markets. A clear distinction is made in this body of literature between interdependency and contagion. Authors such as Ronn (1998), Boyer et al. (1999) define interdependency with due reference to a high correlation between stock market returns and other financial markets. In turn, contagion refers to a situation where monetary and financial shocks are transmitted from one country to the next (Eichengreen and Rose 1999), or where there is an 'excessive' transmission of shocks from one crisis stock market to another (Serwa and Bohl 2005).[7]

These concepts have been applied to a large number of situations, although a tendency has been to analyze interdependency predominantly within spatially confined regional markets (i.e. Asia versus Europe for example). Only a minority of these articles have dealt with interdependency (and contagion) effects across different regions of the world. In this latter group of studies, one should note the work by Jeon and Lee (2002), Fernandez-Izquierdo and Lafuente (2004), Gannon (2005) and Nikkinen et al. (2006). In particular, Jeon and Lee (2002) discuss the way some foreign exchange market coordination policies – e.g. the 1985 Plaza Agreement – have affected co-movement in foreign exchange markets over the period 1973–96, whereas Nikkinen et al. (2006) look at the way macroeconomic news in the USA affect stock markets at world level.

2. Constructing an EU-US-China Vulnerability Index

From a methodological viewpoint, the research in this area lacks both an empirical and a comparative focus. A first step with regard to the methodology is to construct a vulnerability index, which is also the ultimate objective of this article. This index will be a composite index given the multiplicity of macroeconomic variables (monetary and real) that come into play. In light of the discussion above, the variables that matter for the design of a Vulnerability Index (VI) are presented in the five sub-sections below.

---

7 All this being measured and appraised with the help of cointegration techniques (with the Granger causality test, for example, clarifying the direction of causality between two variables).

2.1. Global industrial restructuring

If the three economies are specialized in different product groups (narrowly defined), i.e. if inter industry trade is high (or intra-industry trade is low), mutual dependency is high and vulnerability increases. Conversely, if intra-industry trade (IIT) is high (narrowly defined), vulnerability is low. We use GL indices for the analysis of IIT patterns between the three economies and the results are depicted in Table 2.2. As shown in Table 2.2, there are clear industrial specialization patterns between China on the one hand, and the USA and the EU on the other. These primary data show therefore a clear trade complementarity between China and the USA (with GL indices lower than 0.18), and also between China and the EU. By contrast, given their greater degree of structural similarity, the EU and the USA are engaged mostly in similar two-way trade (with GL above 0.66 over the period).

Data at a disaggregate level are however even more instructive, for they provide information for each type of industry at a fine level of analysis. A cursory look at these data reveals that there are generally very low GL indices between the three countries in the agricultural and food sector (Codes 00-22) except for some categories such as cereals (code 04). This is obviously due to the perishable nature of these products, and the consequent problems of their transport across different regions of the world, as well as to the still relatively protected nature of this sector. The fact that the USA and the EU are structurally similar economies can be seen through high indices in the case of high-tech products such as Medical and Pharmaceutical Products (code 54), Chemical Materials (59), Telecommunication Equipment (76) and Photographic Apparatus (88). In the same vein, the disengagement of the US (and also EU) economies from a number of 'traditional' industries such as Apparel and Clothing (84) and Footwear (85) is apparent.

Table 2.2 Intra-industry trade (1995–2005)

	1995	2000	2005
EU-USA	0.69	0.69	0.66
EU-China	0.31	0.37	0.33
USA-China	0.17	0.17	0.18

Sources: EUROSTAT COMEXT and UN Comtrade for USA-China figures.

Beyond these Ricardian type specialization patterns, one has to note increased IIT between China and the USA/EU in a number of medium-high tech industries.[8] These are the new patterns of industrial specialization with, for example, high GL ratios between China and the EU (and also between China and the USA) in certain types of machinery: (72) and (73) for the USA and (74) and (77) for the EU. Also, Road Vehicles (78) and Other Transport Equipment (79) are other medium-high tech industries for which IIT indices between China and the EU are high.[9] For the construction of the vulnerability index, we will use total GL indices (i.e. for all industries, except services) and for each country pair.

2.2. Dependency on inward foreign direct investment

This is first measured by FDI stock as a percentage of gross fixed capital formation. While inward FDI does confer many economic benefits on the recipient economy in terms of employment, technology transfer and spillover effects, it renders the host economy more vulnerable to international economic forces as inward investment tends to be more footloose than investment from indigenous firms in the economy. A second criterion for the complete measurement of this variable relates to the notion of FDI linkages: the stronger the linkages of inward FDI to the local economy (with local sub-suppliers), the more vulnerable the economy.[10]

The transmission of shocks between the three economies can be gauged from the nature and strength of the links existing within the triad. Table 2.3 shows that there has been an increasing interconnection in terms of FDI stocks as a percentage of the gross fixed capital formation between the three economies over the years. The share, in the EU gross fixed capital formation, of US and Chinese FDI together has increased from 14.33 percent in 1995 to 37.27 percent ten years later. A similar trend can be observed for US gross fixed capital formation, where the share of the two partners' investments more than doubled over the period. The figures relating to EU and US FDI in China (and to their share in the Chinese gross fixed capital formation) appear low, although they are on the rise also. According to official statistics from the PRC Ministry of Commerce, some two-thirds of all inward realized investment by the top ten investors in 2005 was from Asian countries such as Japan, South Korea, Singapore and Taiwan. Nearly 60 percent of

8 Indeed, the correspondence between structural dis-similarity and high IIT (GL) ratios in the case of Japan and neighboring – for the major part developing – Asian countries, was already noted in the work by Wakasugi (1997).

9 On the whole, there are more medium–high-tech industries displaying relatively high GL indices between the EU and China than between the USA and China. This is partly due to a greater disposition by EU firms (and governments) to transfer technology to China (Andreosso-O'Callaghan and Qian 1999).

10 Paradoxically, although linkages increase embeddedness of foreign firms in the domestic economy, they also increase risk due to domestic contagion effects when a foreign owned firm closes down.

Table 2.3 EU-US-China foreign direct investment interdependence (percent)

Inward FDI/GFCF to the EU-15 from		
	USA	**China**
1995	14.320	0.017
2005	37.207	0.067
Inward FDI/ GFCF to the USA from:		
	EU-15	**China***
1995	20.820	n/a
2005	44.845	0.020
Inward FDI/ GFCF to China from:		
	EU-15	**USA***
1995	1.249	1.137
2005	4.059	1.769

Source: EUROSTAT, * Bureau of Economic Analysis, U.S. Department of Commerce, Gross fixed capital formation of China from Asian Development Bank (ADB).

the investment by the top ten was in fact 'round trip' investment flowing through tax havens such as the Virgin Islands, Cayman Islands, Western Samoa, as well as through Hong Kong. In these conditions, it is difficult to have a precise knowledge of the exact contribution of EU and American direct investment to the Chinese economy. If these 'round trip' investments (excluding those from Hong Kong) were redistributed proportionately to the EU and the USA, the ratios at the bottom of Table 2.3 would increase substantially.[11]

2.3. Shifting trade balances in key industries

The trade balance to GDP ratio is particularly relevant when assessed with reference to key industries in line with our earlier discussion. Table 2.4 presents the trade position of each of the countries in the triad and *vis-à-vis* the rest of the world in a selected number of key sectors, such as chemicals, machinery (including computers) and motor vehicles.[12]

11 For the USA, the redistribution of the share of the top ten would increase US FDI from 6 percent to nearly 7 percent.

12 Note that an ideal methodology would consist in taking the trade position of each country in each industry *vis-à-vis* the other two partners, but unfortunately, data

The table shows the spectacular improvement of Chinese trade in the high-tech sector over the period, with a substantial deficit in 1995 turning into a comfortable surplus ten years later. In 2005, the positive trade balance of China in high-tech products represented 1.44 percent of its GDP. Whilst the EU-15 was able to consolidate its trade position on world markets in the three industries, the USA has seen its trade deficit widen in these areas. The US deficit in high tech products represented more than 1.5 percent of US GDP in 2005, up from 0.38 percent 10 years earlier. More generally, the US current account deficit has gone well beyond 6 percent of GDP in early 2005, the largest in the nation's history. At the time, this was already seen as being unsustainable by some observers and analysts (OECD 2005).

Table 2.4 Trade balance/GDP ratio (in percent; calculated with respect to the world)

EU-15*	**Year**	
	1995	2005
Chemicals	0.140	0.164
Machinery	0.540	0.444
Road vehicles	0.444	0.511
Total High Tech	1.124	1.119
USA**	**Year**	
	1995	2005
Chemicals (and other industrial products)	0.289	-0.300
Machinery	0.166	-0.132
Automotive vehicles, engines, and parts	-0.842	-1.131
Total High Tech	-0.387	-1.563
China***	**Year**	
	1995	2005
Chemical products	-0.283	-0.842
Machinery, mechanical appliances, and electrical equipment	-2.760	2.284
Total High Tech	-3.043	1.442

Sources: Derived from * EUROSTAT, ** Bureau of Economic Analysis, U.S. Department of Commerce, and ***Asian Development Bank, Key Indicators 2006.

disaggregated in that way are not available for all three countries.

2.4. Global saving – investment imbalance

The other variables that matter for the design of a vulnerability index are financial macroeconomic indicators. These variables are summarized in Table 2.5. Among these variables, we have identified the savings rate and other variables that are grouped under the 'financial robustness' heading.

An important question at this juncture is to ascertain whether a low saving rate (or in the case of the USA, private indebtedness) is detrimental to investment. Following Keynesian theory (Keynes 1936, Book 2, Chap. 6), a domestic savings rate in line with domestic investment needs allows economic growth, contributes to macroeconomic stability and reduces an economy's exposure (perhaps vulnerability) to unexpected shifts in international financial flows. As documented in several World Bank Development reports, the gap between savings rates in developed and developing countries has widened since the mid-1970s (with a doubling of these rates in East Asia). Does this imply that the USA is much more vulnerable than, say, China?

Bahmani-Oskooee and Chakrabarti (2005) provide a thorough literature review on the saving-investment relationship for the past 30 years or so, following the Feldstein and Horioka study of 1980. Most studies (cross-country, time series and panel) conducted for the different countries (OECD and developing) conclude with a high and significant relationship between the two variables. Using cointegration techniques for 126 countries over the period 1960–2000, Bahmani-Oskooee and Chakrabarti (2005) find both a positive relationship between the ratio of gross domestic investment to GDP and between that of gross domestic saving to GDP, confirming earlier results. Focusing on country size and openness, the authors argue that the saving-investment relationship over the period is stronger for large and high income countries and for relatively closed economies.[13] Although the controversy on the strength of the saving-investment relationship is still open, these additional results would suggest that the USA is a plausible candidate in the select group of high income, large and relatively closed countries. As can be seen in Table 2.5, the savings rate has deteriorated in the USA, whereas it has remained at around the 20 percent mark (of gross national disposable income) in the EU over the period, although the lack of harmonized definitions hampers direct comparisons.

2.5. Economic and financial robustness

This relates to the healthiness of the economy assessed though a number of fundamental macroeconomic and financial indicators. These indicators include:

13 Openness is defined in this study on the basis of the Sachs and Warner (1995) composite index, based on each country's average tariff, non-tariff barriers (NTBs), black market premium, economic system and export marketing.

inflationary pressures (measured by the M2/RES ratio),[14] and a proxy for the financial bubble, the latter being an important factor in China, the USA, as well as in some parts of Europe. Due to statistical constraints, we have selected M2, which measures the extent of money supply, related to international reserves (including gold reserves). The higher the ratio, the more vulnerable the economy to disequilibria. In addition, stock market indices (NASDAQ, Dow Jones, London, and Shanghai) are used in this study, and can serve as a proxy for the bubble. Again, excessive values imply vulnerability.[15] The M2/Reserves ratio has expanded sharply in the case of the USA (partly due to the international role of the

Table 2.5 Financial macroeconomic indicators (1995 and 2005)

	1995			2005		
	EU-15	**USA**	**China**	**EU-15**	**USA**	**China**
1. Savings rate (%)	20.8	4.6	39.0	20.0	-0.4	46.0
2. Financial robustness: M2/Reserves ratio	10.688	41.542	9.567	11.375 (#)	100.322	4.416
FTSE index	100	-	-	153.9	-	-
DJ Indus Average	-	100	-	-	234.7	-
NASDAQ	-	100	-	-	226.9	
Shanghai Composite Index	-	-	100	-	-	228.0
Shenzhen CI	-	-	100	-	-	278.8

Sources: For the EU-15: EUROSTAT. For China: Asian Development Bank, Key Indicators 2006. For the USA : M2/Reserves and Gross savings rate are from the Bureau of Economic Analysis, U.S. Department of Commerce; Federal funds effective rate from the Federal Reserve Board. Sources for stock market data are New York Stock Exchange (NYSE), Dow Jones & Co., Inc., Standard & Poor's (S&P), and NASDAQ Stock Market.

Notes: M2/Reserves data are for the Euro Area-11 only (reserves include also gold reserves); the savings rate is defined as Gross saving/ Gross national disposable income for the EU and as Personal saving/disposable personal income for the USA.

Notes: Stock indices are averages of daily closing prices. For China, the savings rate is defined as the ratio between GDP minus consumption, and GDP.
(#) Value for 2000.

14 M2 comprises broadly all currency in circulation plus various deposit accounts. It does not comprise repurchase agreements and Eurodollars in the case of the USA, the latter being part of M3.

15 The Tobin q (ratio) is certainly one of the most appropriate indicators for measuring excessive (i.e. above normal) values on the stock exchange. Because of data limitations, we unfortunately have to resort to crude indicators. Nevertheless, these indicators are useful in that they show that the increase has been moderate in the EU but important in both the Chinese and US markets.

US$), whereas the same ratio has been rather stable or decreasing in the EU and China respectively. In the case of China, this is explained by an unprecedented accumulation of international reserves, due to its growing trade surplus, during the period under review.

Finally, because of the still limited possibility of arbitrage between the different currencies (namely the US$ and the €), the exchange rate variable is excluded from our analysis.

3. Formulation of the Vulnerability Index – Increasing Global Vulnerability 1995–2005

Having identified the variables that matter for the construction of the VI, a subsequent question is whether a weighting should be placed on them. This is a crucial and rather complex issue. On the one hand, the financial and monetary variables are the classical symptoms or early warnings of the likelihood of an unfolding crisis. On the other, these symptoms mirror directly the disequilibria of the real economy. Consequently, we have opted for no weighting coefficient.

The VI is therefore a composite indicator, the components of which are summarized in Table 2.6. The table also gives an indication of the trend behavior of each component, and therefore an increase in the indicator as a whole is associated with increased vulnerability. The higher the VI, the more likely endogenous and exogenous shocks will jeopardize macroeconomic stability in the system as a whole.

Although we did not weigh the different components (variables) of the vulnerability indicator, we have scaled down those with values varying well beyond the upper limit of the [0,1] interval, such as M2/Reserves but dividing each value by 100. This implies that, although not being confined to the [0,1] interval of variation, the financial indicators do not vary excessively outside this

Table 2.6 Construction of the Vulnerability Index Components

Variable	Trend behavior	Variation interval
Real indicators		
(1-IIT)	increasing	[0,1]
(FDI/GFKF)	"	[0,1]
Financial indicators		
[1-(TB/GDP)]key	increasing	[0, +∞]
(M2/Res)/10	"	[0, +∞]
(1 – savings rate)	"	[0, +∞]
Stock exchange indicators/100	"	[1, +∞]

interval. Again, we use two values for each real variable (for each country pair and year), so as to restore some equilibrium between the relative importance of the real versus the monetary variables. For instance, the first two values of the first column of the final table refer to the component (1-IIT) of the EU *vis-à-vis* the USA and China respectively. Tentative results drawn from such a methodology are shown in Table 2.7 for the years 1995 and 2005. Several instructive conclusions emanate from this exercise.

First, vulnerability has increased for each of the three economies during the 1995–2005 period. Owing to the selection of the different components of the VI indicator, in particular to the variables mirroring interdependency between the three economies, such as IIT and FDI, this reflects the greater impact of openness through globalization in the three economies. Second, the increase of the VI has been less pronounced for the EU-15 than for the other two partner countries. The EU-15 appears, therefore, as being moderately vulnerable over the period under review. It is probable that the creation of a zone of monetary stability through the advent of the Euro has greatly contributed to this performance. By scaling down the monetary variables to bring them in line with the real variables (and even by subtracting in the limit case the M2/Reserves variable as in the last line of the table), an inescapable conclusion holds: in 2005, the USA was more vulnerable than either the EU or China. It should be noted that both the EU and the USA started with comparable vulnerability levels at the beginning of the period, and that during the decade under review an important diverging phenomenon has occurred between the two economies. China stands midway between the two other economies. Its level of vulnerability at the end of the period is substantially higher than that of the EU.

Because of its core role in the system, a vulnerable US economy implies necessary adjustments in the other two economies, through transmission effects, in

Table 2.7 EU-US-China Economic Vulnerability Index (1995 and 2005)

	EU-15		USA		China	
	1995	**2005**	**1995**	**2005**	**1995**	**2005**
(1-IIT)	0.31	0.34	0.31	0.34	0.69	0.67
	0.69	0.67	0.83	0.82	0.83	0.82
(FDI/GFKF)	0.14	0.37	0.20	0.44	0.01	0.04
	0.00	0.00	0.00	0.00	0.01	0.02
[1-	0.99.	0.99	1.00	1.01	1.03	0.98
(TB/GDP)]key	0.10	0.11	0.41	1.00	0.09	0.04
(M2/Res)/100	0.80	0.80	0.96	1.00	0.61	0.54
(1 – savings rate)						
Stock exchange	0.00	0.53	0.00	1.26	0.00	1.28
Indicators /100						
VI	3.03	3.81	3.71	5.87	3.27	4.39
VI (without M2/Res)	2.93	3.7	3.3	4.87	3.18	4.35

spite of their relatively healthier economic, monetary and structural performance. As we have observed since September 2008, a substantial downturn in the US economy has had a relatively important impact on Asia, and in particular on China, the manufacturing platform of the USA. Given the investment and financial linkages existing between the USA and the EU, the latter region (and in particular some countries therein) has also been affected. Already the 2005 figures, as computed above, showed clearly that the US model of easy credit, increased current account deficits, rising indebtedness and – quite puzzlingly – of increasing debt refinancing through Chinese saving is unsustainable.[16] With the arrival of the 2008 crisis and with the disappearance of some US and other European (not only EU) banks from the world's banking market, this model has been showing its limitations to the wider community. Given the new international monetary architecture since the advent of the Euro, this *état-de-fait* invites for a thorough rethinking of economic policy in the leading economy of the world. New policies should address the structural problems of the US economy, such as the increasing current account deficit fuelled in part by an increasing dependence on imported technology, in the light of an increasingly fragile US dollar. In China and in other Asian countries, decoupling through domestic demand-led growth as well as regional financial integration have assumed priority on the agenda, clear proof that the Asian governments wish to maximize growth effects with lower interdependency with the USA in the future. This ultimately implies that these governments are eager to minimize their economic vulnerability to external shocks.

4. Conclusions

With the modern wave of globalization, the advent of the euro and the emergence of China, the interdependency of the different economies of the world has increased. This article looks at the interdependency between three selected major economies of the world, namely the USA, China, and the EU. These three economies represent more than 40 percent and more than 60 percent of world merchandise trade and inward FDI stock respectively, and are highly interlinked. Because of the many linkages between them, the three economies can be viewed as forming an open system, with the USA at its core. It is argued that when mutual dependency is beyond the control of national economic policy, in some critical areas and as explored in this chapter, vulnerability arises. An economy can be vulnerable either to external shocks through transmission effects (in particular on financial markets) or because of inherent imbalances such as in the case of the US economy, the core economy in the system. The main objective of this chapter has therefore been to construct a vulnerability index and to apply it to the three economies under study.

16 This echoes repeated warnings voiced to the US Government by the Bank of International Settlements, the European Central Bank, the World Bank and the IMF, before the crisis.

The VI rests on a number of real and monetary variables such as IIT in all industries except services, inward FDI as a ratio of gross fixed capital formation, the savings rate, M2/reserves and stock exchange indices. In discussing the components of the vulnerability index, particular attention has been devoted to the US economy, given its still driving role in the system.

This index is a tool of economic policy, aimed at informing policy makers about the risks associated with excessive dependency, so that corrective action, – encompassing both financial and structural elements – be taken accordingly *before* a financial and then an economic crisis unfolds. This comparative analysis shows that vulnerability has increased in all three economies during the 1995–2005 period. The increase has been less pronounced for the EU, which appears as being moderately vulnerable. The USA is the most vulnerable economy in the system, with China lying mid-way between these two extremes. Because the USA is the core element in the system, and because of increasing interdependency through globalization, potential contagion effects (not analyzed here) imply that major disequilibria in the USA are likely to diffuse elsewhere. The role of the US dollar as the international reserve currency has, for several decades, dispensed the country from the need of major adjustments. Nevertheless, an accumulation of adverse policy decisions and economic events since 2007 and the current economic crisis have rendered the situation all the more fragile. All this puts to question the regulatory role of the US currency in the system, the US *seigniorage* privilege, and the viability of the USA as the leading economy in the future.

References

Andreosso-O'Callaghan, B. and Qian, W. 1999. Technology Transfer: A Mode of Collaboration between the EU and China. *Europe-Asia Studies*, 51(1), 123–42.

Bahmani-Oskooee, M. and Chakrabarti, A. 2005. Openness, Size and the Saving–Investment Relationship. *Economic Systems*, 29(3), 283–93.

Bertalanfy, L. von. 1968. *General System Theory: Foundations, Development, Applications*. New York: George Braziler Inc.

Boyer, B.H., Gibson, M.S., and Loretan, M. 1999. *Pitfalls in Tests for Cchanges in Correlations*. International Finance Discussion Paper No. 597R, Federal Reserve Board, Washington, DC.

Cameron, D., and Gross Stein, J. 2000. Globalization, Culture and Society: The State Amidst Shifting Spaces, Canadian Public Policy – *Analyse de Politiques*, 26(2), Supplement/Numéro Spécial 2, S15–S34.

Cartapanis, A., Dropsy, V. and Mametz, S. 1999. Indicateurs d'alerte et crises de change: Analyse comparée des économies d'Europe centrale et orientale (1990-1997) et d'Amérique latine et d'Asie de l'Est (1971–1997). *Revue Economique*, 50(6), 1237–54.

De Long, J.B., and Summers, L. 1991. Equipment Investment and Economic Growth. *The Quarterly Journal of Economics*, 106(2), 445–502.

Demas, G. 2002. *Small Economies in the Phase of Globalisation*. Caribbean Development Bank Research Papers, Memorial Lecture, May.

Eichengreen, B. and Rose, A. 1999. Contagious Currency Crises: Channels of Conveyance, in: T. Ito and A. Krueger (eds), *Changes in Exchange Rates in Rapidly Developing Countries: Theory, Practice and Policy Issues*. Chicago: University of Chicago Press, pp. 29–50.

Feldstein, M. and Charles, H. 1980. Domestic saving and international capital flows. *Economic Journal*, 90(358), 314–29.

Fernandez-Izquierdo, A., and Lafuente, J.A. 2004. International Transmission of Stock Exchange Volatility: Empirical Evidence from the Asian Crisis. *Global Finance Journal*, 15(2), August, 125–37.

Field, A.J. 2007. The Equipment Hypothesis and US Economic Growth. *Explorations in Economic History*, 44 (1), 43–58.

FRBSF. 2002. *What's Behind the Low US Personal Savings Rate?* Federal Reserve Bank of San Francisco Economic Letter, March 29th.

Gannon, G. 2005. Simultaneous Volatility Transmissions and Spillover Effects: U.S. and Hong Kong Stock and Futures Markets. *International Review of Financial Analysis*, 14(3), 326–36.

Goldfajn, I. and Valdès, R.O. 1997. *Are Currency Crises Predictable?* IMF Working Paper, WP/97/159.

Guillamont, P. 1999. *On Economic Vulnerability of Low Income Countries*. International Task Force on Commodity Risk Management in Developing Countries.

Hettne, B., Inotai, A. and Sunkel, O. (eds) 1999. *Globalism and the New Regionalism*. London: Macmillan.

Hirschman, A.O. 1958. *The Strategy of Economic Development*. Yale: Yale University Press.

Hogenbirk, A. and Narula, R. 1999. *Globalisation and the Small Economy: The Case of the Netherlands*. Maastricht: MERIT.

Jeon, B.N., and Lee, E.S. 2002. Foreign Exchange Market Efficiency, Cointegration, and Policy Coordination. *Applied Economics Letters*, 9(1), 61–8.

Keynes, J.M. 1936. *The General Theory of Employment, Interest and Money*, (reprinted 1973, London and Basingstoke: Macmillan and St Martin's Press).

Nikkinen, J., Omran, M., Sahlstrom, P. and Aijo, J. 2006. Global Stock Market Reactions to Scheduled U.S. Macroeconomic News Announcements. *Global Finance Journal*, 17(1), September, 92–104.

OECD. 2005. *Economic Survey of the United States 2005*. OECD: Paris, 27th October.

OECD. 2006. *Economic Outlook*. No. 80, USA, 28th November, Paris.

Ronn, E.I. 1998. The Impact of Large Changes in Asset Prices on Intra-market Correlations in the Stock and Bond Markets, *Mimeo*.

Sachs, J. and Warner, A. 1995. Economic Reform and the Process of Global Integration, *Brookings Papers on Economic Activity*, 26(1), 1–118.

Schultz, S. 1977. Approaches to Identifying Key Sectors Empirically by Means of Input-output Analysis. *Journal of Development Studies*, 14(1), 77–96.

Serwa D. and Bőhl, M.T. 2005. Financial Contagion, Vulnerability and Resistance: A Comparison of European Stock Markets. *Economic Systems*, 29(3), 344–62.

Smarzynska Javorcik, B. 2004. Does Foreign Direct Investment Increase the Productivity of Domestic Firms? In Search of Spillovers through Backward Linkages. *The American Economic Review*, 94(3), 605–27.

Sonis, M., Hewings, G.J.D. and Guo, J. 2000. A New Image of Classical Key Sector Analysis: Minimum Information Decomposition of the Leontiev Inverse. *Economic Systems Research*, 12(3), 401–421

Stein, J.L. 2006. *Stochastic Optimal Control, International Finance and Debt Crises*. Oxford: Oxford University Press.

Wakasugi, R. 1997. Missing Factors in Intra-industry Trade: Some Empirical Evidence Based on Japan. *Japan and the World Economy*, 9(3), 353–62.

World Bank (various years) World Development Reports (1999, 2001, 2003, and 2005).

Yang Dexin. 2005. *China's Offshore Investments – A Network Approach*. Cheltenham: Edward Elgar.

Chapter 3

The Twilight of 'Chimerica'? China and the Collapse of the American Model

Guilhem Fabre[1]

Introduction

The rise of China and its impact on the world economy, especially its relationship with the USA, has played a major role in the present global crisis. The early years of the 21st century have seen the development of a close interdependence between the American model of finance-led growth and the Chinese model of export-led growth. This chapter explores the interaction between these two dynamics and the way China may recover from too much dependence on exports. In a first section, this Chapter will propose a concise analysis of the different growth models of the last few decades as epitomized by both the US model of finance led growth and the Chinese model based on exports. The ensuing section will attempt to answer the central question of this Chapter which is, whether and how, the Chinese economy can lift the western world (starting with the USA) out of the current crisis. The third section will discuss a way forward so as to address the adjustment problem, and some conclusions are suggested in a final section.

1. A Typology of Growth Models: The USA versus China

1.1. The US model of finance-led growth...

According to the liberal *credo*, financial markets were supposed to optimize the allocation of resources and to manage risks, while the rules were mainly fixed by the central banks and the national financial regulatory authorities. This *credo* collapsed with the global crisis that erupted in 2008.

The progressive deregulation and globalization of financial markets since the 1980s created an unusual situation where global savings were financing the credit consumption of one of the richest countries in the world, the USA, because of the

1 I am grateful to Professor Victor Rodwin, from New York University, who provided useful comments on this text.

supremacy of the US dollar. As the winner of the Cold war, the USA set the tune with its low inflation and easy money policy, which allowed financial operators in their quest for profit maximization to create asset bubbles, i.e. the internet bubble of 1998–2001, the housing bubble of 2001–2007, and the primary commodities bubble of 2007–2008, which created another surge of global inflationary trends. The collapse of this neo-capitalist model in September 2008 also signals the transformation of what Moritz Schularick at Berlin's Free University and Niall Ferguson at Harvard University have called 'Chimerica', to illustrate the symbiotic relationship between the two giants who were responsible for more than half of the world's economic growth in the years 2002 to 2008. One did the saving and the other did the spending, as China's accumulated international reserves (estimated at $2 trillion as of late 2008) served to finance the US current account deficit as well as keeping Chinese exports affordable. These are the two sides of the same coin: from the end of 2001, which marked the access of China to the World Trade Organization (WTO), to 2008, Americans' personal accumulated debts exceeded the sum of their debts in the previous 40 years, and US savings declined from more than 5 percent of gross national income to practically zero, while Chinese savings rose from less than 30 percent to more than 45 percent.

This relationship was of course not limited to these two countries as the rest of Asia was also export-driven, trade deficits and household indebtedness had also increased in Europe, and energy exporters were also recycling their petrodollars in other western countries, but as Ferguson (2008a) rightly puts it 'Chimerica' was the real engine of the world economy. Thus, it is useful to analyze the origins, consequences and the mutations that the present crisis may generate from a 'Chimerica' perspective.

First of all, we must underline that the market booms of 1998 to 2008 were based on (ir)rational expectations. The digital revolution, comparable in its impact, to the invention of printing, explains the Internet boom. Oil prices have risen more than five-fold between 2000 and 2007, as strong demand from China and India, accompanied by the depreciation of the US dollar pushed commodity exporters to raise their prices. But as Palley (2007) has shown, the character of oil trading has changed substantially over the past decade or so; institutional investors and speculators (i.e. financial institutions and hedge funds) now account for 70 percent of the trade, compared with 37 percent at the turn of the new millennium. Thus, the accumulation of pro-cyclical risks, based on an easily obtainable banking credit, led to irrational expectations (Boyer et al. 2004). In this respect, the collective culpability of central bankers and fiscal authorities, especially in the USA and Europe, is overwhelming, since they voluntarily let develop the expansion of financial globalization with minimum national (not to mention international) regulation. Focusing on the prices of goods and services, they neglected the follow-ups of asset inflation (real-estate and stocks), and of financial innovations, which were supposed to reduce risk, but which were also 'designed to circumvent regulation or taxation',[2] and which finally spread risk to unprecedented levels.

The market for derivatives or credit risk transfers (CRTs), which has grown more than a thousand times in size since the beginning of the 1980s, to insure operators against commodity prices, interest rates or currency exchange fluctuations, was extended to credit default swaps (CDSs). A credit default swap is a contract under which the seller, for a fee, agrees to make a payment to the protection buyer if the referenced security, usually some kind of bond, experiences various 'credit events', such as bond issuer bankruptcy, default or reorganization. In 2000, President Clinton signed the Commodities Futures Modernization Act exempting certain derivative transactions on commodities and swap agreements, including CDSs, from regulation. As CDSs were not subject to state laws or control, the way was cleared for the growth of a market where deals were privately made between two parties, without standards for the solvency of the parties. 'The buyer does not know how much risk the seller is taking on. And there are no requirements for the seller to hold reserves of capital against the risks it is taking on selling swaps'.[3] CDSs were massively used to insure against mortgage default risks and created the illusion of a low-risk environment supervised by the regulators of the Federal Reserve. In May 2006, Alan Greenspan called the CDS 'the most important instrument in finance', adding 'what CDS did is lay off all the risks of highly leverage institutions… on stable American and international institutions' (Baily et al. 2008: 33). It is exactly the reverse that happened.

This unregulated market concerned risks premiums, off the balance sheets, calculated on a notional value of assets which stood at $54.6 trillion at midyear 2008. CDs were the principal cause of the near collapse of the US financial system, as they played a major role in several US financial institutions' financial problems such as AIG, Bear Stearns and Lehman Brothers. The latter was one of the largest over the counter (OTC) derivative dealers. AIG Financial Products, a subsidiary of AIG, active in the derivative market, did not routinely hold reserves of capital, or collateral for the risks it was taking on. It issued transactions covering more than $440 billion in bonds with obligations that it could not cover, until its bail-out by the US Treasury for $180 bn, allowed it to settle its CDS debts, which amounted to $12.9 bn for Goldman Sachs, $11.9 bn for Société Générale, $4.9 bn for BNP

2 The interested reader can refer to an article by Hannes Androsch, Former Finance Minister and Vice-Chancellor of Austria, *Europe's Financial Vulnerability* , www.project-syndicate.org. The fact that regulators are always running behind private sector innovation, does not however explain the neglect of asset inflation, which had been underlined by economists such as Patrick Artus (2007).

3 Superintendent Eric Dinallo, New York State Insurance Department, Testimony to the US House of Representatives Hearing to Review the Role of Credit Derivatives in the US Economy, Washington, November 20, 2008.

Paribas, and $2.3 bn for the investment bank of Crédit Agricole.[4] As early as 2002, the Bank for International Settlements (2002) noted that this market had given rise to a concentration of risk in financial operators less capitalized and less governed by regulation, such as hedge funds, two-thirds of which are located in offshore locations, with a predilection for the Cayman Islands, but which are mostly funded (86 percent) in the US (IMF 2007).

Hedge funds, with their progressive institutionalization after the year 2000, have played a key role in financial innovation and risk-transfer techniques, especially securitization, which is at the origin of the sub-prime crisis. They were responsible for 58 percent of the US credit derivatives market by volume and 45 percent of its emerging markets bonds in 2005. They represented 40 percent and 50 percent respectively of the New York stock exchange and London stock exchange transactions on the eve of the 2008 crisis. Apart from hedge funds, the new surge of private equity funds, spanning from start-up venture finance to leverage buyouts to 'vulture or distressed asset funds', according to the IMF (2007), increased the use of risk-taking and leverage to unprecedented levels, with concrete implications for the operation of restructured or acquired firms. Cross-border mergers and acquisitions by private-equity firms and hedge funds reached more than $100 billion per annum after 2003, and represented more than a quarter, on average, of global foreign direct investment flows, between 2003 and 2007.[5] The Carlyle Capital Corporation, a subsidiary of the US-based Carlyle Group, particularly active in Defense industry contracts in Iraq, was leveraged up to 32 times, or 1 dollar of capital for 32 dollars of liabilities before adverse market developments led to its liquidation in March 2008, with a $16 billion debt.[6]

Far from effective supervision, offshore financial centers in all continents were responsible for half of the activity of international banks and a third of the total of outward foreign direct investment. Their activities also had strong financial implications, since they cost in foregone taxes $350 billion, or 10 percent of US 2008 government fiscal receipts. This represents between 1.7 to 3 percent of GDP

4 www.boursomax.com 16 March 2009. According to the reference mentioned in footnote 3 above, the head of AIG Financial Products (Joseph Cassano), allegedly made $280 million in the eight years up to 2008, and after leaving the company, in February 2008, got a consultancy contract with AIG for $1 million a month. This is apparently much less than the five managers of the US biggest hedge funds, who made on average more than one billion (US$1,000 million) each in 2007 (US Congress Committee on Oversight and Government Reform: Opening Statement of Rep A. Waxman, Chairman, 13 November 2008; www.oversight.house.gov).

5 IMF (2007: 54–57). In relation to the weight of hedge funds in stock-markets transactions, see Aglietta (2008, in Artus et al., 2008) and Hubert Reynier (2008), Director of International Affairs Regulation, at the French 'Autorité des Marchés Financiers', in *Le Monde Economie*, II, 3 October 2006. Statistics on M&A can be found in the *World Investment Report*, 2008, UNCTAD, p. 6. In 2006, hedge funds drove nearly 60 percent of CDS trading volume (see Bailey et al. 2008: 33).

6 Article by Androsch, *ibid.*

in France, or the equivalent of the French annual budgetary deficit. According to Chavagneux (2009), $350 billion represents not only 10 percent of the fiscal receipts but 80 percent of the US fiscal deficit in 2008, estimated at $438 billion. As wealthy individuals in the developing world evade more than $100 billion worth of taxes in their home countries each year (Rodrick 2008), these fiscal issues are a perfect reflection of the current political order.

The crisis which extended to the whole world with the fall of Lehman Brothers investment bank in September 2008, prompted exceptional bail-out plans in the US and Europe. Rising deficits mobilized governments in the US and Europe to support banks and insurance companies. This assistance which may represent 12 percent of GDP in the US and 9.5 percent in the United Kingdom for 2009, raises again the question of this fiscal evasion which has become systemic, creating a kind of 'illegal legality', and exacerbating the speculative tendencies responsible for the local and regional financial crises since the end of the Cold War (Fabre 2003). Profits without limits, nurtured by non progressive taxes and budgetary redistribution, are a powerful creator of inequalities, and together with high incomes, which may represent a few hundred times the average salary, they also encourage speculation. Once set in motion, the spiral of strong inequalities, stimulated by the dynamics of profit maximization and generalized fiscal dumping, does not know any limits, and encourages in turn speculation.

The second side of the crisis was induced by households' indebtedness, linked to asset inflation. As Sachs (2008) underlined, 'the boom in housing and stock market prices increased US households' net wealth by around $18 trillion during 1996–2006. The rise in consumption based on this wealth', which fed global growth, notably in China, 'in turn raised house prices further, convincing households and lenders to ratchet up the bubble another notch'. Sapir (2008) has clearly shown that the gains of growth due to the 'wealth effect' of mortgage credit (under the form of *Home Equity Extraction*) explain the growth performance of the US economy between 2002 and 2007. Without the *Home Equity Extraction* contribution, US growth would have been comparable to and even less important than Eurozone growth. Since the 1980s, home equity loans were advertised by banks as a way for homeowners to "extract wealth" from their home in order to finance credit consumption. Greenspan and Kennedy (2007) estimate that homeowners 'extracted' $747 billion in net equity from their homes at the peak of the housing boom in 2005, up from $229.6 billion in 2000 and $74.2 billion in 1991.

In short, the American model of finance-led growth succeeded in resolving, by way of deregulation and mathematical formulations, one of the issues which arose in the last ten years after the Asian crisis of 1997–1998: how to give to the one percent richest people, particularly active in the financial sphere, rent-seeking incomes comparable to the beginning of the 20th century, while lending to the poor and letting them realize their dream of security by buying their homes. Finance-led growth, built on easy availability of credit, led to a high concentration of wealth and income gains in the hands of a few: between 1980 and 2006, while the share of American corporate profits going to the financial sector, rose from 16 percent to 40 percent, the share of income going to the top 1 percent of the population more than doubled, from 10 to 23 percent (Summers 2008; Johnson 2009). In 2006 alone, the value-added of the US parent companies in the finance (except depository institutions) and insurance sectors increased by 43.8 percent (Mataloni 2008). Behind all the magic of this financial alchemy, the 'shadow banking system' created according to Roubini (2008) 'a housing bubble, a mortgage bubble, an equity bubble, a bond bubble, a credit bubble, a commodity bubble, a private equity bubble, and a hedge fund bubble, which are all now bursting simultaneously.'

The growth of this shadow banking system is itself linked with the 1999 decision to repeal the Glass-Steagle Act of 1933, which effectively prohibited in the US the mixing of banking with securities and insurance businesses, and permitted the emergence of 'broad banking', that was already present in Europe. This encouraged the mixing of different functions, making loans for long-term investments, and securitization. Massive loans were accorded to hedge funds and private equity firms, as the fees earned were enormous. This may explain the extent of bad debts and the duration of the credit crunch, as these liabilities have been transferred to off-balance-sheets vehicles, probably in offshore locations. The cleansing of the banks balance sheets may require between US$3 to $4 trillion of recapitalization, three times the public-private plan sum launched by the US Treasury in March 2009.[7] It cannot be implemented until new accounting rules are put into effect at international level.

Whatever the political consequences of this systemic crisis, which will certainly come with the socialization of losses by the public authorities, it is clear that it will redesign the post Cold war geo-economic balance, perhaps in favor of Europe, but certainly in favor of East Asia, mainly China. Despite the likelihood of a lasting recession in Britain, Ireland and Spain, due to the size of their housing recessions, the State's redistributive tradition in Europe, which was being more and more discredited in Brussels as it was on the other side of the Atlantic as the main symptom of euro-sclerosis, is better suited to face the current economic crisis. Moreover, the existence of the euro, in a zone whose intra-regional trade represents 31 percent of global trade, and whose interregional trade, mainly directed toward Asia and North America, represents another 20 percent of global trade, will certainly raise its global status as a reserve currency, despite the lack of political integration in Europe. Official reserves held in Euro are 27 percent of the 2008 world total, up from 18 percent a decade ago, while the US dollar share has fallen to 63 percent from 71 percent in the same period (Chen 2009).

7 See 'The Deepening Banking Crisis', interview of Simon Johnson, Peterson Institute for International Economics, Washington, 26 January 2009.

1.2. ... versus the Chinese model of export-led growth

The rise of the economic power of East Asia, and especially China, will be the main consequence of this global crisis for a few reasons. First of all, China, with 6 percent of global GDP, and Japan, with 10 percent, are two of the four large economies having huge export surpluses, along with Germany and Saudi Arabia. China and Japan are in a position to lend to other countries, to demand a bigger share of decision-making in international organizations such as the IMF, or to create their own Asian Monetary Fund, with an US$80 billion reserve, as this idea, first launched during the Asian crisis of 1997–1998, has been revived during the fall of 2008. They are also in a position to diversify their portfolio with the fall of commodity and asset prices, which offers new business opportunities in strategic sectors corresponding to their long-term priorities such as the energy, minerals, transport, environment and health sectors.

China has bypassed Japan for the first time to become the largest holder of US Treasury securities, with $727 billion in March 2009, compared with Japan's $626 billion. China's State Administration of Foreign Exchange (SAFE) and commercial banks held $370 billion in debt issued by then struggling US mortgage giants Fannie Mae and Freddie Mac.[8] With low interest rates, it was not profitable and was even loss making for China to invest in US treasury bonds, given the gap between their low-yield and the 20 percent appreciation of the Renminbi to the US dollar since 2005. But it will be more lucrative to buy back the Chinese enterprises' shares held by US companies, and to diversify the Chinese business portfolio. China Investment Corp., the sovereign wealth fund, has incurred large unrealized losses of several billion US dollars, on its stakes in the US private equity firm Blackstone Group and in the Wall Street Bank, Morgan Stanley. It does not intend to take the same steps as Japanese banks and securities firms, which are acquiring stakes in beleaguered US financial institutions. Chinese companies prefer to make strategic investments: since the globalization of the crisis, they have already invested US$25 billion in the construction of pipelines in Russia, to insure their oil supply, more than US$ 20 billion in the Australian mining groups Rio Tinto and Fortescue metals, not to mention copper investments in Congo, oil in Sudan and Nigeria, and industrial acquisitions in Europe (Chalmin 2009).

However, the securing of adequate returns on the $2 trillion of foreign currency reserves has become a daunting task for China as the USA has become its main banker, and there are plans for the Yuan to join other international currencies to be used as foreign exchange reserves. The Chinese government has decided to allow in the next two years the Renminbi to be used for settlements with Hong Kong and Macao, and has signed settlement agreements with Russia, Mongolia, and other ASEAN countries, to use the Renminbi in bilateral trade. This progressive regional convertibility is the first step to realize the full convertibility of the currency, in order to counterbalance the likely depreciation of the US dollar in the

8 *South China Morning Post* website, Hong Kong, 20 November 2008.

coming years, which would be the most convenient way for the US government to decrease its foreign debt.[9]

Secondly, they are signs that the economic integration of East Asia, which was mainly designed to increase the export competitiveness of the region, may turn out to be more self-centered, and thus stronger, as in the case of Europe. The economic regionalization of East Asia was the unexpected result of the G7 Plaza Agreement, in 1985, whereby the forced revaluation of the Yen, and then the Korean won and the Taiwan dollar, was seen as an appropriate monetary response to the trade surpluses of these countries *vis-à-vis* the US and European markets. Facing strong export competitiveness falls, Japan and the four dragons (South Korea, Taiwan, Hong Kong and Singapore) delocalized massively towards Southeast Asia and China, which were then opening up, the manufacturing of their labor-intensive and low-added value products (toys, clothing and consumer electronics), while moving into capital-intensive and higher value-added sectors (automobiles, computers, telecom and audio-video equipment, finance etc.). This process accelerated after 1994, with the *de-facto* fixed exchange rate of the Renminbi to the US dollar, and the strong non-inflationary growth of China, which attracted MNCs. China became not only the axis of the intra-Asian division of labor, but also the world's factory, producing practically everything, except large aircrafts. It survived the Asian crisis, which destabilized for a certain period of time Southeast Asia, by adjusting its internal economy through cost cutting, the transfer of State social welfare to households, and by launching a huge program of highway construction, which now covers the entire nation.

With its accession to the WTO in 2001, a quarter of China's growth was generated by exports and investments linked to exports. But this proportion, based on national figures, is much more important, if we take into account the concentration of most of the foreign direct investment and exports in the high growth and relatively rich coastal regions, and its effects on the construction industry, services, and on inland regions, through commodities demand, outsourcing in small and medium-sized firms, employment and labor migration. The funds sent by migrant workers to their villages of origin represented 38 percent of rural income in 2008, nearly as much as the income from agricultural activities (42 percent) (Ambassade de France en Chine 2009). If we add underground lending, mainly based in coastal regions which is equivalent to almost a third of the loans extended through the banking system (Lardy 2008, Jianzhun 2008),[10] we may reasonably estimate that

9 According to Wu Xiaoling, former Vice-Governor of the Central Bank, in Xinhua, 25 October 2008. On the likelihood of an US dollar depreciation to decrease the US foreign debt, see Yu Yongding (2008) in *Caijing* (Finance Magazine), Institute of World Economics and Politics, Chinese Academy of Social Sciences, Shanghai, 17th December.

10 As for the strong bias in favor of the coastal regions, since the opening up of China in 1984, let us remember that in 2005, with 43 percent of the population, they were responsible for 62 percent of GDP, 86 percent of FDI and 93 percent of exports.

during the early years of the 2000s at least 40 percent of China's growth was directly or indirectly dependent on external demand.

From 2001 to 2007, Chinese exports, growing at an unprecedented yearly average of 28 percent, more than quadrupled while its imports more than tripled. About 45 percent of its trade receipts came from Asia in 2007, while Europe and North America each received 21 percent of China's exports. This dynamic of regional integration is even stronger in the case of Japan. More than half of its exports and nearly half of its imports are made with Asian countries, and China became its main supplier in the early 2000s, with more than 20 percent of its market share (WTO 2008).[11] So, despite an expected sharp decline of Chinese exports to Europe, North America, and to the new emerging markets of commodity exporters that it gained in the early 2000s, such as South America ($39 billion of exports in 2007), Africa ($37 billion), the Middle East ($44 billion) or the Commonwealth of Independent States (CIS; $48 billion), who are suffering from the fall in commodity prices, China has the scope to keep its export status of low-cost products in Asia, especially in Japan, South Korea, Taiwan, Indonesia, Thailand and India, and to appear more and more as an importer's market for equipment, transport goods and other technology intensive products from the USA and Europe.

Since the globalization of the crisis in September 2008, China has renewed and strengthened its relationships with the heavyweights of the Asian region, such as Japan, and South Korea, and has addressed liquidity problems in South Korea, which has seen its currency plunge, as foreign investors have fled from the country's financial markets amid the worldwide credit crunch.[12] Following an agreement between the three Central Banks, Seoul can obtain a combined total of $46 billion from Tokyo and Beijing in case of necessity. An Asian Monetary Fund with an $80 billion reserve available to fight a regional financial crisis is therefore *de facto* taking shape. What is more, China has taken decisive steps towards Taiwan, with the historic agreement of November 2008, expanding cross-straits air services to more than 20 Chinese cities, allowing direct shipping and postal links, as well as setting-up a reporting mechanism on food safety, to enforce quality control after the melamine scandal. This agreement represents a 'giant step in cross-strait relations' according to Taiwanese business leaders who are eager to enhance financial cooperation with China and to set-up a mutual mechanism to manage the strong foreign exchange reserves of the mainland, Taiwan and Hong Kong. In the trade field, there is ample range for further cooperation between the two complementary economies, since 40 percent of Taiwan's exports are shipped to China, especially under the form of processing trade for ICT industries (computers,

11 If we include re-exports through Hong Kong, the real breakdown of China's exports are in 2007, 27 percent for Europe, 22 percent for the US, 9 percent for Japan, 21.6 percent for Hong Kong, Korea and Taïwan and 3.9 percent for CIS-Ukraine (cf. *Missions économiques, MINEFI*, 17 March 2008).

12 Kyodo News Service, Tokyo, 13 December 2008; Chungang Ilbo, Seoul, 13 December 2008.

telecommunication and audio-video equipment), while China accounts for only 12 percent of Taiwan's imports. Two-way trade was $130 billion in 2007, although the traders had to go through a third territory, usually Hong Kong. The same restrictions were limiting Taiwanese investment in the mainland until the new President of Taiwan, Ma Ying-jeou lifted most of these restrictions during the summer of 2008. Around 80 percent of Taiwan's FDI is directed to China, especially in the ICT sector, which has become the driving force of Chinese exports in the early 2000s. Since the late 1980s, Taiwanese companies have pumped at least $100 billion into China, about a fifth of the total realized FDI stock. Four hundred thousand Taiwanese are officially working in China, mainly in the Shanghai (Kunshan district), Fujian and Guangdong regions, but most observers estimate they may be at least twice that number. In 2008, Taiwan-based large banks and stocks and securities firms opened representative offices in Beijing, Shanghai, Kunshan and Shenzhen and hope to quickly engage in meaningful business opportunities 'to overcome the negative effects of the ongoing financial tumult, which is not going to end anytime soon.'[13]

In short, the general concentration on China of Taiwanese businesses, eager to overcome the reduction in their export markets, may lead to the emergence of a real common market of Greater China (China, Hong Kong and Taiwan), which would have tremendous consequences on the global economic order, as well as delicate consequences on China's internal political system, which has always been based on a monopolistic approach.

1.3. China and the global crisis

This does not mean that China will not suffer from the global crisis. First of all, the general climate of increasing living standards, similar to the one prevailing on the other side of the Pacific, began to deteriorate in October 2007, two months after the subprime crisis, with the continuous fall of the Chinese stock market, by almost two thirds in the following year. This has reduced the savings of 60 million middle-class shareholders, who tended to favor investments funds and stocks instead of low-yield bank deposits in an inflationary environment. The real estate boom, which represented around 15 percent of overall investment and an important part of local authorities' revenues, began to decline, after exceptional gains in 2007. This weakness in the building industry in turn caused a slowdown in upstream industries and services, such as steel, cement, electricity, and freight (World Bank 2008).

Secondly, falling demand for exports, higher material costs, stricter labor laws adopted in 2008, and a strong appreciation by 23 percent of the Renminbi to the Euro between July and October 2008 have combined to reduce China's growth in the last quarter of 2008. The greatest impact was on the labor-intensive, small and medium-sized export-oriented enterprises, situated in the coastal areas,

13 Central News Agency Website, Taibei, 3rd, 5th and 6th November 2008.

and vulnerable to market changes. These are major employers, accounting for 70 percent of the 20 million new jobs every year.[14] In the first half of 2008, some 67,000 such companies, each with an annual turnover exceeding 5 million Yuan ($735,000) closed and laid off more than 20 million employees, according to the National Development and Reform Commission.[15] Two-thirds of toy exporters, mainly small-sized businesses situated in Guangdong province, shut down in the first nine months of 2008, according to Chinese customs officials. The Federation of Hong Kong Industries has warned that a quarter of the 70,000 Hong Kong owned firms in Southern China, which employ 10 million people, may go bust. The flows of migrant workers from inland provinces to coastal areas, is reversing. Statistics from the Ministry of Human Resources and Social Security showed that 10 million of China's total 130 million migrant workers went back jobless to their rural place of origin in 2008.[16]

But these developments, which have strong social implications in terms of employment, concern labor-intensive exports and low value-added industries, mainly based in Guangdong or in other coastal provinces (manufacturing toys, shoes, clothing, textiles, accessories, furniture etc.) which were already migrating to Cambodia, Vietnam or Bangladesh in search of lower wages. The situation is less dramatic for the higher value-added sectors, such as machinery, equipment and ICT, which have been slowing with the reduction of external demand since mid 2008. As during the Asian crisis of 1997–1998, national authorities will openly use this opportunity to restructure the economy, this time in favor of higher added value and technology intensive sectors, and to organize the return of migrant workers to their original provinces in order to participate in the development of the poorest regions (Ambassade de France en Chine 2008).

2. From Export-led Growth to Domestic Consumption-led Growth, or 'Where Have All the Savings Gone?'

In the wake of the global financial crisis, the Chinese leadership at last realized that it could no longer rely solely on exports as the engine of economic growth, and that it was urgently needed (and not only rhetorically) to boost domestic demand. This necessity, underlined long ago, became more pressing as the export led growth strategy was undermining the balance of 'Chimerica', and more recently Sino-European trade (Fabre 1994, 1996; Lardy 2006). As half of this trade is linked to FDI and outsourcing by foreign corporations in the quest for low labor costs, Chinese export competitiveness has long been based on the capacity

14 *Xinhua*, Beijing, 1 November 2008.

15 *Xinhua*, 13 December 2008. That figure does not include smaller firms, for which there are no available statistics.

16 *Xinhua*, 3 January 2009; *Xinhua*, 20,21 November 2008; *Nanfang ribao*, Guangzhou, 18 November 2008.

to discipline its workers, especially migrants, by prohibiting workers unions, and routinely violating the international agreements on workers' rights it has agreed to under the United Nations. As US and European businesses, as well as developed Asian ones, were the main beneficiaries of this situation, the USA and Europe never really raised the issue of Chinese workers' bargaining rights, which could have had resulted in a more equal income distribution in China. They preferred to focus on the question of exchange rates, and accused China of 'monetary dumping', which was just the result of severe restrictions on workers' salaries and workers' rights. As Palley (2007) has underlined, 'unions have historically been especially important since they engage in decentralized wage bargaining that tie wages to firms' productivity', and these unions are in a position to 'expand markets in developing countries, which means tackling income inequality and getting income into the right hands.' As China's huge trade surplus with the USA is more a reflection of structural issues than the under appreciation of the China's currency, it cannot be addressed by a change in relative prices. As Justin Lin, from the World Bank, has underlined in the *Wall Street Journal* (2009), an appreciation of the Yuan by as much as 40 percent would increase the price of imports into the USA, with a detrimental impact on Chinese exports, and consequently on the struggling world economy.

The Chinese leadership has chosen rural policy as the main lever of domestic demand. Rural consumption represents about a third of total consumption, although 60 percent of the population still live in the countryside. On October 12, 2008, on the thirtieth anniversary of the historic plenum, which launched Chinese reform in 1978, the Chinese Communist Party Central Committee adopted new reforms extending farmers' leases on land from the current 30-year term to an open-ended one, and protecting land-use rights, including the right of land transfer. As land works as a rural safety-net for 250 million farm households, this new policy, which may allow farmers to use their land as collateral to access credit, or to rent it when they migrate, may stimulate rural incomes thereby narrowing the gap between the rural and the urban sector, stimulating urbanization on a sound basis, and raising productivity growth. In recent years, much farmland had been abandoned or under-cultivated as 130 million migrants flocked to the cities to work in factories or construction sites. A report from Qinghua University revealed that at least 120 million farmers needed loans but only 60 percent of them were able to obtain financing. The recent injection of 130 billion Yuan ($19 billion) in the Agricultural Bank of China, China's third largest Bank, enables it to sell shares to strategic investors and to the general public, with the aim of developing an effective agricultural lending network, through its 24,000 outlets nationwide, which, until now, were mainly diverting rural savings towards urban projects.

The new rural land reform was launched as early as 2006 by a four-year joint project of the United Nations Development Program and the Chinese government, covering eight pilot provinces.[17] Throughout Chinese history, land has always been a strategic resource, as it was the main factor of production in a large population, agricultural land resource poor, country. Today, the economic potential of the transfer of land is considerable, as the value of land assets is greater than that of industrial assets: 119,000 state-owned enterprises have a book value of around $4 trillion while state-owned land is valued at more than $7 trillion.[18] Official statistics show that revenue from the transfer of land amounted in 2005 to 550.5 billion Yuan ($68.8 billion), accounting for one third of the revenue of local governments, and 3 percent of GDP. But as 'two-thirds of land is transferred far from public scrutiny', [19] the potential value of such deals may be at least twice that number ($137 billion) or 6 percent of GDP, a figure that may be compared to the share of agriculture in the GDP at the same time, around 15 percent.

Thus the importance of land requisition or of this grey market, which has developed in a context of quick urbanization, is considerable in terms of resource transfer and rent seeking. It has been the source of millions of complaints and hundreds of violent incidents, which erupted in the period 2000 to 2008 around land requisition and housing demolition and resettlement, and which was the top source of social conflict in China, opposing land grabbers (real estate developers) in collusion with local government officials, in opposition to peasants or local residents. Official figures show that more than 40 million farmers had their farmland partially or wholly used for non-farming purposes, while only six million of them, who became landless in land requisitions, have been compensated by the basic living or old age security programs.[20] Other estimates are much higher: between 80 and 100 million of rural residents, out of a total of 730 million, are landless or do not have access to enough land for subsistence.[21] The real estate boom and land rush in a context of quick urbanization, contributed significantly to social polarization, as 10 percent of the richest Chinese families now own more than 40 percent of total wealth, while the poorest 10 percent share less than 2 percent.[22] According to the newspaper columnist Yao Zhongqiu, 'land acquisition, infrastructure and real estate development contribute profits as well as astonishing economic growth, to bolster the political career of officials. A government's social responsibilities are relegated to a minor place when compared to making profit.'[23]

17 *Xinhua*, 30 December 2007; *Xinhua*, 6 November 2008; and *Xinhua*, 20 December 2006.

18 Chen Zhiwu, Yale School of Management, *South China Morning Post*, Hong Kong, 29 November 2008.

19 *Xinhua*, 22 November 2006.

20 *Xinhua*, 17 November 2006 and 29 December 2006. More than 7 million hectares, nearly 9 percent of the country's total farmland, have been taken over for industrial and other purposes, according to official data (*South China Morning Post*, 6 January 2009).

21 *Wall Street Journal*, 2 December 2008.

22 *Xinhua*, 7 January 2007.

23 Cited by Fiona Tam, *South China Morning Post*, 6 January 2009.

The economic potential of the transfer of land which may raise peasants' income and productivity through a better allocation of land, largely depends on the local authorities, who, in the absence of any independent judicial system, are responsible for implementing laws and policies, fixing the value of land, and providing appropriate documentation ensuring the rights of peasants on land. That is apparently the case for only half the peasants.[24] The paradox of this policy adopted in Beijing, is that it will deprive local governments of a part of their land revenues, which represents at least a third of their income, not to mention the hidden commissions they used to receive for commercial development.[25]

The same logic of delegation to local authorities applies to the stimulus plan, which was announced with great fanfare before the November 2008 G20 summit in Washington. Out of this four trillion Yuan ($585.76 billion) two year plan, 38 percent will go to the building of 17,000 km of new railways lines, new highways, airports and power grids, 25 percent will go to reconstruction following the snowstorms and the Sichuan earthquake of 2008, 9 percent has been earmarked for rural development and infrastructure, another 9 percent for innovation and industrial restructuring, 5 percent for the environment and sustainable development, and 4 percent for social protection. The remaining 5 percent includes spending on health, education and innovation. This stimulus package is expected to improve the infrastructure of the country and to create employment, especially in railway construction, where it would account for 6 million new jobs. However, most beneficiaries of the infrastructure spending are state-owned enterprises rather than small- and medium-sized enterprises that contribute to the largest share of industrial output and to more than 90 percent of employment, according to Prime Minister Wen Jiabao's estimates.[26] The progressive acceptance of the informal banking market, which has been tried-out in Wenzhou, Zhejiang, may help these labor-intensive companies, if the authorities carefully control the liabilities of these financial actors and the interest they can charge. As for the stimulus spending, the central government will apparently just provide less than 30 percent (1.180 trillion Yuan or $173 billion), while local governments and state companies will supply the rest. Provincial authorities have begun to compete to get a share of the pie by drawing-up investment plans that total 10 trillion Yuan ($1.5 trillion), the largest being that of Yunnan province which has drawn-up an annual investment plan of 600 billion Yuan over the next five years, more than its actual GDP. Behind such unrealistic expectations, central authorities have worries about corruption that

24 *International Herald Tribune*, 12 October 2008.

25 The property sector accounts for a quarter of Beijing's tax revenue, according to *Xinhua*, 13 January 2009.

26 For details on these estimates see *South China Morning Post*, 10 December 2008 and *Wall Street Journal*, 14 March 2009. For more on the package, see *Caijing* (Finance Magazine, 6 March 2009), and for its impact on railway construction see *South China Morning Post*, 28 November 2008, Hong Kong.

may develop with the stimulus package, and ritually call for strict control of local cadres, who were responsible for large-scale mass incidents in 2008.[27]

This plan is forecasted to contribute between 1.5 and 1.9 points of GDP growth in 2009. Other measures such as the increase in tax rebates for labor-intensive exports, or the successive large cuts in banks' interest-rates and reserve requirement ratios by the Peoples Bank of China, will improve the growth record in 2009 and 2010, but they do not provide an answer to the structural problems of the Chinese economy. While the central as well as local authorities are focused on strong investment to create economic growth and social mobility in the context of urbanization and the expansion of export markets, household consumption has continued to fall to a low level of 35.3 percent of GDP in 2007. This low propensity to spend can be viewed in conjunction with the high savings rate, which currently represents 25 percent of disposable income and 45 percent of GDP, and which feeds the trend for overinvestment through the state banking system. The restructuring of the state sector in the 1990s under Zhu Rongji, has led to the progressive transfer of health, education, welfare, pensions and housing costs to the urban households, whose motivation for saving has become precautionary in nature i.e. for retirement, illness, education of children, and unemployment purposes. Health expenses are the highest of these costs.

Hu Angang, an economist from Qinghua University, has estimated the extent of what he calls 'health poverty'. Between 1995 and 2005, the number of people suffering from illness increased by 16.5 percent, while those without social medical insurance coverage rose from 900 million to one billion, which is more than 80 percent of the population.[28] In 2004, a think-tank of China's Ministry of Health established that AIDS and Hepatitis B Infection caused by unsafe injections had caused 390,000 premature deaths. Statistics showed that 30 percent of immune injections and 50 percent of therapeutic ones were unsafe, and in western rural areas, more than 70 percent of disposable syringes for single use were reused. Of China's total medical costs, the government's input only accounted for 15 percent and patients paid 60 percent in 2005. As hospital treatment is too expensive for Chinese citizens and only about half of the urban population is covered by basic health insurance, the other half choose not to go to hospital when ill, and about a third give up hospitalization because of expensive medical costs. The medical coverage network has progressed since with a medicare system covering more than 91 percent of China's rural families who have joined the new rural cooperatives.[29] China's State Affairs Council has launched a long-awaited health reform program, which promised to allocate 850bn yuan (US$123 bn) until 2011, to expand health insurance coverage to an additional 400 million Chinese, and to give them near

27 *Financial Times*, 15 December 2008; *Xinhua*, 29 November 2008 ; Zhong Zhuwen, Renmin ribao website, 28 November 2008.

28 Zhongguo Xinwen She, 7 January 2005.

29 *Xinhua*, 5 August 2004; *Xinhua*, 8 December 2005 and *Xinhua*, 2 November 2008.

universal coverage at affordable prices. Yet 11.8 percent of household expenditure goes on health care, while 8 percent of urban household expenditure goes on education.[30]

As lower income people have a higher propensity to consume than to save, any policy aiming to increase domestic demand should relieve health care and education costs which decrease private consumption, not only for the masses of peasants but also for urban dwellers. But despite recent efforts in these fields, which are burdensome, these expenses are only a small part of the stimulus plan. Health care, social security, and unemployment welfare programs were about 15 percent of the 2007 budget and 2.4 percent of GDP, far below the percentage of other developing nations. By way of comparison, Brazil's government spends 4.7 percent of GDP on health care alone, and 5.4 percent on education, against around 3 percent for China (Chen 2008).

Besides, the situation varies greatly as more than 90 percent of these public expenses are managed by local authorities. Local governments manage 91 percent of retirement funds, 87 percent of social security, 99 percent of social assistance, 97 percent of health care, and 94 percent of education funds (Ambassade de France en Chine 2008). In reality, boosting domestic demand requires more than investment plans, as overinvestment has been a recurrent trend of China's economy in the 2000s. Otherwise, China may face the situation of post-bubble Japan in the 1990s, when ten years of public spending in infrastructure created a 'liquidity trap', unable to boost private demand. The widening income gap is responsible for the low domestic consumption rate, as most of the savings are concentrated in the hands of the urban middle class and the few hundred thousands millionaires, who will certainly benefit from the recent opening of a subsidiary of the Bank of China in Geneva, specializing in non-resident Chinese wealth management.[31] Thus, any realistic plan should address the question of income redistribution, not only by way of public goods such as health and education, but with a bold, immediate initiative, which would be able to motivate the population, and to reverse the adverse current situation.

Chen Zhiwu (2008) suggests distributing the remaining state assets equally to China's 1.3 billion citizens, by putting these assets into national wealth funds and distributing the funds to citizens at no cost, and to open the state budgeting process through public hearings in the national legislature and public participation via the media, in order to reorient public spending towards peoples' needs. This would certainly be the best plan to boost domestic demand, when one considers the institutional difficulties of land reform, but it would be a far cry from the dynamic of 'transition', which has been until now characterized by the conversion of the power of decision of the *nomenklatura* into a power of appropriation and appreciation of public assets, in industry, commerce and land. One of the

30 *Xinhua*, 21 January 2009; *Xinhua*, 7 January 2007 and National Bureau of Statistics of China 2005.

31 *Le Figaro*, 28 November 2008.

main ex advisers of former party chief Zhao Ziyang, and former premier Zhu Rongji, the economist Wu Jinglian, popularly known as 'Mr Market', has recently underlined these institutional difficulties. As corruption has infected crucial party organs including the police and the judiciary, 'if the mainland is to become fully modernized', he declared, 'it must introduce three principles: democracy, constitutionalism and the rule of law'.[32] That is word-for-word what the young Wei Jingsheng, who was sentenced to 14 years in prison, wrote in 1979 on the Beijing democracy wall, in his famous wall poster 'the fifth modernization: democracy'.

Whatever the future of Chen Zhiwu's proposition, it is certain that the stimulus plan, based on investment, will not be able to contain the dramatic reversal of the flows which have funded China's growth since the end of the Asian crisis ten years ago, and which are reflected by the return of migrant workers to the countryside. Anyway, if the government sticks to its proposals and neglects the importance of social security, people, especially lower income earners will react negatively and indeed they are already reacting. There are numerous signs that China is now entering a new phase, which has already been passed through by Taiwan and South Korea after 1986, with the revaluation of their currencies, the end of their old fears and anti-communist martial laws, and a phase of strong labor unrest in favor of a better income distribution. In Qingdao for instance, the main port of Shandong, which is the largest economic province in terms of GDP after Guangdong, there were more than 7,800 cases of labor disputes in 2008, up 140 percent from 2007. Half of these dispute cases were about wages, and a third involved social insurance and welfare.[33] Unlike in 1989, this unrest will not be limited to the cities, as in the case of the September and October 2008 strikes of cab drivers in eleven cities to cut the monthly fee they pay to their employers and limit the number of licenses issued. In October 2008, the CCP Central committee decided to enroll for regular training the weakest-link of party management, the 2,000 county-level party secretaries. The week-long program was widely interpreted as one of the latest moves to improve the performance of local officials, who 'were extensively taught on how to deal with mass incidents such as protests and strikes.'[34]

In such circumstances, it is unrealistic to wait for China to redress the world's recession. 'Chimerica' is not going to collapse, as China needs – as long as it has trade surpluses and the Renminbi is not convertible – to recycle its huge foreign exchange reserves and to make its exports to the US affordable by buying US Treasury bonds. Any massive selling of their US Treasury bond portfolio would lower the US $, and raise the relative price of Chinese exports. But Chinese officials, who have an asset portfolio estimated at $1,100 billion in the USA, are worried about the sustainability of these assets. In March 2009, after having lowered the interest rates to practically zero, the US Federal Reserve Board announced that it would buy US$300 billion in treasury bonds and US$750 billion in mortgage

32 *South China Morning Post*, Hong Kong, 3 December 2008.

33 *Xinhua*, 23 November 2008.

34 *Xinhua*, 1 December 2008.

securities over the next six months. This move will lead to an acceleration of the US money supply, and to a further depreciation of the US dollar, not to speak of inflationary tendencies. Zhou Xiaochuan, China's Central Bank Governor, has called for an alternative to the US dollar as a reserve currency, by the creation of a substitution account at the IMF, through which unwanted dollars holdings could be converted into special drawing rights (SDR), the international money created by the fund in 1969. This old idea, proposed again in December 2007 by Bergsten (2007), would certainly ease the tensions between the international status of the US dollar, and the current bad shape of the American economy.[35] The American model of finance-led growth nearly collapsed along with the shadow banking system; its rescue added to existing private debt a soaring public deficit of nearly US$ 1.5 trillion by way of loans, investments and guarantees. As Ferguson (2008b) has underlined, the Treasury may have to issue $2,200 billion new debt in 2009, and it is not surprising that the cost of insuring against a US government default has risen 25-fold in little over a year.

3. The Two Sides of the Same Coin

The problem is not reducible to an adjustment between American 'over-consumption' and Chinese 'over-saving', which will take years to take shape.[36] As noted in 2005 by *The Economist*, the entry of China's vast army of cheap labor into the global system of production and trade has modified the relative prices of labor, capital, goods and assets. It has increased the worldwide return on capital: in 2004, America's corporate after tax profits rose to their highest level as a proportion of GDP in 75 years, while the profit levels in Japan and the Euro area were close to their highest for 25 years. It has reduced the price of many consumer goods, but also the bargaining power of workers in developed economies, by the threat of offshore production. In this sense, the East Asian economies and China have exported wage deflation (the disconnection between growth, wages and productivity), which was largely responsible for developed countries' households running into debt. This point is well illustrated by Sapir (2008) in the case of France. China has also held down interest rates in rich economies, by recycling its foreign exchange reserves in Treasury bonds, indirectly creating a global liquidity

35 Zhou Xiaochuan, 'Reform the international monetary system', People's Bank of China; Bergsten C. F. 2007; www.petersoninstitute.org.

36 As reported by the *Financial Times* (14 December 2008), estimates by M. Pettis, Peking university, show that a decline in US consumption equal to 5 percent of US GDP would require an increase in Chinese consumption equal to 17 percent of Chinese GDP, or a nearly 40 percent growth in consumption.

bubble, which did not translate into goods inflation (thanks to its cheap products) but into asset inflation (real estate and stocks).[37]

Thus, credit consumption in the West largely reflects the long-term fall of wages in the sharing of profits, as well as widening income disparities. In the USA particularly, asset inflation (real estate and stocks) has been combined with the privatization of what is still referred to as public goods in most of the Euro area countries, i.e. health and education. Health insurance costs and education fees inflation accelerated the decline of savings and the demand for credit.[38] Finally, while households' total wealth is less in 2009 than it was in 2001, the average households' debt rose from 75 percent of annual disposable income in 1990 to nearly 130 percent in 2008 in the USA. According to Lardy (2009), the household debt to GDP ratio in the United States is roughly 100 percent, compared with 20 percent in the case of China.

It is striking to see how this picture looks similar to what we have observed in the case of China, where savings, and not credit, in the hands of the urban middle class, mainly finance the failure of public goods supply, such as health and education, which have been largely privatized. But apart from the obvious developmental levels of the two countries, there is a difference in the process of accumulation, which may influence future economic policies. In the USA as well as in the Euro area, the big winners of the last thirty years have been a small financial and entrepreneurial oligarchy, which, with the help of the political elite, have accumulated incomes completely disproportionate to their productivity levels, in their quest for capital profit maximization. In China however, the dynamics of accumulation have been largely under the control of the party-state oligarchy, under the form of a decentralized state capitalism. Chen Zhiwu (2008) has calculated that from 1995 to 2007, 'inflation-adjusted government fiscal revenue increased 5.7 times. In contrast, over the same period, the cumulative increase was 1.6 times for urban residents' per capita disposable income and 1.2 times for rural peasants' per capita income'. So, China's 'socialism with Chinese characteristics' is an economy where an increasing share of national income goes to the state. Here again, the disconnection between growth, wages and the level of wealth redistribution is responsible for under consumption, and overinvestment, as savings are massively reallocated through the state banking system.

Finally, the macro-economic imbalances on the two sides of the Pacific, which are reflected by over-saving and over-investment in the case of China, and credit consumption and leverage investment in the case of the USA, are two faces of

37 *The Economist* 2005. However, it is not relevant to blame China as responsible for the asset inflation in the US. As Baily et al. (2008: 38) and others rightly underline: "Without access to foreign funds, the US economy would have invested less in all kinds of capital. The problem was the diversion of too much investment into housing, that was not productive at the margin, a problem we should blame on ourselves more than on those who lent the money".

38 *Le Monde*, 6 January 2009, 8.

the same coin. They reflect the crisis of an accumulation model tailored for a financial, entrepreneurial or party-state oligarchy, which created an unsustainable model of 'growth with inequity'. The remedies adopted up to now in the West, which tended to add excessive leverage in the public sector to excessive leverage in the private sector, may have controlled the fire, but not the embers, which may inflame again if the structural question of wage deflation and the sharing of profits, which has strong social and fiscal implications, is not addressed (Ferguson 2008b). The privatization of profits and the socialization of losses have created a vicious circle of risks-transfer to the whole of society. State indebtedness will be heavier for a long time, and it will only diminish with the end of the generalized fiscal dumping.

Conclusion

'Chimerica' has been basically built on an international division of labor and capital that is no longer sustainable. On one side, the finance-led growth model has been built on the monetary supremacy of the US dollar, which has created an addiction to debt, in order to sustain a consumerist mode of living. On the other side, the export-led growth model has pushed the gigantic capacities of production, fuelled by investment from developed Asian countries and by MNCs in China, to flood the world. These capacities of production concern practically all sectors, from ICT to naval construction and aeronautics, as Boeing and Airbus have outsourced in China parts of their new programs so to reduce their production costs. In this sense, the vessel of 'Chimerica' may be heading towards twilight, but certainly not *China's* twilight, as these capacities of production will remain, and China, whatever its political and social tribulations, will climb up the technology ladder to become more and more competitive in a more and more interdependent world.

References

Ambassade de France en Chine, 2008. *Bulletin économique Chine*. Pékin: Mission économique. Novembre, 2.

Ambassade de France en Chine, 2009. *Bulletin économique Chine*. Pékin: Mission économique. Janvier, 6.

Artus, P., Betbèze, J.P., de Boissieu, C. and Capelle-Blancard, G. 2008. *La crise des subprimes*. Rapports du CAE, 78. Paris: La Documentation Française.

Artus, P. 2007. *Les incendiaires: Les banques centrales dépassées par la globalisation*. Paris: Perrin.

Baily, M.N., Litan, R.E. and Johnson, M. 2008. *The Origins of the Financial Crisis*. Paper 3, November. Washington: The Brookings Institution.

Bank for International Settlements, 2008. *Annual Report* 2002. Bâle.

Bergsten, C.F. 2007. How to solve the problem of the dollar. *Financial Times*, 11 December.
Boyer, R., Dehove, M. and Plihon, D. 2004. *Les crises financières*. Rapport au Conseil d'Analyse Economique. Paris: La Documentation Française.
Chalmin, P. 2009. L'arme des matières premières change de mains. *Le Monde Economie*, 10 Mars, 3.
Chavagneux, C. 2009. Le boom de la finance offshore. *Alternatives économiques*, 75, 44–5.
Chen, Z. 2008. China's construction fetish. *South China Morning Post*. Hong Kong, 29 November 2008 and Project Syndicate, An association of newspapers around the world, www.project-syndicate.org, November.
Fabre, G. 1994. *Integration Versus Fragmentation? A General Framework for Post Deng Xiaoping Economic Policy*, September. London: Imperial College.
Fabre, G. 1996. *Une politique économique alternative pour l'après Deng Xiaoping*. Cahiers du Centre Chine. Paris: EHESS.
Fabre, G. 2003. *Criminal Prosperity: Drug Trafficking, Money Laundering and Financial Crises after the Cold War*. London and New York: Routledge Curzon.
Ferguson, N. 2008a. *Geopolitical Consequences of the Credit Crunch*. [Online]. Available at: www.niallferguson.org [accessed: 30 September 2008].
Ferguson, N. 2008b. The age of obligation. *Financial Times,* 18 December.
Greenspan, A. and Kennedy, J. 2007. *Sources and Uses of Equity Extracted from Homes?* Discussion Paper 2007–20, March. Washington: Board of Governors of the Federal Reserve System.
IMF, 2007. *Global Financial Stability Report*. April. Washington.
Jianzhun, L. 2008. Irregular credit completely offsets the retrenchment gap. *China Economic Management Report*. July 6, Capital University of Finance and Economics.
Johnson, S. 2009. The quiet coup. *The Atlantic Monthly*. Available at: http://www.theatlantic.com/doc/200905/imf-advice [accessed: 9 August 2009].
Lardy, N.R. 2006. *China: Toward a Consumption-Driven Growth Path*. Washington: Institute of International Economics.
Lardy, N.R. 2008. *Financial Repression in China*. September. Washington: Peterson Institute of International Economics.
Lardy, N.R. 2009. *China's Role in the Origins of and Response to the Global Recession*. 17 February. Washington: Peterson Institute for International Economics.
Lin, J. 2009. Report of the conference organised by the Brooking Institution and the review *Caijing* (Finance). *Wall Street Journal*, 13 January.
Mataloni, Raymond, J., Jr, 2008. US multinational companies' operations in 2006. *Survey of Current Business*, November, 31.
Palley, T.I. 2007. Humpty Dumpty and global financial imbalances. *US-China Economic and Security Review Commission*. Project Syndicate.

Palley, T. 2008. *Speculators at the Pumps*. [Online, 26 August]. Available at: www.project-syndicate.org [accessed: 26 August 2008].

Rodrick, D. 2008. *Let Developing Nations Rule*. Project Syndicate, December. Available at: www. project-syndicate.org.

Roubini, N. 2008. *From Financial Meltdown to Global Depression?* Available at: www.project-syndicate.org.

Sachs, J. 2008. *Boom, Bust and Recovery in the World Economy*. Available at: www.project-syndicate.org.

Sapir, J. 2008. *Les sources internationales de la crise actuelle*. Novembre. CEMI/EHESS.

The Economist 2005. How China runs the world economy. *The Economist*, 30 July, 65–7.

UNCTAD. 2008. *World Investment Report*, 6.

World Bank. 2008. *Quarterly Update*. December. Beijing Office.

WTO. 2008. *World Trade Developments* 2007, 5.

Chapter 4
De Facto Trade Integration and Exchange Rate Policies in East Asia

Françoise Nicolas

Introduction

Economic integration in East Asia has proceeded along very different lines from the European Union experience. While *de facto* and *de jure* regional trade integration have gone hand in hand in the latter case, economic interlinkages have kept deepening throughout East Asia in the absence of institutionalized regionalism. Moreover, Europe has gradually emerged as a stable well-structured currency area while exchange rate policies in East Asia are both heterogeneous and uncoordinated. In Europe, monetary cooperation graduated to monetary integration because exchange rate stabilization appeared necessary for the completion of the Single Market. In other words, government-led trade integration was clearly instrumental in paving the way for monetary integration. Although such a sequence cannot be expected in East Asia, the chapter argues that *de facto* trade integration has had an impact on exchange rate policy decisions in East Asia so far and will continue to do so in the future. In this respect, the change in the nature of intra-regional trade patterns can also be expected to influence the exchange rate debate in this part of the world.

The objective of the chapter is twofold, first to explain why and how intra-regional trade patterns impact exchange rate policy decisions in East Asia, and second to examine whether and how the recent global financial crisis may change the current situation.

The remainder of the chapter is divided in four sections; the first two sections describe the evolution of trade patterns in East Asia, from the so-called 'flying geese' structure to the emergence of vertically-integrated regional production networks. In the process, the two sections propose an analysis of the impact of these trade patterns on the exchange rate choice. The next section examines the potential impact of the current global economic crisis on the regional division of labor as well as on the changing rationale for exchange rate cooperation in East Asia. A final section concludes with policy implications for the rest of the world economy, and in particular for the European Union.

1. East Asia Until the Mid-90s: Rising Intra-regional Trade Under the Dollar Peg

It is a well-known fact that despite the quasi absence of institutionalized regionalism (so-called *de jure* regional integration), economic interactions have kept deepening throughout East Asia since the 1980s. Intra-regional trade rose from 35 to 43 percent of total trade over the period 1985–1997. This is still lower than the level observed in the EU15 (with about 52 percent in 1980 rising to over 60 percent in the late 1990s) but it is increasing at a faster rate, and is quite comparable to that of the North American Free Trade Area (NAFTA, 46 percent).[1] The present section examines the links between the nature of *de facto* intra-regional trade and investment linkages and *de jure* cooperation, with a special focus on exchange rate issues.[2]

1.1. East Asia under Japanese firms' leadership

Interestingly enough, in the 1980s and early 1990s the progress in intra-regional trade remained extremely modest within the only Asian institution-based economic grouping, namely the Association of South East Asian Nations (ASEAN).[3] The expansion of intra-regional trade was at first primarily due to a sharp increase in trade linkages between Japan and the rest of East Asia incorporating ASEAN and the Newly Industrialized Economies or NIEs[4].

In East Asia, economic integration has long been a "spontaneous" process fuelled by the private sector and by the quest for efficiency on the part of multinational firms (primarily of Japanese origin), seeking to build up marketing and supply chain networks to exploit economies of scale arising from the division of labor and specialization (Barrell and Choy 2003). In contrast to what can be observed in Europe, the movement of firms to low-cost locations is more common in East Asia than in Europe where firms tend to move close to the final consumer markets. Japanese firms played a leading role in the early stages of regional integration when they established region-wide production structures, resulting in a multi-tier division of labor. This pattern corresponds to the so-called "flying geese" model,

1 Calculations based on the IMF's *Direction of Trade Statistics*. All figures on trade shares are taken from this source.

2 For further considerations on the interaction between *de facto* and *de jure* regional integration in East Asia, including the trade dimension, see Nicolas (forthcoming).

3 The bulk of ASEAN countries' trade is conducted with Asian countries, but usually outside ASEAN. The intraregional trade ratio for ASEAN increased from 16 percent in 1980 to 16.9 percent in 1990, and to about 23 percent in 2005 (IMF, Direction of Trade Statistics). However, intra-ASEAN trade as a proportion of total trade of member countries is likely to be vastly overestimated as a result of Singapore's *entrepôt* role, of the trade in petroleum products, and bilateral trade between Singapore and Malaysia.

4 Hong Kong, South Korea, Singapore and Taiwan.

with Japan as the "lead goose" which industrialized first, followed by the NIEs and eventually by the ASEAN countries. In this context, the regional organization of production is based on conventional changing comparative advantages (Athukorala and Yamashita 2005).

Japan's exports to the rest of East Asia, which was 24 percent of the total in 1980 increased to 44 percent by 1996, and its share of imports from Asia rose from 22 percent to 42 percent over the same period of time. Similar developments can be observed for South Korea, whose exports to the rest of Asia rose from 14 percent in 1980 to 39 percent in 1997.

The interactions between trade and direct investment flows account for the deepening of economic linkages in the region. Japanese firms started relocating part of their production facilities in the first-tier NIEs (Taiwan, Singapore and Hong Kong) in the early 1980s. The movement gained further momentum with the strengthening Yen in the wake of the 1985 Plaza Agreement, but the rise in labor costs in the NIEs, in parallel to ASEAN's relatively low labor and production costs, helped to divert foreign direct investment (FDI) flows toward ASEAN.[5] In a secondary move, capital started flowing from the NIEs to the new low-cost sites.[6] In these countries trade liberalization ensued largely as a result of increased confidence in outward orientation made possible by FDI flows from Japan, and eventually Hong Kong, Taiwan and South Korea. This move was clearly instrumental in fuelling the development of regionalization in East Asia.

As a result of these tight interconnections, East Asia was perceived (and rightly so) as a relatively coherent region prior to the 1997–98 financial crisis. While this pattern of interdependence was part and parcel of the so-called East Asian miracle, it eventually proved to be negative as financial difficulties easily spread from one country to another at the time of the financial crisis.

1.2. The rationale for the de facto dollar peg

The rising trade integration highlighted above was associated in East Asia with a persistently high level of outward-orientation, making the region less economically self-contained than Europe (Glick 2005). In other words East Asia was at the time substantially dependent on the rest of the world, with obvious implications in terms of exchange rate policy.

During this first pre-1997 crisis period, intra-regional exchange rate stability prevailed by chance rather than by design. Because of their strong export-orientation (sometimes referred to as export fetishism), East Asian economies were faced with a prisoner's dilemma. Although domestic macroeconomic conditions should have induced them to let their currencies appreciate, they chose to intervene to

5 A number of pull factors also played a role, in particular a stable macroeconomic environment and the increased liberalization of ASEAN economies.

6 The loss of preferential access to major developed markets for the NIEs is an additional factor increasing the available supply of FDI (OECD 1999).

avoid an appreciation lest they might lose competitiveness *vis-à-vis* their major regional partners. They thus all ended up managing their exchange rates and *de facto* pegging their currencies to the dollar.

As rightly pointed out by Jomo (1998: 1570), despite "official fictions of exchange rates moving with the baskets of the currencies of major foreign trading partners", in reality East Asian currencies were pegged to the dollar. The effective weight of the dollar in the basket of currencies was so high that exchange rate policies can be characterized as an implicit peg to the dollar. This is confirmed by a number of authors who showed that the weight of the dollar in the reference basket of East Asian economies was much higher than what would have been implied by trade flows (Goldberg and Klein 1997, Frankel and Wei 1994). As a result of these policies, most East Asian currencies proved extremely stable *vis-à-vis* the dollar in nominal terms for most of the period 1985 through August 1997; by contrast, they depreciated *vis-à-vis* the Yen and most European currencies over the period 1985–95, and appreciated in the last two years before the Asian financial crisis.

Intra-regional exchange rate stabilization was deemed important for Asia at the time in order to avoid the distorting impact of exchange rate fluctuations on competition for exports to important third markets. For instance, ASEAN countries were mutual competitors on third markets: they used to compete in sectors such as textiles and apparel and machinery and electrical appliances in the US market, while they competed in machinery and electrical appliances in the Japanese market. Preventing the exchange rate from appreciating *vis-à-vis* the dollar was certainly instrumental in maintaining export competitiveness in East Asian economies when the dollar was weak relative to both the Yen and most European currencies, namely during the decade following the Plaza agreement. The Yen appreciation turned out to be positive for those economies which pegged their currencies to the dollar because it made their products more price-competitive *vis-à-vis* competing Japanese products.

Pegging (like fixing) the exchange rate also reflects the search for more stability, a factor deemed fundamental to attract foreign investors. This objective appeared of the utmost importance for Southeast Asian countries whose major objective was to boost FDI-related exports. The *de facto* dollar peg strongly influenced trends in FDI in the four major ASEAN countries (Indonesia, Malaysia, Philippines and Thailand).[7] Pegging to the dollar at a time when the Yen was appreciating *vis-à-vis* the dollar undoubtedly helped maintain FDI inflows from Japan. Goldberg and Klein (1997) underline the importance of pegging to the dollar for the expansion of trade and FDI linkages within the region, which is one feature of the so-called Asian miracle.[8]

7 For more details, see OECD (1999).

8 The tight interdependence which had developed between the economies of the region turned out to be a liability because these links provided a channel for the contagion to spread throughout the whole of East Asia, making the recovery process more problematic.

Although this exchange rate policy served most countries in the region rather well for some time, it became increasingly rigid and monetary authorities proved unable to adapt to changing circumstances. Such was the case because of the pressures exerted by various groups with vested interests in the preservation of the peg.

2. East Asia From the Mid-90s Onwards: The Rise of China

The lack of effective cooperation within the region, and a non-optimal way of pegging the currencies explain the 1997–98 meltdown in a context of insufficiently supervised banking. Also, the crisis exposed the limitations of the traditional dollar tracking exchange rate policy (Barrell and Choy 2003) and prompted interest in exchange rate cooperation. The positive side of the *de facto* dollar peg in most countries of the region was the absence of beggar-thy-neighbor devaluations, while the negative side was susceptibility to contagion. The contagion mechanism and the spillovers underline the regional dimension of the crisis and the need for a collective approach.[9] While it seemed to be in the interest of all the countries in the region to opt for more active cooperation, all efforts undertaken at the time (such as the Chiang Mai Initiative) fell short of any genuine monetary cooperation (Nicolas 2008). It will be argued below that the rise of China played an important role in explaining the absence of monetary cooperation.

2.1. The emergence of the East Asian "integrated circuit"

Despite the disruptions caused by the 1997–98 financial crisis, intra-regional trade and investment kept deepening in East Asia, in the absence of any formal arrangement. The share of intra-regional exports and imports reached 57 percent in 2006.[10] Since the mid-1990s, the further rise in intra-regional trade has been fuelled by the integration of China in regional production networks as well as by the increasing fragmentation of the production process in a number of important sectors such as the electronics sector.

As a result of its open-door policy, China has been increasingly integrated with the global trading system and has become the fourth largest trading nation worldwide. A major consequence of China's economic "normalization" is its active participation in the regional production networks. The country's exports and imports have surged since the early 1990s, with the USA, Japan and the EU

9 It is worth stressing at this stage that China was not part of the so-called Asian miracle. Moreover, China remained unscathed by the 1997–98 Asian financial crisis thanks, in particular, to the controls it maintained on capital flows.

10 Compared to 43 percent before the crisis.

(in that order) as major export destinations, and with Japan, the EU and emerging East Asia as major suppliers of imports.[11]

The specific role played by China in the expanding regional production networks shapes the pattern and nature of intra-Asian trade. A substantial share of Chinese imports from the rest of the region (from industrial and emerging economies alike) is for processing and re-exporting.[12] China primarily imports electronic goods (electronic components and computer equipment) from the major ASEAN member countries (with the exception of Indonesia). In the latter industry, there have been major changes in the structure of imports from ASEAN, with a rise in the share of machinery and electrical goods, mainly components and parts. The trade structure between ASEAN and China is characterized by intra-industry trade: computers, machinery and electrical equipment make up 38.2 percent of ASEAN's exports to China and 46.6 percent of ASEAN's imports from China (Hefeker and Nabor 2002: 14). Similarly South Korean electronic exports to China have shifted from consumer electronics to electronic components, telecommunication equipment and more recently computer equipment. These are clear indications of the existence of cross-border production-sharing systems based on the fragmentation of production processes[13] in sectors which are particularly amenable to a modularization (or fragmentation) of the production process. As a result, the rise of China has been accompanied by an explosive increase in the trade of machinery parts and components which accounts for close to 65 percent of East Asia's total intra-regional trade in 2007.

It is worth stressing at this stage, however, that the rise in intra-East Asian trade has been much stronger in imports than in exports,[14] thus reflecting the persistence of a strong outward orientation for the region as a whole despite the rise in intra-regional trade. Moreover, the share of components in intra-regional imports is much larger and has increased at a faster rate in total imports compared to exports, reflecting the greater reliance of the region on the rest of the world as a market

11 Over the period 1990–2006, the share of East Asia as a destination for Chinese exports has decreased (from 67 to 39 percent) while its share as a source of imports has risen (from 55.4 to 58 percent). In 2003, China surpassed Japan as the major export destination for East Asian countries: China imported $168 billion from this region and Japan only $152 billion (IMF, Direction of Trade Statistics).

12 On the export side, so-called processing trade accounts for the bulk of China's trade. In the electronics and information/technology (IT) industry processing trade has accounted for approximately 90 percent of China's total exports since 1995 (Gangnes and van Asche 2008).

13 By contrast to what can be observed in other regions, the geographic coverage of these regional networks is quite large with most East Asian countries being involved, with the exception of the least advanced of them, such as the CMLV countries (Cambodia, Myanmar, Laos and Vietnam).

14 In 2006, intra-regional exports accounted for 52 percent of total East Asian exports and intra-regional imports for close to 60 percent of total imports (IMF, Direction of Trade Statistics).

for final goods. The USA (and to a lesser extent the EU) remains a very important partner for a number of East Asian economies at the individual country level, and trade among East Asian countries is largely based on the segmentation of the production process with the USA and the EU as the ultimate destinations. Moreover, as explained by Thorbecke and Yoshitomi (2006: 6) "starting in the 1990s, China also became an important recipient of FDI. After the Asian financial crisis of 1997–98, new flows to Southeast Asia slowed. Meanwhile, China's accession to the WTO in 2001 increased investor confidence and resulted in a surge of investment." These two developments are closely related since foreign invested enterprises (FIEs) account to a large extent for China's stellar export performance. As stressed by Gilboy (2004), in 2003 foreign firms accounted for 79 percent of China's exports in high-tech sectors such as industrial machinery, 92 percent of its exports of computers, components, and peripherals and 74 percent of its $89 billion exports of electronics and telecommunications equipment.

The reorganization of the production process at the regional level has given rise to a triangular trade pattern, with parts and components being produced in countries such as Japan, Taiwan, South Korea, even Malaysia (and other ASEAN countries where multinational corporations – MNCs – are located), and eventually exported to China (and some ASEAN countries such as Vietnam or the Philippines) for assembling, with the USA, the EU and Japan as final destination markets.[15] This has been described as the "Asian integrated circuit". The existence of such an indirect trading relation is confirmed by Figure 4.1 which shows the very close correlation between the change in South Korea's exports to China and that of China's exports to the USA.[16] This is one of the major reasons why East Asia could not easily decouple from the rest of the world.

As a result of China's integration in the regional production networks as a low end assembling and exporting platform, Chinese value-added in processed exports is extremely low.[17] According to various estimates (Koopman, Wang and Wei 2008) the share of domestic content in China's processed exports is about 25 percent, and it can even drop to 20 percent in sectors that are likely to be labeled as relatively sophisticated such as computers, telecommunication equipments and electronic devices. Lastly, FIEs also tend to have lower domestic content in their exports than do Chinese domestic firms. As explained below this impacts directly on the exchange rate policy choice debate.

15 The high complexity of the resulting networks is underlined by Thorbecke (2006).

16 This is in line with the idea that external demand is a major determinant of Chinese imports.

17 The fragmentation of the production process has led to a redistribution of industrial activities within the region: the high value-added stages of production (both upstream – conception and development of prototypes, etc. – and downstream – brand and services) remain in the most advanced economies, while low value-added stages (assembling) are relocated in China.

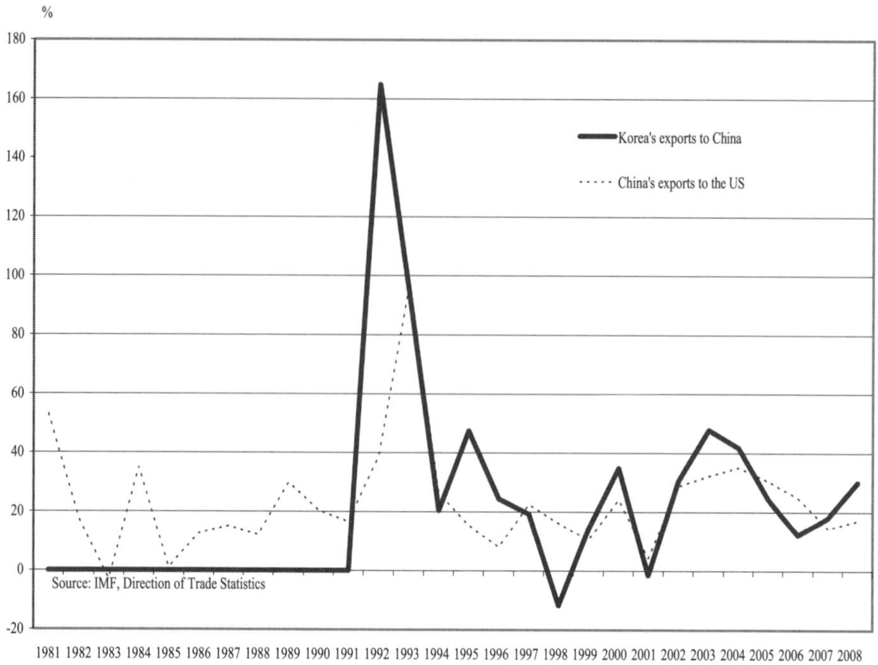

Figure 4.1 Changes in China's and Korea's exports
Source: Direction of Trade Statistics, IMF.

2.2. Implications for exchange rate policy

East Asia's current experience with trade integration departs from Europe's experience on two major counts. First, the rise in intraregional trade is still associated with a strong outward orientation. Although intra-regional trade is on the rise in East Asia, exports to the rest of the world remain extremely dynamic. Second, economic integration in East Asia is increasingly based on intensive vertical intra-industry (even intra-product) trade.[18] East Asian countries exchange primarily intermediate products, parts and components while consumer goods only account for a marginal share. By contrast, intra-industry trade within the EU15 is primarily horizontal in nature with countries of similar development levels and of similar productive structures exchanging end-use products with varietal differences, in particular differentiated types of consumer goods, such as automobiles. The rationales for intra-industry trade in these two configurations are totally different: in the latter case (EU15), firms seek to satisfy consumers' love for variety, while in the former (East Asia) firms take advantage of the differences in factor endowments prevailing between developing, emerging and

18 East Asian intra-industry trade is comparable to intra-industry trade between the USA and Mexico.

industrial economies and fragment the production process accordingly.[19] As a result, the European experience with exchange rate coordination is of limited value, as explained below.

As suggested by Mundell (1961) in his optimum currency area theory, two countries may be induced to form a monetary area or to stabilize their bilateral exchange rates either if they are unlikely to be subject to asymmetric shocks (in other words if they do not need the exchange rate as an adjustment instrument) or if they have other adjustment instruments at hand (such as labor or capital mobility).

When trade intensification leads to inter-industry specialization, it is traditionally thought to exacerbate cyclical asymmetries, thus enhancing the case for flexible exchange rates as a means of adjustment. In contrast, when the increase in trade gives rise to intra-industry specialization, it is expected to foster business cycle synchronization, making the case for flexible exchange rates less compelling (and the case for fixed exchange rates more compelling) because the chance of asymmetric shocks is very low. The former situation usually prevails with economies at different levels of development, while the latter is more common among economies at similar levels of development (as in the case of the EU15).

In East Asia, given the intra-regional pattern of production described earlier, the implications in terms of exchange rate policy are more complex. First, intra-industry trade prevails although the economies concerned are rather dissimilar in terms of levels of development, leading to potential diverging interests. Moreover, as stressed earlier, intra-regional trade in East Asia is dominated by vertical intra-industry trade and not by horizontal intra-industry trade. As a result, intra-regional trade flows can be shown to be relatively insensitive to exchange rate changes under specific circumstances. Empirical evidence by Obashi (2008) confirms that intra-East Asian trade in parts and components is far less sensitive to exchange rate fluctuations than trade in finished products[20] suggesting that exchange rate stabilization is less of an issue (and priority) in this part of the world. Lastly, the persistent dependence on external markets despite a rise in intra-regional trade makes the situation even more complex.

The specific position of China within the East Asian integrated circuit and the magnitude of processing in China's total trade impose different constraints on the conduct of its exchange rate policy, compared to other countries in the region. While pegging to the dollar (or manipulating the currency in order to avoid an

19 With the increase of the EU to 27 member countries, heterogeneity can be expected to rise within the EU. The pattern of intra-industry trade is likely to evolve, with a rise in the fragmentation of the production process. As Arndt (2001: 14) aptly puts it 'the major gains from entry will not come from freer trade along established patterns but from the reorganization of production and the consequent integration of those economies into the production networks of the EU." As a result, there may be a rising convergence in the way production networks are organized in East Asia and in the EU27.

20 This has probably to do with the substantial intra-firm nature of such trade.

appreciation) may still be appropriate for most East Asian economies which seek to preserve their competitiveness,[21] it is more debatable for China. First, given the importance of processing in China's trade, a unilateral appreciation of the renminbi *vis-à-vis* the US dollar is unlikely to have a large impact on China's exports to the US because the loss of competitiveness of Chinese exports will be partially offset by the decline in inputs costs resulting from the renminbi appreciation against East Asian component suppliers. By the same token, if the renminbi depreciates both *vis-à-vis* the dollar and *vis-à-vis* the currencies of the component-supplying countries, the gain in competitiveness on the US market will be offset by the rise in input costs but there will be no major loss in competitiveness (Thorbecke 2006, Rahman and Thorbecke 2007, Cheung, Chinn and Fujii 2009). Of course the situation would be different if ordinary exports were dominant; in the latter case a renminbi appreciation is found to cause a large decline in ordinary exports.[22]

Results by Garcia-Herrero and Koivu (2007 and 2009) are partly in contradiction with this hypothesis. They show that a renminbi's appreciation impacts Chinese exports negatively while also depressing Southeast Asian exports to China. This suggests that Chinese imports from Southeast Asia are more sensitive to lower external demand induced by a real appreciation of the renminbi than to a rise in purchasing power. It remains, however, that the negative impact of a renminbi's appreciation on some Southeast Asian economies would, in principle, be larger if Southeast Asian currencies were to follow the renminbi's upward trajectory.

As a matter of fact, if the renminbi and the currencies of the component supplying countries appreciate together *vis-à-vis* the dollar, the traditional negative impact of an appreciation will be felt on Chinese processed exports without any offsetting mechanism (Rahman and Thorbecke 2007). This situation may be particularly negative for other East Asian economies which may be losing on both fronts (through the fall of their exports to China and through the fall of their own exports to the rest of the world).

The pivotal role now played by China in the region suggests that the need for exchange rate co-operation/stabilization *vis-à-vis* the currencies of the final markets is probably stronger for East Asian economies (excluding China) and that the appropriate anchor remains the dollar, or a basket including the dollar, the euro and possibly the Yen. In this context some flexibility in the dollar/renminbi exchange rate may turn out to be less problematic than often claimed. What is certain is that East Asian economies do not have a strong interest in having their currencies move in line with the renminbi.

Intra-East Asia (excluding China) cooperation is desirable but difficult to obtain because of the persistent prisoner's dilemma configuration highlighted earlier. In spite of various post-crisis financial cooperation schemes in the region

21 This is referred to as the "fear of floating" or rather the "fear of appreciation" (Pontines and Rajan 2008).

22 Such differentiated impacts are obtained by Marquez and Schindler (2006), and Thorbecke and Smith (2007).

(such as the Chiang Mai Initiative in particular), there is currently no formal effort at exchange rate coordination among East Asian economies. Not much has been done in concrete terms beyond discussions and consultations about the feasibility, difficulties and challenges of going ahead with monetary integration (Nicolas 2008). Until recently, despite allegations to the contrary,[23] most East Asian countries tended to continue to smooth their exchange rates against the dollar. As a result, there was an apparent return to the *de facto* dollar peg that prevailed prior to the crisis in a number of countries in the region, as well as a more formal peg in some others, in particular in Malaysia (Volz 2007). A major benefit of the *de facto* dollar peg is to help maintain a consistent exchange rate policy throughout the region and thus to avoid beggar-thy-neighbor phenomena. Yet this convergence (or quasi-coordination) still prevails by chance rather than by design and is thus vulnerable to major external shocks. Although a number of signs have suggested that exchange rates are increasingly managed more flexibly, this move was not matched by a rise in regional coordination and individual strategies remained the norm.

3. Crisis-induced Changes in Regional Production Networks and Exchange Rate Policies

The present global economic crisis can be expected to induce major changes in the way the world economy operates, with East Asia as a case in point. In particular the crisis may pave the way for a deep shift in strategy leading to new conditions for monetary cooperation in East Asia.

3.1. The East Asian version of the crisis

With the bankruptcy of Lehman Brothers in September 2008, the then exclusively US sub-prime credit crisis was turned into a global financial and economic crisis. While there were initially good reasons to believe that most East Asian economies would remain unscathed, in particular because of the low exposure of their banks to the so-called sub-prime credits, most East Asian economies were severely hit by the turmoil with sharp drops in their growth rates.

The major channel of contagion was through the real economy and through trade, and the existence of regional production networks proved to be key in this development.[24] In contrast to what a number of people have argued, East Asia could not remain immune to the global financial and economic turmoil and the

---

23 A number of countries in the region have officially adopted a flexible exchange rate since the financial crisis.

24 Another channel of contagion is FDI on which East Asian economies tend to be heavily dependent. At the time of writing, i.e. summer 2009, foreign investors tend to adopt a wait and see attitude and contribute to holding back economic activity.

so-called "decoupling" hypothesis was soon found to be a myth. This argument for decoupling, which is essentially based on the traditional notion of horizontal specialization (Athukorala and Kohpaiboon 2009), is primarily founded on the observation that the share of intra-regional trade in East Asia's total trade has risen significantly since the 1997–98 crisis and that the share of extra-regional trade has fallen accordingly, together with the belief that business cycle co-movements are a function of trade linkages.[25]

In reality, as explained earlier, the sharp rise in intra-Asian trade has been fuelled by rapidly growing trade in parts, components and intermediate products that is a reflection of greater vertical specialization and the dispersion of production processes across borders. Moreover, the rise in intra-East Asian trade has been much stronger in imports than in exports, thus reflecting the persistence of a strong outward orientation for the region as a whole. Because the USA was still China's main export market, it should not have come as a surprise that the collapse in US demand immediately impacted the Chinese economy. In this respect, the current global economic crisis hit export-dependent China much harder than the 1997–98 Asian financial crisis. This direct impact was soon followed by an indirect one on the rest of East Asia. The production networks are organized in such a way in East Asia that a drop in the demand for final goods could be expected to reverberate on the whole production chain, including assemblers and parts suppliers in the rest of the region (Thorbecke 2008). The remarkably synchronized nature of the trade contraction across East Asian countries is consistent with their respective common positions within regional production networks.

Interestingly enough, the drop in China's imports from the rest of East Asia proved to be much sharper than the drop in its exports to the USA (Athukorala and Kohpaiboon 2009). This can be explained by a large de-stocking of imported parts and components by Chinese firms in anticipation of a protracted slack in the demand for processed exports.

All East Asian countries have not been affected to the same extent by the slowdown in Chinese imports. Taiwan, South Korea and Japan have suffered the highest rates of contraction in exports to China compared to the other countries in the region reflecting their greater dependence on that market.

---

25 Representative of this view are statements by Anderson (cited in Eichengreen and Park 2008: 11) about China, to the effect that "there is no reason to argue over whether the mainland is decoupling from the global cycle – as far as macro growth is concerned the economy is and always has been effectively "decoupled", and China has little to fear from a global demand slowdown." It is worth stressing that this argument had proven to be true in the early 1990s when China remained unscathed by the US recession. This time around however, the situation is different.

3.2. East Asia's response to the crisis: a possible shift in development and growth strategies

In East Asia, as in the rest of the world, the immediate response to the economic slowdown took the form of standard stimulus packages. In a longer-term perspective, however, another part of the response lies in potentially fundamental shifts in economic strategies.

The present global economic crisis will no doubt induce major changes in the way the world economy operates. In the EU, a major challenge has been to define the most appropriate cooperative response to the financial difficulties. In East Asia, the challenge is substantially different: while the region spent the last 30 years building up its global supply chain to cater to Western consumers' needs, the crisis points to the need to accelerate the development of individual Asian markets as well as of a strong intra-Asian market. In parallel, the alleged surplus savings, which Asia is being criticized for,[26] should be increasingly channeled within the region rather than outside. These changes may imply major shifts in the direction of East Asian countries' development strategies as well as in the nature and form of intra-regional economic linkages.

A major lesson to be derived from the current global economic crisis and from its contagion to East Asia is the need to reduce the region's vulnerability to external demand shocks. In addition, as aptly stressed by Lamberte (2009), Asia has never been able to pull itself out of recession through export growth at a time of weak growth in the USA. For Asia, there is no alternative other than to change its growth strategy. As explained by Masahiro Kawai in a speech delivered at the Asian Development Bank Institute (ADBI) in July 2009 "Asian economies benefited tremendously from export-led growth centered on US and European markets in recent decades. This growth model can no longer be relied upon to sustain the region's economic growth beyond the crisis."[27] A major post-crisis objective is to turn the region into an integrated consumer market. This would definitely contribute to shield the region against another global crisis since an expanded East Asian market would cushion it against falls in global trade.

In response to the current crisis, East Asian economies are indeed starting to take the appropriate steps to shift partially away from export-led growth to more balanced growth strategies giving higher priority to the promotion of domestic and regional demand, as well as of intra-regional trade of final-demand goods. By shifting their export-led production structure away from the advanced economies to the regional market, East Asian economies will be given opportunities to expand trade and investment in unexplored and potentially strong markets such as China,

26 This refers to the "savings glut hypothesis" (developed by Ben Bernanke in particular), according to which the US current account deficit was driven by a saving glut in the rest of the world, in particular in China.

27 Available at: http://www.adbi.org/files/speech.2009.16.07.welcome.remarks.kawai.gfc.architecture.pdf.

India or the whole of East Asia. The development of an Asia-wide consumer market requires finding effective ways to mobilize Asia's high level of savings to support spending in the region. This includes further promoting the development of a regional bond market and taking appropriate steps to facilitate funds transfers among Asian countries.[28]

Although the dependence on exports and foreign investment is often deemed to be a source of vulnerability that needs to be corrected, a point of clarification is in order as to what is being meant by the need to rebalance growth. Strengthening domestic demand does not imply abandoning the export-led growth strategy altogether (He, Cheung and Chang 2007) but merely requires a better balance between the different engines of growth. This implies in particular removing obstacles to stronger domestic spending (by building stronger social protection systems for instance), altering the composition of aggregate demand in favor of domestic demand, and facilitating changes in the production structure in favor of non-tradable goods and services.

3.3. Post-crisis intra-regional trade and investment linkages

The most dramatic impact of the current crisis can probably be expected by China, with the expansion of its domestic market and the upgrading of its productive structure.[29] These developments will have two major consequences for the rest of the region: first the outward orientation of the region as a whole will decrease, and secondly intra-regional competition is likely to increase.

More competition can be expected between China and some advanced East Asian economies as a result of China's upgrading. As a result of the increasing domestic sourcing by Chinese firms, there will be less systematic complementarity between China and its neighbors, and, in particular, the presence of FIEs will be less important in China, or at least their role will be less substantial in China's export performance. As a result, competition is likely to increase as complementarity declines.

In addition, if China's upgrading strategy succeeds, the level of Chinese value-added is likely to rise in a number of sectors. As a result, the breakdown of Chinese exports between processed exports with low domestic value-added and ordinary exports can be expected to tilt inexorably in favor of the latter rather than the former. This change in the pattern of Chinese exports will be accompanied by the rising influence of bilateral exchange rates on Chinese exports. As shown by Thorbecke and Zhang (2008), the impact of bilateral exchange rate changes is

28 The ADB-sponsored Asian Bond Market Initiative goes precisely in this direction.

29 The objective to move away from export-led growth was already part of the 11th Five-Year Plan issued in 2006. The recent session (March 2009) of the National People's Congress has made clear that China is not backing down from this plan.

indeed more substantial in the case of labor-intensive and ordinary exports than in the case of processed exports.

At the same time, the gradual emergence of an East Asian consumer market will be associated with a decline in extra-regional export dependency (or in outward orientation). A decline in Chinese exports will further strengthen the rising importance of bilateral exchange rates. Another impact of the shift in China's development strategy is the potential gradual erosion of regional production networks with a rise in domestic-sourcing. Although regional production networks will certainly not be dismantled, their importance is likely to decline and, more importantly, the markets for end-products will no longer be located primarily outside the region. Even before the outbreak of the current global financial crisis, a number of developments hinted at the gradual erosion of the Asian integrated circuit (Cui and Sayed 2007), with export-oriented Chinese firms increasingly seeking to source domestically rather than abroad.

All these developments point to a much stronger need for exchange rate cooperation and stabilization.

3.4. Implications for exchange rate cooperation in East Asia

As East Asian economies gradually shift from a primarily export-driven growth strategy to a domestic (or regional) demand-driven strategy, they will also have to opt for more exchange rate flexibility *vis-à-vis* the rest of the world. Yet they will have to do it in a coordinated manner, so as to be able to maintain intra-regional stability. In the case of East Asia, the need to contribute to correct unsustainable financial global imbalances may thus turn out to be a strong incentive to go ahead with closer regional economic cooperation.

With the expansion of a region-wide consumer market, the importance of intra-regional exchange rate coordination will automatically rise. With the objective of completing an integrated East Asian market gaining ground, swings in bilateral exchange rates within the region can be expected to be particularly detrimental. First, in the absence of cooperation, the risk is high that countries may engage in beggar-thy-neighbor policies. Secondly, exchange rates can also be used to enhance a country's attractiveness for foreign investors, also leading to beggar-thy-neighbor policies.

In addition, the development of a region-wide consumer market may be facilitated by the creation of a region-wide free trade agreement (East Asian Free Trade Agreement). While this was not perceived as necessary so far, given the nature of intra-regional trade, the case for an FTA is made potentially more compelling under these new circumstances. If such were the case, the pressure for intra-regional exchange rate stabilization would further intensify since exchange rate disagreements are known to be detrimental to the successful development of free trade agreements (Fernandez-Arias, Panizza and Stein 2002).

So far, the division of labor within the region has been based on the complementarity of trade based on vertical integration. In the wake of the current crisis, however, trade patterns in East Asia can be expected to become increasingly competitive. As a result, divergent movements in exchange rates in the region can be highly disruptive and conflictual. In addition, empirical evidence shows that such movements can become particularly intensive at times of severe external shocks and instability of trade and capital flows. In particular some countries may be tempted to respond by beggar-thy-neighbor exchange rate policies.

For all these reasons, it is important to engage in intra-regional consultations on exchange rate policies and to explore more durable regional currency arrangements. A further implication of the crisis is the perceived need by China to shift away from an exclusive dollar peg since the USA will no longer be the major outlet for Chinese exports. Overall, in the wake of the crisis there is a much stronger case for exchange rate coordination in order to avoid beggar-thy-neighbor policies.

4. Conclusions and Policy Implications

East Asia is unlikely to emerge in the near future as a coherent and a well-structured institutional grouping comparable to the EU. In addition, because of the difficulties highlighted earlier, the pursuit of regional integration cannot be taken for granted in East Asia, and the exact shape that formal regional cooperation may take is still to be defined.

However, with the emergence of a more inward-oriented East Asian market, the conditions for institutional cooperation will no doubt improve and the relationships with the rest of the world will no doubt become increasingly competitive.

This change will have different sets of implications for the rest of the world and in particular for the "West". First, the emergence of East Asia as a better structured economic bloc will challenge mainstream economic thinking. Because it is unique, the East Asian experience will deeply affect the way of looking at, and thinking about, regional economic integration. In East Asia, *de facto* trade integration initially fuelled by the expansion of regional production networks and eventually by deepening intra-regional competition seems to pave the way for monetary cooperation. In the EU by contrast, *de jure* economic integration prevailed ahead of, or together with, de facto integration and *de jure* trade integration went hand in hand with *de jure* monetary cooperation.

Secondly, and more importantly, policy responses in the "West" will need to be adapted to those changing circumstances and to the rise of East Asia as an increasingly independent and self-sustained actor. The plausible gradual erosion of the importance of the dollar is one possible consequence of these new circumstances. In early 2009, there have been repeated calls in East Asia for a major reform of the international currency system to reduce dependency on the US dollar.[30] In particular it was suggested that the IMF's Special Drawing Rights should be used to settle international trade payments as a substitute for the US

30 The People's Bank of China's Chairman launched a proposal along these lines.

dollar. Beyond exclusively monetary considerations, the rise of the East Asian bloc as both a competitor as well as a market will also deeply affect the way Western economies interact with it.

Lastly, and as a corollary, the organization of global economic governance will also be substantially affected by the emergence of East Asia as a partner on equal footing with its two major Western partners. The participation of four major East Asian economies (China, Japan, South Korea and Indonesia) in the G20 is indicative of the shift in the global economic balance of power. It remains to be seen however, whether East Asia will manage to speak with one voice in the absence of a full-fledged regional organization. If the EU's experience is any guide, this is certainly a challenging task. Will East Asia be up to the task ? Only the future can tell.

References

Ando, M. and Kimura, F. 2003. The Formation of International Production and Distribution Networks in East Asia. *NBER Working Paper*, No 10167, December.

Ando, M. and Kimura, F. 2008. Fragmentation in East Asia: Further Evidence. *Mimeo*, January.

Arndt, S. 2001. Regional Enterprise in Preference Areas. *Mimeo*, July.

Arndt, S. 2005. Cross-Border Production Sharing and Exchange Rates in East Asia. *Mimeo*, July.

Arndt, S. 2008. Production Networks and the Open Macro Economy. *Singapore Economic Review*, 53(3), 509–21.

Athukorala, P.-C. and Arshanun, Kohpaiboon. 2009. Intra-Regional Trade in East Asia: The Decoupling Fallacy, Crisis, and Policy Challenges. *Working Papers in Trade and Development*, No 9, ANU, Canberra, August.

Athukorala, P-C. and Yamashita, N. 2005. Production Fragmentation and Trade Integration: East Asia in a Global Context. *Mimeo*, Australian National University, January.

Barrell, R. and Choy, A. 2003. Economic Integration and Openness in Europe and East Asia. *Mimeo*, NIESR, March.

Bénassy-Quéré, A. and Lahrèche-Révil, A. 2003. Trade Linkages and Exchange Rates in Asia: The Role of China.CEPII Working Paper No. 2003–21.

Cheung, Y.-W., Chinn, M. and Fujii, E. 2009. China's Current Account and Exchange Rate. *CESifo Working Paper*, No 2587, March.

Cui, L. and Syed M.H. 2007. The Shifting Structure of China's Trade and Production. *IMF Working Paper* No. 07/214, September.

Dean, J., Fung, K.C. and Wang, Z. 2008. How Vertically-specialized is Chinese Trade. *BOFIT Discussion Papers*, Bank of Finland Institute for Economies in Transition, No 31, December.

Eichengreen, B. and Park, Y-C. 2008. Asia and the Decoupling Myth. *Mimeo*, May.

Fernandez-Arias, E., Panizza, U. and Stein, E. 2002. Trade Agreements, Exchange Rate Disagreements. *Mimeo*, Inter-American Development Bank.

Frankel, J. and Wei, S.-J. 1994. Yen Bloc or Dollar Bloc?: Exchange Rate Policies of the East Asian Economies, in Ito, T. and Krueger, A. (eds), *Macroeconomic Linkage: Savings, Exchange Rates, and Capital Flows*. Chicago: University of Chicago Press.

Gangnes, B. and van Asche, A. 2008. China and the Future of Asia's Electronics Trade. *CIRANO Working Paper Scientific Series*, 2008s–05, February.

Garcia-Herero, A. and Koivu T. 2009. China's Exchange Rate Policy and Asian Trade. *BIS Working Paper*, No 282, April.

Gilboy, G.J. 2004. The Myth Behind China's Miracle. *Foreign Affairs*, 83(4), July–August.

Glick, R. 2005. Does Europe's Path to Monetary Union Provide Lessons for East Asia? *FRBSF Economic Letter*, No 2005–19, August 2005.

Goldberg, L. and Klein, M. 1997. Foreign Direct Investment, Trade and Real Exchange Rate Linkages in Southeast Asia and Latin America. *NBER working paper*, No 6344.

He, D., Cheung, L. and Chang, J. 2007. Sense and Nonsense on Asia's Export Dependency and the Decoupling Thesis. Hong Kong Monetary Authority, *HKMA Working Paper*, No 03/2007, April.

Hefeker, C. and Nabor, A. 2002. Yen or Yuan? China's Role in the Future of Asian Monetary Integration. *HWWA discussion paper*, 206, Hamburg: Institute of International Economics.

Hummels, D., Ishii, J. and Yi, K. 2001. The Nature and Growth of Vertical Specialization in World Trade. *Journal of International Economics,* 54, 75–96.

James, W.E. et al. 2008. The US Financial Crisis, Global Financial Turmoil, and Developing Asia: Is the Era of High Growth at an End? *ADB Economics Working Paper Series*, No 139, December.

Jomo, K.S. 1998. Financial Liberalization, Crises, and Malaysian Policy Responses. *World Development*, 26(8), 1563–74.

Koopman, R., Wang, Z. and Wei, S-J. 2008. How Much of Chinese Exports is Really Made In China? Assessing Domestic Value-Added When Processing Trade is Pervasive. *NBER Working Paper*, No 14109.

Lafrance, R. 2008. China's Exchange Rate Policy: A Review of the Literature. *Discussion paper*, Bank of Canada, 2008–5.

Lamberte, M. 2009. Some Positive Consequences of the Global Economic Crisis. *EABER Newsletter*, June.

Mundell, R. 1961. A Theory of Optimum Currency Areas. *American Economic Review*, 51, 657–65.

Nicolas, F. (forthcoming). *De Facto* and *De Jure* Regional Economic Integration in East Asia – How Do They Interact. *Singapore Economic Review*, forthcoming.

Nicolas, F. 2008. The Political Economy of Regional Integration in East Asia. *Economic Change and Restructuring*, 41(4), 345–67.

Obashi, A. 2009. Stability of Production Networks in East Asia: Duration and Survival of Trade. *ERIA Discussion Paper Series*, No 2009–03, Jakarta, March.

OECD. 1999. *Foreign Direct Investment and Recovery in Southeast Asia (Four Case Studies: Indonesia, Malaysia, Philippines and Thailand)*. (with Thomsen, S.), Paris: OECD.

Pontines, V. and Ramkishen, R. 2008. 'Fear of Appreciation' not 'Fear of Floating'? Foreign Exchange Market Intervention in Emerging Asia. *Mimeo*, November.

Rahman, M. and Thorbecke W. 2007. How Would China's Exports be Affected by a Unilateral Appreciation of the RMB and by a Joint Appreciation of Countries Supplying Intermediate Imports? *RIETI Discussion Paper Series* 07-E-012, March.

Thorbecke, W. 2006. The Effect of Exchange Rate Changes on Trade in East Asia. *RIETI Discussion Paper Series*, 05-E-009, March.

Thorbecke, W. 2008. The Effect of Exchange Rate Changes on China's Labor-Intensive Manufacturing Exports. *RIETI Discussion Paper Series*, 08-E-038, September.

Thorbecke, W. and Yoshitomi, M. 2006. Trade – FDI – Techology Linkages in East Asia. *Mimeograph*, RIETI, Tokyo, July.

Thorbecke, W. and Zhang, H. 2008. The Effect of Exchange Rate Changes on China's Labor-Intensive Manufacturing Exports. *RIETI Discussion Paper*, No 08 E–038, September.

Volz, U. 2007. Integration? What Integration? Monetary Cooperation in East Asia, the Rise of China, and Implications for Korea, in Nicolas F. (ed.), *Korea in the New Asia: East Asian Integration and the China Factor*. London and New York: Routledge.

Chapter 5
Economic and Financial Integration in East Asia: Status and Perspective

Woosik Moon and Hwanhee Oh

Introduction

Since the early 1990s, there has been a rapid increase in cooperation among East Asian countries as they have been continuously liberalizing and deregulating their goods and financial markets. For instance, over the last two decades, East Asian economies[1] have achieved substantial liberalization of trade and foreign direct investment (FDI). The resulting expansion of trade and FDI has become the engine of economic growth and development in East Asia, and rendered the economies of the region to become integrated into the global market as well as amongst themselves.

The increasing financial market liberalization in East Asia has contributed to rapid economic growth by attracting both long-term and short-term capital and, together with trade and FDI openness, has deepened market-driven economic interdependence in East Asia. However, financial openness increased instability too. The culmination of such increasing financial instability was the 1997 currency crisis. The crisis was a watershed for regional cooperation by prompting Asian economies to realize the importance of closer economic cooperation amongst themselves; it led these economies to embark on closer regional cooperation in all areas of trade, investment, money and finance, and consequently gradually distancing themselves from the main Western economies.

The European Union (EU) has, nevertheless, traditionally been a model for East Asia but compared to the EU, the progress in enhancing regional cooperation has remained slow in East Asia. It took the EU more than half a century to deepen, enforce and extend its integration, a process that was greatly stimulated by successful institutionalization. In contrast, the economies in East Asia have just started their integration within the background of increasingly intensified economic ties among them.

1 In this chapter East Asia refers to ASEAN+3 countries, unless otherwise specified. The Association of South East Asian Nations (ASEAN 10) includes Brunei, Indonesia, Malaysia, Philippines, Singapore, Thailand, Cambodia, Laos, Myanmar and Vietnam, while ASEAN+3 refers to ASEAN 10 plus Korea, Japan and China.

This chapter proposes an overview of the current state of economic and financial integration in East Asia and an examination of its future development in light of the process of institutionalization. The 1997 Asian crisis stimulated a change in attitude towards closer regional integration in East Asia; the financial and economic crisis starting in the Autumn of 2008 seems to have reiterated the need for such change. East Asian countries are indeed well aware that regional integration is the key to continued economic growth while securing stability in their economies. All countries including China, let alone Korea and Japan which have traditionally been the active proponents of regional integration, are now moving closer to achieve deeper real and financial integration; there is no doubt today that this has been quite successful at least on the side of monetary and financial cooperation. Nevertheless, these countries are not yet translating their efforts into common institutions. Although compared to the case of the EU, the lack of formal institutionalization may be seen as a blatant weakness in East Asian integration, it might be that current efforts at integrating in East Asia, in particular in the financial and monetary area, might overcome some of the deficiencies inherent in the process of monetary integration in Europe, the latter being seen as a broad model from which refinements are possible.

The content of this chapter is as follows. Section 1 overviews the trade and FDI integration and the recent trend of free trade area (FTA) arrangements in East Asia. Section 2 traces out the history of regional monetary and financial cooperation in East Asia. Section 3 concludes with some predictions on the prospects of East Asian economic and financial integration.

1. Trade and FDI Integration

1.1 Background for regional economic integration in East Asia

East Asian economies have achieved remarkable growth over the past decades. This growth is largely attributed to market driven expansion of trade in the region as East Asia leads the world growth of trade and accounts for about one-quarter of its total (Table 5.1).

East Asian trade is intra-regional as well as inter-regional. In fact, East Asian countries started their industrialization relying largely on the US and world markets and therefore their economies were intimately integrated ('coupled') with the global economy, in particular with the USA. However, they realized that it would leave them overly dependent on one economy and its consequent cyclical fluctuations and they tried to diversify their export markets. Thus, although the US and global markets are still very important, the intra-regional market has grown steadily from the late 1970s and has become the dominant market. Geographical proximity, common life styles and intercultural understandings all contributed to intensifying intra-regional trade. In the latter half of the first decade of the 2000s, intra-regional trade accounted for more than half of total trade in East Asia, while

Table 5.1 Regional Trade as a percentage of World Exports and Imports

	1980	1985	1990	1995	2000	2001	2002	2003	2004	2005	2006
As a % of World Imports											
East Asia	7.0	10.1	16.38	19.34	19.74	18.86	19.73	19.91	20.57	20.82	20.82
EU 25	46.1	40.5	46.9	38.9	34.8	35.7	36.1	37.3	38.0	39.3	37.8
NAFTA	16.8	23.9	19.1	19.2	23.6	22.8	22.8	21.0	21.8	21.7	20.1
As % of World Exports											
	1980	**1985**	**1990**	**1995**	**2000**	**2001**	**2002**	**2003**	**2004**	**2005**	**2006**
East Asia	7.0	10.8	13.37	16.43	15.99	15.46	15.94	16.52	16.99	17.18	17.46
EU 25	42.6	42.0	46.8	41.4	35.5	37.4	38.5	39.8	35.9	39.4	38.2
NAFTA	15.9	17.3	16.1	15.9	17.1	16.6	15.5	14.0	14.9	14.5	14.1

Note: East Asia includes Hong Kong and Taiwan as well as ASEAN+3 (Korea, Japan and China).

Source: IMF Direction of Trade Statistics, ADB FTA Database, Asia Regional Integration Center.

trade with the USA and the EU accounted for about one third of total trade. The rise of China is an important factor in explaining increasing intra-regional trade because it accounts for one third of intra-regional exports. Table 5.2 summarizes this trend over the period 1980 to 2006. It demonstrates that intra-regional trade as a share of East Asia's total trade has risen from 36.8 percent in 1980 to 54.5 percent in 2006. The current share of intra-regional trade in East Asia is however still lower than that in the EU, although it exceeds that of NAFTA.

The increase in FDI in East Asia is another important factor accelerating interdependency among East Asian countries. Global multinational companies and East Asian firms have formed international production networks and supply chains throughout East Asia through FDI. Cross border production and trade networks explain the rapid increase in both trade and FDI inflows to and between Asian countries. According to Ando and Kimura (2003), international production networks account for a significant share of trade flows of most countries in the region and are spreading over a large number of countries.

The appreciation of Asian currencies against the US dollar was initially the most important factor accelerating the relocation of labor intensive production into low wage countries in the region (Naughton 1997). From the mid-1980s, however, changes in the development strategies and trade policies of developing ASEAN countries started to play a pivotal role in the expansion of international production

Table 5.2 Intra-regional trade share (%)

Region	1980	1985	1990	1995	2000	2001	2002	2003	2004	2005	2006
ASEAN	17.9	20.3	18.8	24.0	24.7	24.1	24.4	26.6	26.7	27.2	27.2
ASEAN+3	30.2	30.2	29.4	37.6	37.3	37.1	37.9	39.0	39.2	38.9	38.3
ASEAN+3 +Hong Kong +Taiwan	36.8	39.0	43.1	51.9	52.1	51.9	53.8	55.4	55.9	55.4	54.5
NAFTA	33.8	38.7	37.9	43.1	48.8	49.1	48.4	47.4	46.4	46.1	44.3
EU(15)	60.7	59.8	66.2	64.2	62.3	62.2	62.5	63.0	62.2	60.4	59.5
EU(27)	61.5	60.0	66.8	66.9	66.3	66.7	67.4	68.1	67.6	66.2	68.5

Source: IMF Direction of Trade.

networks, as these countries facilitated inward FDI in export-oriented businesses. Japan and newly developed economies such as Korea gradually moved parts of their production capacities into these countries. This has promoted a dynamic evolution of intra-regional division of labor and led to the rise of vertical intra-industry trade in parts, components, and semi-finished and finished manufactured products (Kawai and Urata 1998, 2004). Furthermore, the rapid growth of a very large emerging market economy, China, was another important factor that contributed to closer economic linkages and the increase in FDI among East Asian economies. China plays a major role in these production networks and supply chains as its expanding exports require imports of industrial materials, parts, components, and other intermediate products from its neighboring economies. China has become a manufacturing assembly for East Asian economies and has developed its comparative advantages in manufacturing industries. These evolutions of specialization patterns in East Asian countries confirm the accuracy of the 'flying geese' model developed by Akamatsu (1961). In the other East Asian countries, the industrial structures are characterized by the lack of a dominant domestic manufacturing sector and by a high dependence on multinational companies.

Table 5.3 shows the trend of cumulative FDI shares for various groups of East Asian economies from 1990 to 2005. It shows deepening regional integration in East Asia through intra-regional FDI. For instance, East Asian economies including ASEAN+3, Hong Kong and Taiwan invested half of their FDI to their region in 2005, compared to 37.6 percent in 1995.

1.2 Recent Trends of economic integration in East Asia

East Asia was a latecomer in the move towards regional trade arrangements compared to other regions in the world such as the USA and Europe. The first FTA in East Asia was concluded in 1976, and the number of FTAs in East Asia

Table 5.3 Cumulative FDI shares from ASEAN+3, Hong Kong and Taiwan (%)

Region	1995	2000	2001	2002	2003	2004	2005
ASEAN+3+HK+Taiwan	37.63	47.16	47.47	49.06	51.21	50.86	50.85
ASEAN+3	37.63	41.98	41.82	42.94	44.85	44.18	43.69
ASEAN	8.99	8.42	8.43	8.66	9.10	8.70	8.47
China	27.98	31.87	31.75	32.65	34.15	33.72	33.33

Note: Cumulative FDI share is the percentage of regional FDI inflows to total FDI from ASEAN+3, Hong Kong and Taiwan.

Source: Integration Indicators Database, Asian Regional Integration Center, Asian Development Bank.

remained as low as 11 until 2000. However, since then East Asia has been rapidly catching up with the global trend. By the end of 2007, there were 103 FTAs, of which 37 FTAs were concluded, 40 under negotiation, and 26 proposed. Table 5.4 summarizes the growth trend of FTAs in East Asia.

It is important however, to note that FTAs in East Asia are more extra- regional than intra-regional. For instance, of all the FTAs concluded, negotiated and proposed in East Asia, the number of extra-regional FTAs reaches nearly four times the number of intra-regional FTAs (Kawai and Wignaraja 2008). Regional economic integration among Asian countries is not yet a top policy issue, although its economic and political importance has been stressed over a long time.

This trend is particularly pronounced for Northeast Asian countries, which have seen their FTA activities increasing at an unprecedented speed. Table 5.5 summarizes the status of the FTAs of Korea, Japan, and China.

Northeast Asian countries have traditionally relied on multilateralism and the WTO for trade liberalization but due to the slow pace and progress of the Doha Round, they had to shift towards bilateralism and FTAs as a means of trade liberalization. Furthermore, bilateralism was considered as an effective instrument to promote regional economic cooperation and domestic economic growth. For instance, the Korean government set its aim as an FTA hub in the region. It concluded its first FTA with Chile in 2004. Since then, it has embarked simultaneously on various bilateral and multilateral trade arrangements. By expanding its market through FTAs, new investment opportunities were made for companies willing to invest in Korea as a base for production operations. Since access to the domestic market and the investment environment are important factors in attracting FDI, Korea has tried to use these FTAs to increase the incentive for foreign companies to invest in Korea through better market access to its domestic markets while Korean industries secure access to the markets of its FTA members. By taking advantage of the country's geo-political position in Northeast Asia, the

Table 5.4 Growth of FTAs in East Asia, 1976 to 2007 (cumulative)

		Status of FTAs		
Year	**Number of FTAs**	**Concluded**	**Under Negotiation**	**Proposed**
1976	1	1	0	0
1986	1	1	0	0
1996	4	3	0	1
2000	7	3	1	3
2001	10	5	2	3
2002	14	6	4	4
2003	23	9	5	9
2004	42	14	16	12
2005	67	21	30	16
2006	96	31	42	23
2007	103	37	40	26

Source: Kawai and Wignaraja (2008).

Table 5.5 Status of FTAs of Korea, Japan and China (as of June, 2009)

		Within the region	**Outside of the region**
Korea	Concluded (Entered into force)	Korea–Singapore (2006.3.2) Korea–ASEAN (Goods, 2007.6.1) Korea–ASEAN (Services, 2009.5.1)	Korea–Chile (2004.4.1) Korea–EFTA (2006.9.1)
	(Not in effect)	Korea–ASEAN (Investment, 2009.6.2)	Korea–United States (2007.6.30) Korea–EU (2009.7.1)
	Under negotiation	Japan	Canada India Mexico GCC Australia Peru New Zealand
	In preparation	China ASEAN+3 ASEAN+6	MERCOSUR Turkey Russia

continues on next page

Japan	Concluded (Entered into force) (Not in effect)	Japan–Malaysia (2006.7.13) Japan–Singapore (2006.11.30) Japan–Thailand (2007.11.1) Japan–Indonesia (2008.7.1) Japan–Brunei (2008.7.31) Japan–ASEAN (2008.12.1) Japan–Philippines (2008.12.11) Japan–Vietnam (2008.12.25)	Japan–Mexico (2005.4.1) Japan–Chile (2007.9.3) Japan–Switzerland (2009.2.19)
	Under negotiation	Korea	GCC India Australia Peru
	In preparation	ASEAN+3 ASEAN+6	Canada
China	Concluded (Entered into force) (Not in effect)	China–ASEAN (Goods, 2003.7.1) China–Hong Kong (2004.1.1) China–Macau (2004.1.1) China–ASEAN (Services, 2007.7.1) China–Singapore (2009.1.1)	
	Under negotiation		Australia GCC Iceland Norway South Africa
	In preparation	Korea Peru ASEAN+3 ASEAN+6	India Costa Rica

Note: ASEAN+6 refers to ASEAN+3 plus Australia, New Zealand and India.

Source: Ministry of Foreign Affairs and Trade, Korea, Ministry of Economy, Trade and Industry, Japan, and WTO RTA Database.

Korean government has also decided to further regional economic integration and cooperation. To achieve this objective, various industries such as those in the manufacturing, finance, energy and environment sectors need to cooperate with each other to establish rules and systems to stabilize the different factors that influence the Korean economy and society.

In Japan, the government normally promotes economic partnership agreements (EPAs) which include and go beyond the elements of FTAs. The objectives of these EPAs are to achieve deeper integration with Japan's trading partners on a formal basis, to go beyond reductions in border restrictions while pursuing investment liberalization, to promote greater competition in the domestic market, and to harmonize standards and procedures. Japan's first FTA was with Singapore which was enacted in November 2002. This FTA was a comprehensive agreement to liberalize and facilitate trade and investment while promoting bilateral cooperation in various sectors such as small- and medium-sized enterprise developments.

For China, the FTA is an instrument to confirm its commitment towards trade liberalization and at the same time a tool for commercial diplomacy. China did not start FTA negotiations until 2001, when it became a member of the WTO. Compared with many other countries, it is a late comer in the FTA arena as well as in other aspects of economic globalization. The FTAs of China are less comprehensive than the FTAs of other countries since they typically exclude issues such as dispute settlement mechanisms, intellectual property, the environment and labor. Instead, the FTAs focus primarily on liberalizing trade in goods and services and the agreements take into account particular bilateral or regional commercial and strategic interests. China takes different approaches when cooperating with its neighbors since the development level and economic structure of other economies are different for each country. If China manages to successfully implement FTAs, this would be an important stepping stone towards economic integration through trade liberalization in the region.

FTAs can help achieve deeper economic integration through agreements that are not covered by the current WTO agenda and in areas where it is difficult to make substantial progress through a multilateral framework. With or without the conclusion of the Doha Round, the trend for more FTAs is likely to continue. These FTAs will be as much extra-regional as intra-regional. The reason is that East Asian countries urgently need to use these FTAs as a way towards greater liberalization of trade and FDI. Deeper regional integration such as that existing in a Customs Union is however not envisaged at all. Indeed, the dominance of the FTA as a mode of integration over Customs Union has been the unique feature of Asian regionalism. The reason is that, unlike in Europe where 'fortress Europe' often threatens multi-lateralism, East Asia has pursued open-regionalism from the start and multi-lateralism continues to prevail.

2. Monetary and Financial Integration

2.1. Background for monetary and financial integration

Given the magnitude of intra-regional trade, even small exchange rate misalignments can disturb trade and investment flows and create trade frictions among the region's economies, resulting in economic instabilities which can be detrimental for many developing countries in the region. This is why regional mechanisms and arrangements for greater stability in intra-regional exchange rates are important.

Indeed, the scale of interdependence among East Asian economies has risen to a level almost matching that in Europe in the 1980s–90s. Given the heightened interdependence of economies in the region and their decreasing interdependence with the US market, it may be argued that these East Asian countries should aim to stabilize intra-regional exchange rates through policy coordination rather than through stability with the US dollar. As pointed out, increasing intra-regional trade and investment explain the closer linkages among East Asian economies, proof of 'decoupling' from the West. Despite the close and rising interdependence of East Asian economies, however, there was no such exchange rate policy coordination in East Asia. Moreover, the region's exchange rate regimes were in serious disarray. In contrast to the pre-crisis period, when many emerging market economies in East Asia maintained US dollar-pegged regimes, the exchange rate regimes after the 1997 crisis exhibited greater diversity. The two giant economies in the region, Japan and China, adopt different exchange rate regimes as Japan has a free floating one while China has a heavily managed peg system.

Given the importance of exchange rate stability in East Asia, there is a strong need for a common action in setting up appropriate exchange rate regimes. A valid reason for common action in coordinating the exchange rate is because individual efforts will not be effective in stabilizing the exchange rate. The cost of intervention in the exchange rate market is huge and intervention itself could be very dangerous as witnessed in the 1997 crisis and more recently in the current global financial crisis. Collective action for self-protection is the only possible alternative in the current state of international financial integration. Indeed, according to the so called 'impossible trinity theorem', there are only three possible options under such a situation: free floating, complete peg or capital controls. Given that capital market integration is one important step to be taken in the future to circulate the savings of East Asia to the region, capital controls are not desirable. No sovereign East Asian country is implementing a complete peg. Free floating is not acceptable for developing East Asian countries because they need exchange rate stabilization to continue their economic development. Indeed, East Asian countries have been pursuing exchange rate policies to promote growth, trade, and investment. For them, an intermediate exchange rate arrangement like a soft peg or a managed float was naturally attractive because it helped them to minimize the negative impact of exchange rate appreciation on their exports, which for them was the motor for economic growth. Therefore, despite the bitter experience of the currency crisis, East Asian economies never gave up on the policy of stabilizing their exchange rates. Even Japan, which was officially adopting free floating, intervened quite frequently in the foreign exchange market to prevent the appreciation of its yen against the dollar until 2004. This is the reason why many East Asian countries continued to intervene to stabilize their currencies. It suggests the need for a collective regional monetary arrangement as an alternative to the deadlock of the individual country choice of exchange rate regimes.

One such idea for a collective arrangement is a common exchange rate arrangement among Asian countries which can be modeled after the European Monetary System (EMS) or the snake system that was present during the early 1970s in Europe. The idea starts with setting up a monetary system that enables defending the exchange rate parities between regional currencies, while jointly floating *vis-à-vis* the US dollar. Given the little progress made in achieving monetary and financial cooperation in East Asia, such a collective exchange arrangement will be certainly a long term goal but it is also true that the ever increasing economic and financial linkages and interdependencies among East Asian countries call for immediate action.

A common exchange arrangement, however, requires deciding on what the parity should be and on the mechanism that is to be used to stabilize foreign exchange rates.

First, concerning the parity, a basket currency parity was proposed. There were generally two types of basket currency proposals. The first one was to include the US dollar, euro and Japanese Yen in the basket. But this system has two weaknesses. First, this proposal does not take into account the increasing economic interdependence among East Asian countries and the importance of intra-regional exchange rate stability. Second, and more importantly, it does not refer to the burden of responsibility for maintaining the pegging system, especially for interventions in a fixed exchange rate system. It is clear that even if Asian countries were to adopt a basket peg system on the basis of the US dollar and the euro, neither the USA nor the euro area of the EU would be interested in maintaining stable exchange rates between the basket and their currencies. It implies that Asian countries would have to rely on unilateral intervention, not bilateral cooperative intervention, if the exchange rate of the Asian Currency Unit (ACU) and the dollar deviates from its target value. More seriously, Japan, which would be expected to play the most important role in maintaining a stable exchange rate, not only between the dollar and ACU but also between the Yen and the national currencies of the region, would not have any obligation or responsibility for maintaining such exchange rates. Thus, other Asian countries would not be willing to adopt this basket system without gaining strong commitment from key currency countries to support them in emergency situations. The only feasible exchange rate system for East Asian countries would consequently be to construct the basket only on the basis of regional currencies, e.g. a local currencies-based ACU. This was in fact what happened in the case of European monetary integration. The European Currency Unit (ECU) was a basket composed only of regional currencies. This option would lead to further economic policy coordination and cooperation. Secondly, when it comes to the question of how to maintain such a basket system, one essential precondition is that it would have to be accompanied by an emergency liquidity provision system to cope with speculative attacks. In fact, in order for Asian countries under the pressure of a crisis to be provided with sufficient liquidity, an emergency liquidity facility that lends without limit would have to be setup. In the case of the EMS, the financial solidarity mechanism, which was one of the three components of the EMS, was aimed at fulfilling this role. Although the Chang Mai Initiative (CMI) was the first step in this direction in the case of East Asian countries, it is far from fulfilling all the objectives of such a facility.[2] As argued by Moon, Rhee and Yoon (2000), such need for international cooperation is all the stronger, given the magnitude of current capital movements. In this regard, the European monetary cooperation experience could provide a very good guide. In the case of the EMS, the facility for the provision of liquidity known as the Financial Solidarity Mechanism and comprising a Very Short Term Financing Facility (VSTFF) was one of the most important cornerstones for European monetary cooperation. Indeed, in the whole history of monetary cooperation in Europe, the facility for the provision of liquidity has been constantly strengthened and constituted one of the most important instruments for monetary cooperation.[3] Despite these improvements, this provision was far from being a perfect one, for this system could not work properly when large scale instabilities happened. In such cases, European countries had to resort to the realignment of their parities within the EMS.

2.2 Initiatives and trends of regional monetary and financial arrangements

The East Asian financial crisis has spawned a number of proposals for institutional reform. Some of these envisage reforming existing institutions, particularly the IMF, while there are other suggestions for new institutions to stand alongside the IMF or to replace it. Just as multilateral trade reform and multilateral trade institutions have been joined by an increasing array of regional trading arrangements, it has also been suggested that regional financial crises may be better handled by regional monetary funds. Specifically, the Asian financial crisis has focused attention on the idea of establishing an Asian Monetary Fund (AMF).

In September 1997, the Japanese Ministry of Finance proposed the creation of an AMF to support the countries in crisis. Although this particular proposal was scuttled, the idea of a common regional fund on which East Asian governments might draw in times of financial turmoil survives. But the notion received strong

---

2 The insufficiency of the CMI is explained in the next section.

3 The credit mechanism existing when the EMS was launched in the late 1970s amounted to Ecus 25 billion. This was a substantial improvement over the liquidity available under the 'snake' arrangement, whereby the US$2–3 billion liquidity available to European banks was less than half of the daily fluctuations in these banks' reserves.

opposition from the US government on the grounds that the AMF would be a duplication of the IMF and would only exacerbate the moral hazard behavior of borrowing countries. However, three arguments can be provided for regional financial arrangement in East Asia. The first is that an international institutional response is not speedy enough to nip a crisis in the bud. The transaction costs to arrange a cooperative response may be lower at the regional level because the number of participating governments is smaller and the countries involved are more cohesive (Eichengreen 2001: 40). When significant problems appear within a region, which are clustered because of intra-regional interdependence, a regional institution could redirect its resources better than a truly international institution. Second, financial assistance from an international organization might not be encompassing enough in comparison to what ought to be achieved. For example, the IMF is not only concerned with East Asian matters but must be and is concerned with other regions as well. Third, the decisions of an international institution do not take account of regional peculiarities but are based on general rules. It is well known that the IMF conditionality clause imposed on the crisis-stricken East Asian countries was too harsh compared to other regions. The fact that East Asian countries share common problems does not justify that all regional peculiarities must be got rid off, as connoted by the statement that the Asian crisis was a "punishment for Asian sins" (Krugman 1998). To the extent that East Asian peculiarities matter, there is an obvious case for a regional arrangement. Finally, debates over the AMF proposal have revolved around distributive political issues rather than of economic efficiency, which in the end led to the Chang Mai Initiative (CMI).

In 2001, East Asian governments and central banks met each other at Chiang Mai, Thailand and they agreed to create a set of bilateral swap arrangements (BSAs). The CMI was designed to address short-term liquidity needs in the event of a crisis or contagion and to supplement the existing international financial arrangements. In fact, one of the important features of the BSAs is that members requesting liquidity support can immediately obtain short term financial assistance. Although the CMI is undeniably an important step in establishing a regional monetary cooperation, the CMI is far from such a regional arrangement. First of all, the bilateral facility was too small to be effective. Moreover, because of its bilateral nature, the CMI requires a country to negotiate with all member countries when it needs emergency liquidity, and consequently, it is not speedy enough to prevent a crisis by early intervention. Also, the provision of liquidity in times of crises could not be decided without the prior consent of the IMF. The provision of funds is linked up to 80 percent of its amount to IMF's approval. This conditionality is another important hurdle preventing the effectiveness of the CMI. Thus, Asian countries have tried to expand the facility on the one hand, and to transform BSAs into a more comprehensive multi-lateral facility on the other. The most recent development of the CMI was the expansion of its funds and its multilateralization.

At the 12th ASEAN+3 Finance Ministers' Meeting held on 3 May 2009 in Bali, Indonesia, ASEAN+3 countries reached an agreement on all the main components of the Chiang Mai Initiative Multilateralization (CMIM), including the individual countries' contribution, borrowing accessibility, and surveillance mechanism. The multilaterized arrangement will be governed by a single contractual agreement. The total size of the CMIM fund was also expanded to US$ 120 billion with the contribution proportion between ASEAN and the 'Plus Three' countries at 20:80 (Table 5.6). Furthermore, on the decision-making mechanism of the CMIM, it was agreed that fundamental issues such as the size of the fund and membership would be decided through the consensus of all ASEAN+3 members, while the lending issues would be decided through a majority.

Table 5.6 The Structure of CMIM

Country	Contribution (US$ billion)		Borrowing Multiplier
Brunei	0.03		5
Cambodia	0.12		5
China	38.4	China (Exclude Hong Kong, China) 34.2	0.5
		Hong Kong, China 4.2	2.5*
Indonesia	4.77		2.5
Japan	38.4		0.5
Korea	19.2		1
Lao PDR	0.03		5
Malaysia	4.77		2.5
Myanmar	0.06		5
Philippines	3.68		2.5
Singapore	4.77		2.5
Thailand	4.77		2.5
Vietnam	1.00		5

Source: Joint Media Statement of the 12th ASEAN Plus Three Finance Ministers' Meeting, Bali, Indonesia, 3 May 2009. Available at: http://www.aseansec.org [accessed: October 2009].

**Note*: Hong Kong, China's borrowing is limited to IMF de-linked portion because Hong Kong, China is not a member of the IMF.

Asian officials hope that such a facility could underpin exchange rate cooperation and monetary integration in the region, although such proposals remain for the moment a long-term vision. As well as the CMIM, Asian countries have considered creating a common currency basket. On May 3 2006, finance ministers from Korea, China, and Japan announced that they would take steps to coordinate their currencies in a way that would ultimately produce a common regional currency similar to the euro. They also added steps to study all related issues, including the creation of a Regional Currency Unit (RCU) that had often been referred to as the ACU. The creation of a RCU could play a pivotal role for monetary stability in Asia and speed up the road to create a monetary union in Asia.

Asian governments also launched what is called the Asian Bond Markets Initiative (ABMI). The reason for this initiative was that despite various attempts and ideas for monetary cooperation in Asia, they were unfeasible in the near future. Thus, initiatives to develop regional bonds markets have attracted special interest. First, the development of regional bond markets was considered to help solve the double mismatch problem, which, for many, seemed one important cause of the currency crisis in East Asia. Second, the post-1997 crisis accumulation of foreign reserves in US dollars, incomparable in its magnitude, prompted a discussion on bond market development. The development of regional bond markets has since been at the center of discussions in many ASEAN+3 and APEC meetings.

In this context, a number of initiatives have been undertaken to develop regional bond markets. These can be grouped into two main initiatives, each falling under the auspices of a major regional multilateral organization. The first of these initiatives falls under the Executives' Meeting of East Asia-Pacific (EMEAP) Central Banks and takes the form of bond funds aimed at channeling a small portion of the very large official reserves held by the Asian economies into the region. The first of these funds – the Asian Bond Fund I (ABF1) – was launched in June 2003 and is now fully invested in US dollar-denominated bonds issued by sovereign and quasi-sovereign issuers in the EMEAP economies. Following the successful launch of the ABF1, the EMEAP Central Banks have also launched the second fund, the ABF2, which invests in local currency-denominated sovereign and quasi-sovereign issued bonds in the eight Asian EMEAP countries. Both of these funds are aimed at promoting the development of index bond funds in regional markets and, at the same time, enhancing both the domestic and the regional bond market infrastructure.

The second set of initiatives, under the ASEAN+3 forum, involves a variety of studies known as the Asian Bond Market Initiative (ABMI) on issues such as new securitized debt instruments, issuance of debt by international financial institutions, regional credit guarantees and enhancement facilities, and the establishment of local and regional credit rating and credit enhancement agencies. This initiative was first endorsed at the ASEAN+3 Deputies Meeting in Chiang Mai, Thailand on 17 December 2002. Six working groups were since established to further the development of Asian bond markets. At the 12th ASEAN+3 Finance

Ministers' Meeting, the importance of the ABMI in promoting the local currency bond markets and enhancing the recycling of regional savings towards developing regional bond markets was stressed. It was agreed to enhance the ABMI Roadmap taking into account the outcome of the 1998 London Summit. The establishment of the Credit Guarantee and Investment Mechanism (CGIM) as a trust fund of the Asian Development Bank (ADB) with an initial capital of US$500 million, which could be increased once the demand was fully met, was also endorsed during the meeting. The objective of the CGIM is to support the issuance of local currency-denominated corporate bonds in the region. This initiative would contribute to developing regional bond markets. Issues regarding the establishment of the CGIM such as its business scope, leverage ratio and country limit are to be further discussed at working level in order to make the mechanism effective by the 2010 ASEAN+3 Finance Ministers' Meeting.

3. Concluding Remarks and Prospects

The EU has traditionally been seen as a model of monetary integration for East Asia. It is worth noting that it took the EU more than half a century to deepen, enforce and extend its integration, thanks to a successful level and type of institutionalization from the outset. In East Asia, the progress for enhancing regional cooperation remains slow. Indeed, the East Asian economies have just started their integration within the background of increasingly intensified economic ties amongst themselves, economic crises, but with very little or no institutionalization.

East Asian countries are nevertheless well aware that regional integration is the key to continuous economic growth while securing stability in their economies, and greater independence *vis-à-vis* the Western economies. All countries including China, let alone Korea and Japan, which have traditionally been its active proponents, are now moving closer to achieving deeper real and financial integration, and no doubt this has been quite a remarkable achievement. Nevertheless, these countries are not yet translating their efforts into common institutions, and there is a strong need for formal institutionalization. One serious constraint for this institutionalization has been that the countries in the region have failed to clearly articulate the ultimate objectives of regional arrangements. Regional identity is weak and regional solidarity remains to be developed. The lack of political leadership, which was so critical in Europe as a determining force of integration, is another serious problem. There are two countries in East Asia that are capable of providing such a leadership role. These are China and Japan, given that they are the largest economic and political forces in the region, but, due to their rivalry, they have not been able to reach a consensus on a number of issues related to regional integration. As far as trade integration is concerned, their disagreements look more serious. Japan and China might have different interests and hence different strategies for economic integration in East Asia. Japan and

China have been for a long time opposed to regional trade arrangements with each other. Japan might have been afraid of losing its leadership status in cases where China is involved. For China, economic integration with ASEAN members was also a priority to rival Japan. In fact, Japan is the most advanced economy in East Asia, while China is still a developing economy with a huge gap to narrow in terms of technological and industrial sophistication compared to Japan, although it is a major military power. These differences in the economic and military status of the two countries suggest that, even if they manage to reconcile their troubled memories of the past, China and Japan may find it difficult to work together as equal partners for regional integration in East Asia.

In spite of these political difficulties, some sort of institutionalization is emerging slowly, in particular in the area of monetary and financial integration. The development of CMI into CMIM throws a very bright perspective on the emergence of common institutions in East Asia. Compared to monetary and financial integration, institutionalization in the real sector is not yet on the agenda or at best is very slow. There has been little discussion on the appropriate form of regional integration in East Asia. The main discussion so far has focused only on opening markets, dismantling the barriers that prevent market access and implementing the many FTAs in East Asia. Asian regionalism was from the start open regionalism and it was geared toward multilateralism, which explains why the process of setting up a common institution in the real sector has been delayed.

The issues discussed in this Chapter show that East Asian countries seem to be opting for a different type of integration, when compared to the case of the EU. The major instabilities brought about by the 1997 crisis, and the imbalances spilling over into these economies with the 2008 crisis, have nurtured the need for monetary and financial integration in East Asia. In short, integration in East Asia seems to be a pragmatic response to major regional and world imbalances. In terms of financial and monetary integration, the EU serves as a rough model upon which refinements such as the CMIM initiative, are possible.

References

Asia Development Bank FTA Database, Asia Regional Integration Center (www.aric.adb.org).

Akamatsu, K. 1961. A Theory of Unbalanced Growth in the World Economy. *Weltwirtschaftliches Archiv*. Hamburg, 86 (2), 196–217.

Ando, M. and Kimura, F. 2003. The Formation of International Production and Distribution Networks in East Asia. *Mimeo*. Tokyo, Japan: Keio University.

Bergsten, F. and Chul Park, Y. 2002. *Toward Creating a Regional Monetary Arrangement in East Asia*. ADBI Research Paper Series (50).

Eichengreen, B. 2001. *Hanging Together? On Monetary and Financial Cooperation in Asia*. Available at: http://www.econ.berkeley.edu/~eichengr/.

Hummels, D., Rapoport, D. and Yi, K.-M. 1996. Vertical Specialization and the Changing Nature of World Trade. *Federal Reserve Bank of New York Economic Policy Review*, June 1998, 59–79.

Kawai, M. and Urata, S. 1998. Are Trade and Direct Investment Substitutes or Complements. An Empirical Analysis of Japanese Manufacturing Industries. In Lee, H. and Roland-Holst, D.W. (eds), *Economic Development and Cooperation in the Pacific Basin: Trade, Investment, and Environmental Issues*. Cambridge: University Press, 251–93.

Kawai, M. and Urata, S. 2004. Trade and Foreign Direct Investment in East Asia. In de Brouwer, G. and Kawai, M. (eds), *Economic Linkages and Implications for Exchange Rate Regimes in East Asia*. London and New York: Routledge Curzon: 15–102.

Kawai, M. and Wignaraja, G. 2008. Regionalism as an Engine of Multilateralism: A Case for a Single East Asian FTA. *Working Paper Series on Regional Economic Integration*, No. 14. Asian Development Bank.

Krugman, P. 1998. *Will Asia Bounce Back?* A Speech for Credit Suisse First Boston, Hong Kong, March 1998. Available at: http://web.mit/krugman/www/suisse.html.

Moon, W. 2006. Asian Bond Market Initiatives: A Korean Perspective. *Asia-Pacific Journal of EU Studies*, 4 (2), 167–84.

Moon, W. and Rhee, Y. 2007. Regional Currency Unit and Exchange Rate Coordination in East Asia. *The Kyoto Economic Review*, 76 (1), 53–66.

Moon, W. and Rhee, Y. 2009. Financial Integration and Exchange Rate Coordination in East Asia. In Chung, D.K. and Eichengreen, B. (eds), *Fostering Monetary and Financial Cooperation in East Asia*, Singapore: World Scientific.

Moon, W., Rhee, Y. and Yoon, D. 2000. Asian Monetary Cooperation: A Search for Regional Monetary Stability in the Post Euro and the Post Asian Crisis. *Bank of Korea Economic Paper,* 3(1), May.

Naughton, B. 1997. The *China Circle: Economics and Technology in the PRC, Taiwan, and Hong Kong*. Washington, DC: The Brookings Institution.

Ng, F. and Yeats, A. 2003. *Major Trade Trends in East Asia: What are their Implications for Regional Cooperation and Growth*. World Bank Policy Working Paper 3084.

Pangestu, M. and Gooptu, S. 2003. New Regionalism: Options for China and East Asia. In *East Asia Integrates*, (eds), Kathie Krumm and Homi Kharas. Washington: World Bank.

United Nations Conference on Trade and Development, 1996. *World Investment Report 1996: Investment, Trade and International Policy Arrangements*. New York and Geneva: United Nations.

United Nations Conference on Trade and Development, 2007. *Trade and Development Report 2007: Regional Cooperation for Development*. New York and Geneva: United Nations

Zebregs, H. 2004. Intraregional Trade in Emerging Asia. *IMF Policy Discussion Paper*. Washington: International Monetary Fund.

Chapter 6
Land, Biofuels and Food Security: Another 'Impossible Trinity Theorem'?

Bernadette Andreosso-O'Callaghan and M. Bruna Zolin

Introduction

Recent events in agricultural and energy world markets suggest that the well-known tri-lemma in monetary policy, according to which it is impossible to have simultaneously a fixed exchange rate, perfectly mobile capital and an independent monetary policy, might find an equivalent outside the sphere of monetary economics.

The 1980s and 1990s have been characterized by a sort of indifference in the field of commodities. Due to general over production and the decreasing importance of agricultural output in countries' GDP, security of supply assumed a low priority for both users and public authorities. Consequently, there was also very little interest in these issues on the part of speculators who preferred investing in the fields of information technologies and of high value-added (and sophisticated) services. The developed countries pursued a process of 'dematerialization' in the sense that a decreasing volume of raw material was needed per unit of value added.

However, the 'dot.com' crash of the early 2000s introduced a radical departure from the belief that *only* knowledge-based economic activities should be accorded the primary role in modern economic development. The rise in energy, primary commodities and food prices revealed the possible vulnerability of economies solely based on some types of knowledge-based services. The early 2000s also saw the entry into primary commodity markets of firms originating from emerging economies, e.g. China in African mineral resource markets.

Today's world is therefore facing a new important tri-lemma: to what extent is securing food and energy through biofuels for an increasing growing population compatible with exploiting finite land resources? What policy responses have been proffered so far? Are not the current signals emanating from the emerging countries of Asia, in particular, strong enough to stimulate a higher degree of cohesion between the EU Energy and Common Agricultural Policy? Starting with a brief reference to some crucial agricultural economic laws, this chapter will first raise a number of important questions by depicting the recent trends perceptible on the global agricultural markets. It will then analyze the challenges brought about by the development of biofuels, and it will explore whether the signals sent to the European Union by the emerging economies of the world, in particular by

Asian countries, are being echoed in EU policy making. A few final remarks will be proposed in a concluding section.

1. Theoretical Underpinning and Recent Trends in the Global Agricultural Market

From the early 2000s, the world economy has started realizing the difficulty in reconciling three apparently conflicting objectives in terms of agricultural and energy policies:

i. addressing energy (fossil fuel) shortages by developing biofuels,
ii. feeding a growing population with more diversified consumption patterns, and
iii. maximizing land efficiency (a factor in limited supply).

The global economic crisis that started unfolding in Autumn 2008 is temporarily making the global rise in energy and food prices a latent phenomenon. When growth will resume, in Asian countries and other regions with emerging markets, increasing inflationary pressures (see Chapter 1 in this volume) will start putting a strain again on food and energy prices. Partly because of dampening pressures exercised on producer prices, the supply of food products, and in particular of crops, finds it difficult to keep pace with increased demand. The land factor, the availability of which is quasi-finite, is indeed increasingly used for crops that are destined for non food consumption ends. In addition, the below expectations returns derived from Genetically Modified Organisms (GMOs), combined with the law of non-proportional yields (Turgot 1766)[1] seem to give some grounding to Malthus's pessimistic insight according to which agricultural outputs are unable to keep pace with population growth trends (Malthus 1803). This pessimism was further echoed by Ricardo (1809) who stated that in order to increase output from agriculture, farmers would have to farm less fertile land or farm with more intensive methods (law of rent).

If it is assumed that food security remains a primary objective of all governments, land, a rarer factor of production should not be used for bringing about a solution to our countries' energy problems.

In this new 'impossible trinity theorem' this chapter focuses on some of several recent phenomena, in particular on the rising food prices and on possible explanations for such rises.[2] These explanations are: (i) The emergence of new global actors (exerting a strain on energy consumption) as well as changing

1 This law is more widely known as the law of diminishing returns.

2 The issue of how arbitrage on international markets (speculation) affects food and energy prices (as mentioned in Chapter 3 of this volume) is not included in the analysis of this chapter.

consumption patterns; (ii) A high level of uncertainty in the agricultural markets, except for a probable upward adjustment of food prices. These two factors will be briefly analyzed in turn.

1.1. The emergence of new global actors and changing consumption patterns

The economic development of the BRICs (Brazil, Russia, India and China) translates itself by an overall increasing imbalance between world supply of and demand for agricultural and energy products.[3] In Brazil, the pace of growth in the demand for soybeans, beef, pork, poultry, sugar, and even cotton is unprecedented.

China tackles its status as a non-food-sufficient country by importing large volumes of food products. It has experienced significant increases in its imports in almost every single commodity whereas Brazil has increased its exports. India is a major producer of many crops and milk, yet the country is almost absent from world agricultural markets because of its present tariff structure. The economic development of the BRICs is of paramount importance because it creates a radical shift in the world agriculture, food and energy equilibria. This developmental factor has had but a relatively small effect so far, but it is expected to exert more pressures in the future. In addition to the BRICs, Argentina is an important agricultural trader; its exports cover cereals and many dairy products. Other growing exporters in the developing and transition economies include the Ukraine (and Russia) for coarse grains, Vietnam and Thailand for rice, Indonesia and Thailand for vegetable oils, and Thailand and Malaysia for poultry.

On the supply side, short-term changes such as short-term supply shocks due to adverse weather conditions (droughts in Australia, poor crops harvests in the EU and Ukraine), support for the production of renewable energy (a new market for agricultural/non food products), higher oil prices with their impact on the prices of agricultural inputs (such as fuel and fertilizer), previously low international prices (which may have reduced production incentives), and the entry of speculators in the commodity world all explain the recent trends in global food markets. On the consumption side, the demand for direct consumption for food (or for cereals, or for grain) is relatively income-inelastic. Feed grain demand for energy purposes (especially maize in the United States and wheat in Europe) is dependent on public support, while the livestock sector is much more sensitive to changes in income.

What Figure 6.1 and 6.2 suggest is that it is more the relative wealth of households rather than the increase in the population *per se* that seems to exert

3 Agricultural products cover a large range of goods from unprocessed commodities (such as wheat, rice, soybeans) to highly processed, high-value foods and beverages. Agricultural products are normally for food consumption (either through final demand or through intermediate inputs as in the case of meat production, bearing in mind that 8 kg of grain are required to produce 1 kg of beef); the rise of biofuels has led to the non-food use of agricultural products and land.

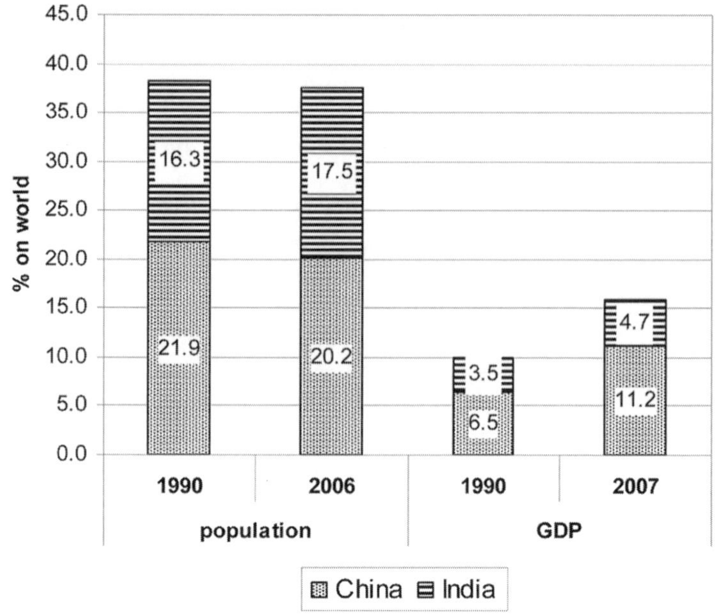

Figure 6.1 Share of China and India in world population and GDP

Source: FAO Stat, Rome and Worldbank, Washington.

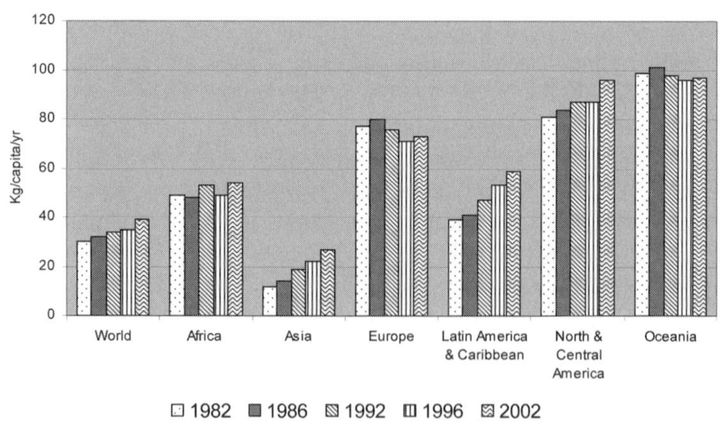

Figure 6.2 Growth in per capita meat consumption across the major world regions (selected years)

Source: FAO, Rome.

pressure on food markets. Figure 6.1 provides evidence of increasing GDP *per capita* levels in two of the BRICs (China and India). Higher levels of wealth lead to changing consumption patterns, with a shift towards high income elasticity of demand products such as meat. The issue of changing food consumption patterns alongside increasing *per capita* incomes, appears neatly from Figure 6.2. Although dietary concerns explain the perceptible decrease in *per capita* meat consumption in Europe over time, other regions have experienced sharp increases over the last 20 years under review. The increase in *per capita* meat consumption is particularly notable in Latin America and Asia, where rising incomes have propelled demand for this income elastic product.

Beside meat, dairy products have shown a strong growth in both total production and prices until 2007. According to OECD and FAO data (OECD and FAO 2009) the demand for dairy products is expected to increase in developing countries (due to income and population growth, changes in diet and dietary diversification strengthened by a large urbanization process). The increase is primarily expected in Asia (China, India and Pakistan).

The impact of these changing food consumption patterns is visible from Figure 6.3, which shows that quasi-stagnant resources in terms of arable land have to cater for a growing world population with a diet shifting towards protein-based food products.

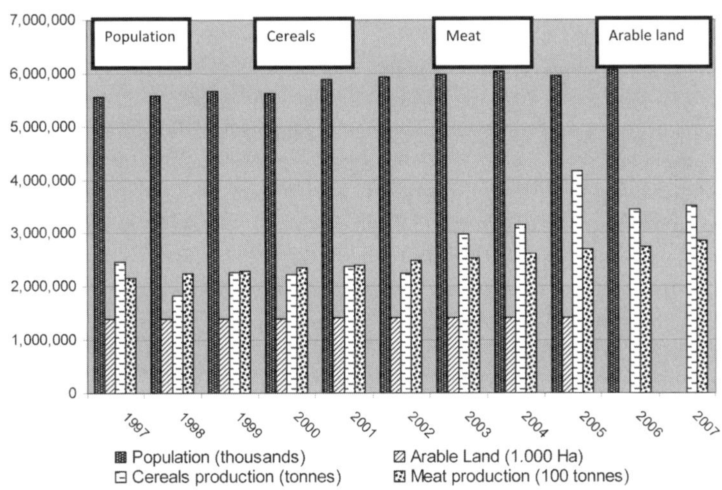

Figure 6.3 Major world trends in the agricultural sector (1997–2007)

Note: The percentages shown in the boxes refer to the growth over the period 1997/07.
Source: FAO Stat, Rome.

1.2. A high level of uncertainty in the agricultural markets, except for a possible upward adjustment of food prices

Before delving into the issue of food prices, this sub-section will very briefly discuss the possible implications for the EU of the entry of new players, particularly from Asia, in the agricultural market.

Implications for the EU of the entry of new players from Asia As a major producer of many crops and milk and as a relatively absent trade partner, India expects some positive impact arising from further liberalization, in particular from the planned EU-India Free Trade Area (FTA). In the case of China, according to official Chinese sources,[4] in 2000 the demand for grain was the equivalent of 385 kg per person. With shifting food consumption patterns as explained above, this demand is expected to reach 390 kg per person by 2010, and 400 kg per person in 2030. More than half of the 400 kg will be used for staple foodstuffs, while the rest will be used for producing food of animal origin. Consequently, given the tremendous need to meet food demands in China, grain production was overemphasized in some areas of the country, to the detriment of product diversification.

For the EU, the consequences arising from the entry of new players into the market are numerous and diverse. A major implication is the marginalization of the EU on world agricultural markets. Although still a sizeable trader by world standards, the EU has lost substantial market shares in many agricultural segments. The entry of new players, particularly from Asia, does not however fully explain this loss. It is also the result of a reform process that has led to lower surpluses in cereals and beef, to quotas that have kept production stable in dairy and sugar, and to increased competitiveness as a result of the cereal policy reform (for pork and poultry). Further reform of the Common Agricultural Policy (CAP), such as the decoupling of aids, dairy and sugar reforms, and in the CAP 'health check' will only accelerate this trend in the future (CEC 2007c, and Council of the European Communities 2009). Although a qualitative move is perceptible, with the EU progressively withdrawing from bulk commodity markets and increasing its share of value added exports, the EU is less and less an important agricultural world actor. The marginalization of the EU can be seen for example in the area of milk production, which remains nevertheless a rather sideline activity in Asian countries (Figure 6.4). As the figure shows, the EU share in world milk production was about 40 percent of the total in 1980; this share gradually dropped to roughly a quarter in 2006.

By way of comparison, the results for the USA are more mixed. While the country has retained a significant presence in bulk commodities, it has lost some of its market share in wheat and soybeans, but it continues to dominate in maize. The US market share has increased significantly in cotton and in meat. The issue

4 State Statistics Bureau, PRC, Beijing, various years.

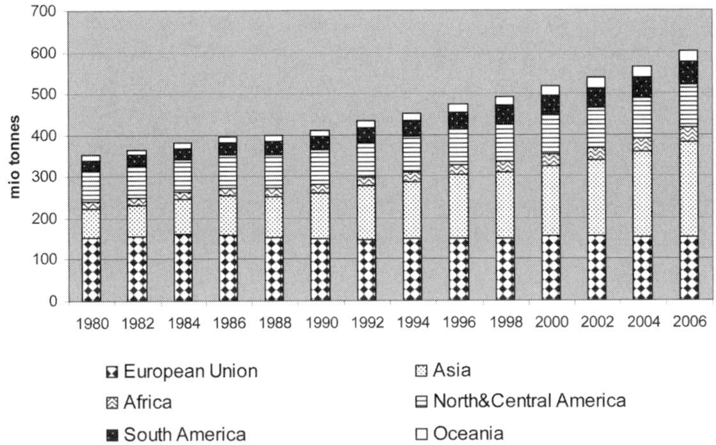

Figure 6.4 World milk production (1980–2006)
Source: FAO Stat, Rome.

of marginalization seems to concern primarily the EU; a question that needs to be addressed at this point is therefore the question of compatibility of this new trend with the objectives of CAP (in particular that of 'regular supply of food products' or food security). Uncertainty of food supply increases food insecurity.

Food and agricultural price trends Over the very long term (1850–1970s), food/agricultural prices have been stable (Federico 2005). They have trended upwards in the 1970s and they stabilized again and fell at the end of that decade. The downward price pressures exercised during and after the last GATT round (1986–1993/4) explain why the price levels were low up to the early 2000s. Since 2002, the increase in the prices of all fuels and some metals exercised an upward pressure on many agricultural commodities. The linkages existing between crop and energy prices affect the supply of agricultural production through direct and indirect effect. Table 6.1 depicts the evolution of the Food Price Index during the latest decade, and as the table shows, there has been a marked increase in food prices since 2005–2006.

In particular, it can be seen that cereal prices increased more than three times over that period. With the exception of sugar, the growth starts from the second half of 2007. The percentage of the food component in the Consumer Price Index (CPI) is estimated at being between 10 to 20 percent in high income countries, and 40 to 60 percent in low and middle income countries. It should be noted that, as in the case of food, energy prices have a much larger share in the CPI of emerging economies than in those of advanced economies. The relatively large

Table 6.1 FAO Food Price Indices (total index and index for different products; 2000–April 2008)

FAO Food Price Index							
		Food Price Index*	**Meat**	**Dairy**	**Cereals**	**Oils and Fats**	**Sugar**
2000		92.7	100	106	87	72	105
2001		94.5	100	117	89	72	111
2002		94.1	96	86	97	91	88
2003		102.3	105	105	101	105	91
2004		114.4	118	130	111	117	92
2005		117.3	121	145	106	109	127
2006		127.4	115	138	124	117	190
2007	January–March	157.4	121	247	172	174	129
2007	April	141.7	119	213	148	150	125
	May	144.4	119	222	150	161	121
	June	151.2	120	252	159	170	119
	July	155.8	120	277	160	175	131
	August	161.6	123	287	171	181	126
	September	171.4	124	290	195	190	125
	October	175.3	122	297	201	202	128
	November	180.6	126	302	203	221	130
	December	187.3	123	295	224	226	137
2008	January	196.3	126	281	238	250	154
	February	215.8	128	278	281	273	173
	March	218.4	132	276	280	285	169
	April	218.2	136	266	284	276	161

* The Food Price Index is defined as the average of six commodity group price indices mentioned above weighted with the average export shares of each of the groups for 1998–2000: in total 55 commodity quotations considered by FAO Commodity Specialists as representing the international prices of the food commodities noted are included in the overall index.

Source: FAO, Rome.

share of food in the CPI of low-income and emerging economies mirrors the fact that food expenditure still represents a relatively large component of total expenditure of the average income in these countries. Moreover, food expenditure represents a larger share of total expenditure in the case of low income households in all countries of the world, when compared with higher-income groups (FAO 2008). This implies that rising food prices threaten social cohesion, including in mature economies such as those of the EU. Rising food prices might fuel the pauperization of vulnerable social groups in the EU and other countries, for an increasing income share has to be devoted to food expenditure at the expense of non-food items. Low-income households lose much on the food side if food prices increase and they gain little on the energy side if energy prices decrease. In light of what has been mentioned before, which is, that food products compete with non-food agricultural crops for the finite land and water resources, these questions raise an ethical issue: is it acceptable, from an economic policy standpoint, to have rising food prices, bearing in mind that an important explanatory factor for this rise is the production of biofuels? The extent of this new tri-lemma has led to a number of estimates by, *inter alia*, the International Food Policy Research Institute. Using the IMPACT model 2007/08, Rosengrand (2008) elaborates two scenarios based on two main assumptions: demand is a function of prices, income and population growth; supply is determined by both crop prices and the rate of productivity growth.[5] Taking 2000 as the baseline year, the first scenario is based on the real investment plans in biofuels already made by many of the countries in the world; it also assumes a development potential of countries that have not yet elaborated such investment plans, but that could do so in the near future. Still with 2000 as the baseline year, scenario two assumes a greater expansion of biofuel production, when compared with the first scenario, by multiplying by a factor of two the utilization levels envisaged in scenario 1. According to scenario 1, grain and oilseed prices would increase by 26 and 18 percent respectively by 2020. In scenario 2, the increases would be of 72 and 44 percent respectively. Another outcome of both scenarios would be a decrease in the supply of and access to food products, with an overall reduction in calorie absorption, particularly in sub-Saharan Africa (-8 percent according to scenario 2).

An unanswered question is as follows: what would happen if the production of biofuels does become more competitive, with respect to food production, from a supplier point of view, and when more and more land, water and capital are diverted away from food production and towards biofuels? Table 6.2 shows the outcomes in terms of arable land usage.

Before we analyze the extent to which the not yet inevitable outcomes of these scenarios are being taken into account by policy makers in the EU, we will more fully explain the challenges brought about by the development of biofuels as a possible solution to our growing energy requirements.

2. Biofuels and Land Resources

World energy consumption has been increasing rapidly over the years; it is still now mainly satisfied by fossil fuels, raising a series of issues such as the scarcity of fossil resources, their growing cost, their impact on the environment in terms of greenhouse gas emissions and climate change. A solution can be found in

5 The International Model for Policy Analysis of Agricultural Commodities (IMPACT) was developed in the 1990s.

Table 6.2 Land used for biofuels (% of arable land)

	2004	2030 (scenario 1*)	2030 (scenario 2**)	2030 (scenario 3***)
USA and Canada	1.9	5.4	9.2	10.2
EU	1.2	11.6	14.5	15.7
Latin America	0.9	2.4	2.9	3.4
Africa and Asia	n.a.	0.3	0.3	0.4
World	1.0	2.5	3.8	4.2

* Situation in 2030 if current trends remain unchanged.
** Situation in 2030 if countries adopt all the policies they are currently considering related to energy security and CO_2 emissions.
*** Situation in 2030 in which some biomass for biofuels production comes from non arable land and residues.

Source: FAO, Rome and International Energy Agency, Vienna.

renewable energy,[6] which is an unlimited and non-polluting energy; in addition, it has a much lower environmental impact than conventional sources and several other benefits.[7]

Our chapter focuses on biomass (particularly on biofuels) as one type of renewable energy, because of its influence on land use. Biomass resources are the biodegradable fraction of products, waste and residues from agriculture (including vegetal and animal substances), forestry and related industries including fisheries and aquaculture, as well as the biodegradable fraction of industrial and municipal waste.[8] If the vegetable biomass is the result of the photosynthesis process of plants,

6 Energy from renewable resources means energy from renewable non-fossil sources, namely wind, solar, aerothermal, geothermal, hydrothermal and ocean energy, hydropower, biomass, landfill gas, sewage treatment plant gas and biogases.

7 Such as stimulating the economy (through research activities, new technology developments, etc.) and creating job opportunities. In particular, renewable energy could represent a solution to the problem of dispersed population and ensuing economic and social disadvantages in rural and remote areas of developed countries. In developing countries, the use of non-conventional resources could be a solution to the provision of electricity and services to the populations, in a sustainable way (both from an economic and environmental point of view) and so, it could contribute to improve the standards and quality of life in these areas.

8 Biomass excludes organic material which has been transformed by biological processes into substances such as coal or petroleum.

it can be equally applied both to animal and vegetable derived material.[9] Burning biomass (biopower)[10] is not the only way to release energy. It can be converted into biofuels, for use in the transport sector and bioproducts for everyday use such as plastics, glue, etc.

The most common form of biomass is wood, a product that has a long-standing tradition in rural areas due to its availability, sustainability and the fact that it is an environmentally friendly and a renewable natural resource. Wood also represents a significant source of income for forest owners in the context of forest restitution processes. In this case, an increase in demand for forest products could see a decrease in forestation. A study by Foster and Rosenzweig (2003), which examined the connection between economic growth and the growth of forests in India, concluded that as a result of several of India's policies (economic incentives, conservation methods, trade measures that limited the importation of forest products) forest owners have been given an incentive to increase the supply of trees. Another source of biomass is municipal solid waste.

In addition to the utilization of waste and residues, biomass can be produced by growing crops which are dedicated to energy production. Biofuel is produced by biomass.[11] Some biofuels currently in use are: biobutanol, biodiesel (it is the most common biofuel in Europe, obtained by soybean oil, sunflower, palm oil); bioethanol (the most common biofuel worldwide, particularly in Brazil and it is obtained by fermentation of sugar derived from wheat, corn, sugar beets, etc.). The main advantages of biomass can be summarised as follows:

- It is, in many ways, more environmentally friendly than most fossil fuels;
- It is an inexhaustible fuel force;
- It cuts back on waste and supports agricultural products. In fact biomass fuel from agricultural waste could be a by-product which adds value to agricultural crops;
- Less money is spent on fossil resources.

9 Although fossil fuels originate from ancient biomasses, they are not considered to be biomasses because they contain carbon that has been out of the carbon cycle for a very long time.

10 This process can satisfy three areas of energy demand: domestic use for the production of heat; industrial use (fire wood and agrifood for the production of electricity and heat); and use by local authorities and districts.

11 The use of biofuels as an additive to petroleum-based fuels can also result in cleaner burning with less emission of carbon monoxide and particulates. Ethanol produced by fermenting the sugars in biomass materials such as corn and agricultural residues is known as bioethanol. Bioethanol is used in internal-combustion engines either in pure form or more often as a gasoline additive. Biodiesel is made by processing vegetable oils and other fats and is also used either in pure form or as an additive to petroleum-based diesel fuel. Biogas is a mixture of methane and carbon dioxide produced by the anaerobic decomposition of organic matter such as sewage and municipal waste by bacteria. It is used especially in the generation of hot water and electricity.

The disadvantages are:

- The economic performance is low;
- It is still an expensive source, both in terms of producing biomass and converting it into alcohols. On a small scale, there is more likely to be a net loss of energy;
- It could significantly contribute to global warming and pollution if burned;
- It is not economically viable to transport biomass fuels over long distances; therefore power plants are usually located near biomass sources;
- There is a lack of technologies able to ensure high energy performance during the conversion processes; some biomass conversion projects concern animals and are relatively small and therefore limited;
- Research and public support are needed to reduce production costs;
- Low levels of public awareness;
- The land used for energy crops may be in demand for other purposes, such as agricultural use (mainly for food), conservation, housing and resorts;
- It contributes to exert an upward pressure on food prices.

Among the disadvantages, the issue of food security has been one of the most central issues in recent years, and to make matters worse, the upward pressure on food prices has affected the situation of many poor countries. Solutions could be the strengthening of the agricultural sector's capacity to meet the rising demand for food, through investments so as to improve agricultural productivity and expand production. But how much resources does this process need in terms of land?

Currently, according to FAO data (FAO 2007), the world's total cultivated land is about 1.6 million hectares; over 60 percent is located in the developing countries with Asia accounting for 36 percent of the total. More than 75 percent of the harvesting area for producing biofuels feedstock is concentrated in developed countries, with Asia accounting for 7.2 percent (Table 6.3). A substantial share of maize in the USA, wheat and rapeseed in the EU, as well as sugar in Brazil is used for ethanol and bio-diesel production and less than half of the harvest area of six major crops for producing biofuels feed stocks is located in North America (Tables 6.4 and 6.5).

The growing demand for biofuel production will strengthen the need for more land. Expanding the land resource, through for example land reclamation or an improvement in land quality, is theoretically possible only in developing countries, where this resource has not yet been completely exploited. However, in these countries, insecure property rights, land and labor distribution and allocation as well as inequality in the access to land and credit, all create large inefficiencies.

Table 6.3 Biofuel feedstocks land in global land use (2007)

	Cultivated land Mha	Harvested area of six major* crops					
		For food, feed and biofuels			For producing biofuels feed stocks only		
		Mha	% on cultivated land	% on world	Mha	% on cultivated land	% on world
North America	230	75	32.6	22.2	11.4	5.0	45.4
Europe & Russia	305	24	7.9	7.1	7.2	2.4	28.7
Oceania & Polinesia	53	2	3.8	0.6	0.4	0.8	1.6
Asia	559	105	18.8	31.1	1.8	0.3	7.2
Africa	244	48	19.7	14.2	0.2	0.1	0.8
Central America & Carib.	43	12	27.9	3.6	0.2	0.5	0.8
South America	129	71	55.0	21.0	4	3.1	15.9
Developed countries	591	101	17.1	29.9	18.9	3.2	75.3
Developing countries	972	237	24.4	70.1	6.2	0.6	24.7
World	**1,563**	**338**	**21.6**	**100.0**	**25.1**	**1.6**	**100.0**

* Sugar cane, maize, cassava, oil palm, rape and soybean.

Source: Authors' elaboration based on International Institute for Applied Systems Analysis, *Biofuels and food security – Final Report,* 2007.

Table 6.4 World biofuels production (1.000 liters)

	Ethanol		Biodiesel		Total	
	1,000 liters	%	1,000 liters	%	1,000 liters	%
Brazil	19,000	37.0	227	2.0	19,227	31.0
Canada	1,000	2.0	97	1.0	1,097	2.0
China	1,840	4.0	114	1.0	1,954	3.0
India	400	1.0	45	0.0	445	1.0
Indonesia	0	-	409	4.0	409	1.0
Malaysia	0	-	330	3.0	330	1.0
USA	26,500	50.0	1,688	17.0	28,188	44.0
European Union	2,253	4.0	6,109	60.0	8,362	13.0
Others	1,017	2.0	1,186	12.0	2,203	4.0
World	52,010	100.0	10,204	100.0	62,214	100.0

Source: Derived from F.O. Licht 2007, data from the OECD–FAO AgLink-Cosimo database.

As a consequence, the increase in the availability of arable land meets many constraints.[12]

From the point of view of the developed countries, located mainly in temperate areas, and bearing in mind that ethanol and bio-diesel productions are not economically viable without public support, a different combination of technologies, crude oil prices and renewable resources policies could change the current situation. Because of the relatively high costs in the EU for both land and labor, biomass production is actually more expensive per unit of energy produced than that produced by available residues and wastes.

Table 6.5 Harvested areas of selected first-generation biofuel feedstocks, million hectares and % of total cultivated land (2007)

	Sugarcane		Maize		Cassava		Rape		Soy bean		Palm oil		Total
	Mha	%	Mha	%	Mha	%	Mha	%	Mha	%	Mha	%	Mha
North America	0.4	0.2	36.4	15.8	0	0.0	6.3	2.7	31.7	13.8	0	0.0	74.8
Europe & Russia	0	0.0	13.9	4.6	0	0.0	8.2	2.7	2	0.7	0	0.0	24.1
Oceania & Polynesia	0.5	0.9	0.1	0.2	0	0.0	1.1	2.1	0	0.0	0.1	0.2	1.8
Asia	9.7	1.7	48.8	8.7	3.8	0.7	14.5	2.6	19.4	3.5	8.9	1.6	105.1
Africa	1.6	0.7	29	11.9	11.9	4.9	0.1	0.0	1.3	0.5	4.3	1.8	48.2
Central America & Carib.	1.8	4.2	10	23.3	0.2	0.5	0	0.0	0.1	0.2	0.2	0.5	12.3
South America	8	6.2	19.7	15.3	2.7	2.1	0.1	0.1	40.4	31.3	0.4	0.3	71.3
Developed countries	0.8	0.1	50.4	8.5	0	0.0	15.6	2.6	33.7	5.7	0	0.0	100.5
Developing countries	21.2	2.2	107.5	11.1	18.7	1.9	14.7	1.5	61.2	6.3	13.9	1.4	237.2
World	**22**	**1.4**	**157.9**	**10.1**	**18.7**	**1.2**	**30.2**	**1.9**	**94.9**	**6.1**	**13.9**	**0.9**	**337.6**

Source: Authors' elaboration based on International Institute for Applied Systems Analysis, *Biofuels and Food Security – Final Report,* 2007.

12 According to FAO terminology, arable land is land under temporary crops (double-cropped areas are counted only once), temporary meadows for mowing or pasture, land under market and kitchen gardens, plus land temporarily fallow (less than five years). The land abandoned resulting from shifting cultivation is not included in this category. Cultivated land is the sum of arable land and the land under permanent crops. Land under permanent crop refers to land cultivated with crops that occupy the land for long periods and need not be replaced after each harvest.

In this context, support by the public authorities is essential (Menanteau et al. 2003). Without such aid, market forces would result in the limited diffusion of renewable energy in limited niche markets. Public involvement can be justified as a means for correcting negative external effects, which result from the use of fossil fuels, and for increasing efficiency by stimulating technical change. Renewable energy contributes to the preservation of a public good. Due to the non-excludable and non competitive characteristic of air and climate stability as a public good, private actors are not interested in investing in something which everyone can acquire free of charge. Government intervention is therefore essential in this area.

3. EU Energy Policy and CAP

The main issue to be addressed in this section is whether the EU energy policy can be reconciled with the reformed CAP, in light of the recent or current signals sent in particular by the fast growing economies of Asia, which are summarized by our new 'impossible trinity theorem'. More specifically, this section will try to analyze whether the development of biofuels are compatible with the objective of reasonable food prices in the EU and further afield.

Policy targets for renewable energy exist in almost seventy countries worldwide, including all 27 European Union countries (REN21 2007) and at least sixty countries have some type of policy to promote renewable power generation.

Worldwide, the most common renewable energy promotion policy is represented by feed-in schemes.[13] This policy was enacted for the first time by the United States in 1978. Feed-in policies were next adopted in Denmark, Germany, Greece, India, Italy, Spain and Switzerland in the early 1990s. The EU energy policy is a relatively new policy and it has the aim to drive sustainable processes, leaving the individual Member States to deal with specific areas of intervention. The European guidelines and support are more complex and thorough, and yet, at the same time, more lenient, than national ones. Currently, the main EU guidelines and regulations concerning energy and renewable energy are summarized in a number of documents (EP 2008; CEC 2005, 2006a, 2006b, 2007a, 2008; EP and Council 2009).

The January 2007 Communication from the Commission to the European Council and the European Parliament entitled *An energy policy for Europe* represents a strategic review of the European energy situation and it introduced a complete set of European Energy Policy measures (the so called 'energy' package). The new European energy policy includes main topics and objectives which have

13 This is an incentive structure to encourage the adoption of renewable energy through government legislation: the electricity utilities are obligated to buy renewable electricity at above market rates set by the government.

been suggested in various Commission documents (CEC 2005b, 2006a, 2006c). The main established objectives are:

1. Establishing the internal energy market.
2. Ensuring a secure energy supply, minimizing the EU's vulnerability concerning external energy dependency, through measures supporting strategic oil stocks and increasing security of electricity supply.
3. Reducing greenhouse gas emissions, through the so called initiative "20-20-20".
4. Developing energy technologies, by strengthening the European Strategic Energy Technology Plan which will cover the entire innovation process, from the initial research to entry into the market.[14]
5. Considering the future of nuclear energy.
6. Implementing a common international energy policy, in particular by strengthening the European Energy Charter,[15] and taking the initiative in an agreement on energy efficiency.

In 2009, with the Directive *on the promotion of the use of energy from renewable sources*, the EU established a common framework for the promotion of energy from renewable sources and committed itself to completing the initiative "20-20-20".

In particular, the Directive establishes that each Member State shall ensure that the share of energy from renewable sources, in gross final consumption of energy in 2020, is at least equal to its national overall target for the share of energy from renewable sources in that year (set out in Annex 1 of the Directive).[16] With regard to transport, each Member State shall ensure that the share of energy from renewable sources in all forms of transport in 2020 is at least 10 percent of final consumption of energy in transport in that Member State. As far as biofuels are

14 This strategic plan will support the Seventh Framework Programme for Research, which foresees a 50 percent increase in spending on research in the energy sector, along with the Intelligent Energy for Europe programme.

15 Council and Commission Decision 98/181/EC, ECSC, Euratom of 23 September 1997 *on the conclusion, by the European Communities, of the Energy Charter Treaty and the Energy Charter Protocol on energy efficiency and related environmental aspects*. The Energy Charter Treaty establishes a framework for international cooperation between European countries and other industrialised counties with the aim of developing the energy potential of central and Eastern European countries and of ensuring security of energy supply for the European Union. The Protocol on energy efficiency and related environmental aspects aims to promote energy efficiency policies that are compatible with sustainable development, to encourage more efficient and sound use of energy and to promote cooperation in the field of energy efficiency.

16 These mandatory national targets are consistent with a target of at least a 20 percent share of energy from renewable sources in the Community's gross final energy consumption in 2020.

concerned, with effect from 2017, the greenhouse gas emission savings from the use of biofuels and other bioliquids shall be 50 percent. After 2017 it shall be 60 percent for biofuels and bioliquids produced in installations whose production has started from 2017 onwards. Finally, Member States shall introduce in their building regulations and codes appropriate measures in order to increase the share of all kinds of energy from renewable sources in the building sector. With regard to biomass, the recommendations of the Commission must not be overlooked (CEC 2005a, 2006a). The biomass action plan presents measures aimed at intensifying energy production from wood and agricultural waste by offering incentives based on market mechanisms and the elimination of barriers that hinder the development of the market. These incentives will enable Europe to reduce its dependence on fossil fuels, curb greenhouse gas emissions and stimulate economic growth in rural areas. The EU's strategy on biofuels has three main aims:

i. to promote the more widespread use of biofuels within EU states and in developing countries, and to guarantee that their use is compatible with the environment, and respecting the Lisbon objectives while addressing the issue of competitiveness;
ii. to provide conditions for the wide-scale use of biofuels and enhancing their competitiveness with regard to cost, optimizing the production of the raw materials, encouraging research into "second generation" biofuels by promoting them on the market and consequently increasing the number of demonstration projects and eliminating non-technical barriers;
iii. to examine the opportunities available to developing countries – including those affected by the EU's CAP sugar reform – thanks to the production of raw biofuel materials and the biofuels themselves, as well as defining the EU's potential role in the development of sustainable biofuel production.

In addition, the 2003 mid-term reform of the CAP introduced aid for energy crops and within the instrument envisaged for this purpose, it maintained the opportunity to grow non food crops. The Council Regulation (EC) No 73/2009 of 19 January 2009 on the modifications to the Common Agricultural Policy abolished compulsory set aside facilities as well as specific support for energy crops due to recent developments in the bio-energy sector and, in particular, to the strong demand for such products on international markets and the introduction of binding targets for the share of bio-energy in total fuel by 2020.[17] This implies that European Union public support is now more decoupled than in the past, and that farmers can make their choices in response to market signals aiming at improving

17 This was done by amending Regulations (EC) No 247/2006, (EC) No 320/2006, (EC) No 1405/2006, (EC) No 1234/2007, (EC) No 3/2008 and (EC) No 479/2008 and repealing Regulations (EEC) No 1883/78, (EEC) No 1254/89, (EEC) No 2247/89, (EEC) No 2055/93, (EC) No 1868/94, (EC) No 2596/97, (EC) No 1182/2005 and (EC) No 315/2007.

their competitiveness, whether they produce feed or energy crops. On the one hand, the EU underlines that its primary vocation is the production of food and feed. On the other hand, the second pillar of the policy (rural development policy) implies the support of the environmental use of land and water, as well as the promotion of ecosystem management, afforestation and renewable energy measures. The objectives of food and energy production as embraced in EU policy making might therefore be in conflict; indeed, if the price of energy increases, farmers will shift their cultivation towards biofuel feeedstocks, thereby exacerbating the competition between food and fuel. The trade-off between food and fuel may be accelerated when biofuels become more competitive compared to food.

The latest developments in terms of EU policy making show that the EU energy and agricultural policies are becoming more intimately intertwined, and that developments in one area (energy markets) do have an impact on the other area (food crops). The integration of these two policies at EU level does not seem, however, to lead to a compatibility of the objectives enshrined in these two policies. In the case of the EU, more resources for producing energy from renewable sources inevitably imply a diversion of the same resources (land in particular) from traditional agricultural areas (food crops). This is an inescapable conflict that does not seem to have been properly addressed in EU policy making so far.

4. A New "Impossible Trinity Theorem"? Some Concluding Remarks

The new challenges facing the world agricultural and energy systems are explained by a combination of three different forces: first the entry of new players (in particular of China) into agricultural markets; second, sustained growth in the emerging economies of Asia and elsewhere, leading to an unprecedented energy demand; and third, changing food consumption patterns in the emerging economies, with a shift towards meat consumption and its concomitant effect on demand for grain as animal foodstuff. These three forces, the intensity of which has only temporarily been suspended by the current economic crisis, exert an increasing pressure on arable land requirements, a production factor in quasi fixed supply and prone to diminishing returns. The current enthusiasm for the development of biofuels (biomass) as an alternative to oil and as a solution to the world's energy problems leads yet to another "impossible trinity theorem". This theorem refers to the difficulty (perhaps the impossibility) of reconciling three apparently conflicting objectives, namely: (i) addressing energy (fossil oil) shortages by developing biofuels; (ii) feeding a growing population with more diversified consumption patterns; (iii) and maximizing land efficiency.

The use of arable crop land for producing fuel remains a highly controversial topic, as biofuels compete with food products for scarce resources such as land, water, as well as for fertilizers and pesticides. The competition between food and energy for land and water can be seen in the increasing co-movement of agricultural commodities and energy prices (Peňaranda and Rupérez-Micola 2009), and can be best summarised by the following FAO quote (FAO 2007: 1):

> International cereal prices remain high and volatile, reflecting sustained demand, in particular from the fast growing bio-fuels industry, coupled with historically low levels of stocks and insufficient increases in the 2007 production.... Rises in international prices have translated into higher retail prices of basic food in many countries. Most affected by the food inflation are those developing countries that depend heavily on imports to cover their cereal consumption requirements.

In turn, this competition raises the issue of compatibility between food security and energy security in a context of sustainable development, an issue that has not yet sufficiently been tackled by government policy in general (Berndes et al. 2003). The specific case of EU policy analyzed in this chapter reveals that, in spite of it being regarded as a progressive actor in terms of delineating and implementing a well developed agricultural policy, the EU cannot currently be seen as providing a solution to resolving this 'impossible trinity theorem'. Its energy policy is nascent and weak, and although it does attempt at connecting CAP and energy policy, the EU seems to prefer ignoring the very existence of this theorem. It might, therefore, be that only exacerbated trends in the emerging markets in general, and in particular in Asia, will ultimately provide real policy change in the EU.

There are indeed a number of ways forward that ought to be used as guidelines for designing better intertwined agricultural and energy policies in the future at both EU and world levels. These encompass: (i) limiting the development of biofuel products, and developing alternatives to biofuels, particularly in the transport area, through R&D; (ii) re-regulating international trade in key food products so as to protect them from speculation and introducing a ceiling on the volume of oil open to hedging practices on international markets; (iii) controlling the power of the distributive trade sector, particularly in the developed economies and (iv) stimulating food grain supply (particularly in emerging countries such as in the Association of South East Asian Nations – ASEAN).

These few guidelines are aimed at placing food production and consumption at the centre of economic activity, and at having food security as the policy core objective at the world level. These guidelines are essential ingredients for the design of a new world economic order, and for economic growth and stability.

References

Antle, J.M. and Heiderbrink, G. 1995. Environment and development: theory and international evidence. *Economic Development and Cultural Change*, 43 (3), 603–25.

Aqeel, A. and Butt, M.S. 2001. The relationship between energy consumption and economic growth in Pakistan. *Asia-Pacific Journal*, 8 (2), 101–110.

Berndes, G., Hoogwijk, M. and van der Broek, R. 2003. The contribution of biomass in the future global energy supply: a review of 17 studies. *Biomass and Bioenergy*, 25, 1–28.

CEC 2004. *The Share of Renewable Energy in the EU*. Commission of the European Communities, Brussels.

CEC 2005a. *Biomass Action Plan*. Commission of the European Communities, Brussels.

CEC 2005b. *Green Paper on Energy Efficiency or Doing More with Less*. Commission of the European Communities, Brussels.

CEC 2006a. *Action Plan for Energy Efficiency: Realising the Potential, Saving 20% by 2020*.October, Commission of the European Communities, Brussels.

CEC 2006b. *An EU Strategy for Biofuels*. Commission of the European Communities, Brussels.

CEC 2006c. *Renewable Energy Road Map. Renewable Energies in the 21st Century: Building a More Sustainable Future*. Commission of the European Communities, COM (2006) 848 final, Brussels.

CEC 2007a. *An Energy Policy for Europe*. Commission of the European Communities, Brussels.

CEC 2007b. *Intelligent Energy Programmes*. Commission of the European Communities, Brussels.

CEC 2007c. *Preparing for the "Health Check" of the CAP Reform*. Commission of the European Communities, Brussels.

CEC 2008. *Second Strategic Energy Review. An EU Energy Security and Solidarity Action Plan*. Commission of the European Communities, Brussels.

Council of the European Union 2009. *Council Regulation (EC) No 72/2009 of 19 January 2009 on modifications to the Common Agricultural Policy by Amending Regulations (EC) No 247/2006, (EC) No 320/2006, (EC) No 1405/2006, (EC) No 1234/2007, (EC) No 3/2008 and (EC) No 479/2008 and repealing Regulations (EEC) No 1883/78, (EEC) No 1254/89, (EEC) No 2247/89, (EEC) No 2055/93, (EC) No 1868/94, (EC) No 2596/97, (EC) No 1182/2005 and (EC) No 315/2007.*

European Parliament's and Council Directive 2009a. 2009/28/EC: *Promotion of the Use of Energy from Renewable Sources and Amending and Subsequently Repealing Diresctives 2001/77/EC and 2003/30/EC.*

European Union and Council of European Union. Directive 2001/77/CE on *Electricity Production from Renewable Energy Source*. Brussels.

EIA 2007. *International Energy Outlook*. World Energy and Economic Outlook, Energy Information Administration, Washington DC.

FAO 2006. *Statistical Yearbook*. Food and Agriculture Organization of the United Nations, Rome. Available at: http://www.fao.org/statistics/yearbook/default.asp.

FAO 2007. *Crops Prospect and Food Situation*. December 2007. Available at: ftp://ftp.fao.org/docrep/fao/010/ah877e/ah877e00.pdf.

FAO 2008a. *Production Statistics* (ProdStat). Food and Agriculture Organization of the United Nations, Rome. Available at: http://faostat.fao.org/site/526/default.aspx.

FAO 2008b. *Population Statistics* (PopStat). Food and Agriculture Organization of the United Nations, Rome. Available at: http://faostat.fao.org/site/452/default.aspx.

FAO 2008c. *Consumption Statistics*. Food and Agriculture Organization of the United Nations, Rome. Available at: http://faostat.fao.org/site/345/default.aspx.

FAO 2008d. *Bioenergy, Food Security and Sustainability – Towards an International Framework. Information Paper No. 3 for the High Level Conference on World Food Security: The Challenges of Climate Change and Bioenergy*. HLC/08/INF/3. Food and Agriculture Organization of the United Nations, Rome. Available at:http://www.fao.org/fileadmin/user_upload/foodclimate/hlcdocs/hlc08-inf-3-e.pdf.

Federico Giovanni. 2005. *Feeding the World – An Economic History of Agriculture, 1800–2000*. Princeton: Princeton University Press.

Foster, A.D. and Rosenzweig, M.R. 2003. Economic growth and the rise of forests. *Quarterly Journal of Economics*, 118 (2), 601–37.

Institute for Applied Systems Analysis 2007. *Biofuels and Food Security – Final Report*. Available at: http://www.opecfund.org/publications/pdf/BiofuelAndFoodSecurity.pdf.

Malthus, T.R. 1803. *An Essay on the Principle of Population*. Penguin Books Limited, 1988 edition.

Menanteau, O., Finon, D. and Lamy, M.L. 2003. Prices versus quantities: choosing policies for promoting the development of renewable energy. *Energy Policy*, 31 (8), 799–812.

MNES 2006. *Annual Report 2005–2006*. New Delhi: Ministry of Non Conventional Energy Sources.

OECD and FAO 2009. *Agricultural Outlook 2009–2018*. Organisation for Economic Co-operation and Development and Food and Agriculture Organization of United Nations.

OECD-FAO. *AgLink-Cosimo Database Statistics*. Available at: http://www.oecd.org/document/6/0,3343,en_36774715_36775671_40969158_1_1_1_1,00.html.

Peñaranda, F. and Rupérez-Micola, A. 2009. The Emergence of Biofuels and the Co-movement between Crude Oil and Agricultural Pprices. Economics Working Paper 1174, October, Universitat Pompeu Fabra).

Ricardo, D. 1817. *On the Principles of Political Economy and Taxation*. First Edition. London: John Murray.

Rosegrant, M.W. 2008. *Biofuels and Grain Prices: Impacts and Policy Responses*. Statement prepared for presentation to the Committee on Homeland Security and Governmental Affairs, U.S. Senate. May 7. Available at: http://www.ifpri.org/pubs/testimony/rosegrant20080507.pdf.

Suri, V. and Chapman, D. 1998. Economic growth, trade and energy: implications for the environmental Kuznet curve. *Ecological Economics*, Washington: Elsevier.

Turgot, R. 1766. *Réflexions sur la formation et la distribution des richesses*. (from Schelle, G. 1914. Œuvres de Turgot. Paris: Alcan, Tome II.)

World Bank 2005. *World Bank Group Progress in Renewable Energy and Energy Efficiency: 1990–2004*. Washington D.C., USA.

World Bank. 2009. *Key Development Data & Statistics*. Available at: http://web.worldbank.org/website/external/datastatistics.

PART II
Firm and Industry Level Issues

Chapter 7
Chinese Businesses in Japan: An Emerging Phenomenon

Reinhard Drifte and Jacques Jaussaud

Introduction

Between 2004 and 2005, the Chinese Lenovo group took-over the PC division of IBM, and TCL both acquired the consumer products business of Thomson and took control of Alcatel`s mobile phone business. Such acquisitions showed the astonishing emergence of major Chinese companies as world class competitors, a phenomenon that has been thoroughly analyzed by scholars such as Wang (2002), Rui and Yip (2008) and Deng (2009). These huge operations followed the signature in 2002 of a comprehensive strategic alliance between Haier, a major Chinese household appliances maker, and Sanyo Electric of Japan. With these and many other foreign acquisitions and joint ventures, it has become clear that some major Chinese corporations have been able and willing to seize opportunities provided by China's entry into the World Trade Organization (WTO) in December 2001, although the competitive advantages of Chinese firms may differ considerably from each other.

As stated by Hayashi Yasuo (2007), the number of Chinese firms operating abroad exceeded 10,000 in 2006 according to figures released by the Chinese authorities. That year, the country's overseas investment exceeded $US16 billion, which was around one quarter of China's inward Foreign Direct Investment (FDI). In cumulative terms, China's overseas investment totalled $US73.3 billion as of the end of 2006, which was around 10 percent of China's cumulative inward FDI. Yet, academic literature has mainly focused on China's inward FDI, that is to say foreign business in China (Beamish 1993, Calantone and Zhao 2001, Ding 1997, Isobe et al. 2000, Jaussaud and Schaaper 2006a among others). These figures would suggest, however, that Chinese business investing abroad ought to be addressed as a new and important research issue.

In fact, the idea of investing abroad or "going out" (*zou chuqu*) by Chinese companies was already conceived by 18 researchers of the Chinese Academy of Social Sciences in 1984. In order to limit increasing trade frictions with the USA and Europe resulting from the ballooning Chinese trade surpluses with the two entities, the Chinese government advised companies to move factories abroad (Yomiuri and Chugoku Shuzai Dan 2006). As early as 2002, the Chinese government facilitated the expansion of companies towards foreign markets by strengthening tax relief measures for such companies.

Chinese companies, particularly the major ones, had come to realize their weaknesses in product development, branding and sales network. Acquiring market share in China in the face of the competition from multinational companies (MNCs) was neither easy nor enough (Pan 2009). Obtaining market share abroad is a way of strengthening their competitive advantages, including through economies of scale. In some industries, such as construction, Chinese companies have targeted emerging countries, as they could bid at lower prices. In other industries, such as telecommunications equipment, they have targeted both emerging and developed countries, including the most advanced ones. How they succeed, facing the most powerful competitors, particularly in highly developed markets, is still a question to be carefully addressed.

To the best of our knowledge, only limited attention has been devoted in academic research to firms from an emerging country such as China investing in developed markets. Most of the contributions relate mainly to investments by firms from developing countries, e.g. China, in other developing economies (Lecraw 1977, Khanna and Palepu 2006), with some exceptions such as Yang (2005) who uses a network approach to explain Chinese outward investment in both developing and developed markets.[1] Chittoor and Ray (2007), however, from an investigation on firms in the Indian pharmaceutical industry, find that when they combine the exploitation of their present competitive advantage on one side and exploration strategies of new products and new markets in developed countries on the other side, firms from emerging economies may succeed in competing with major multinational corporations from the developed world. How can they do this successfully still remains an under-researched question.

In order to contribute to this research question, we focus in this chapter on Chinese businesses in Japan, which is widely known as one of the most difficult markets to enter. Japan, although affected by the ongoing worldwide crisis of 2008–2009, is a huge market which is geographically close to China. With regard to Chinese strategies, successes and failures in this market can help us understand the rationale for Chinese businesses investing abroad, their strengths and weaknesses, in respect of their internationalization strategies.

Such a question is a crucial one as it may contribute to the understanding of economic integration in Asia, a process which may lessen both political and trade frictions between neighbors in the region. It is also a question of interest for the West, in particular for the European Union, where economic integration

1 The reader interested in this issue can refer to the chapter by Balcet and Bruschieri (Chapter 8) in this volume, where a literature review of direct investment theories from developing and emerging economies is provided. As shown by Balcet and Bruschieri, there is indeed a long tradition of theories dealing with outward FDI from developing and emerging economies, such as South Korea and Taiwan, with the case of China having only been marginally dealt with.

has proceeded rather smoothly, thanks to a high level of institutionalization of economic integration in Europe. By contrast, foreign multinational firms seem to have been a catalyst for economic – and perhaps political – integration in other regions of the world, above all in Asia (see Chapter 4 in this volume). This chapter's emphasis on two major players in Asia, e.g. China and Japan, brings to the fore the increasing level of interconnections existing between the two countries through the activities of Chinese firms. From that point of view, among others adopted in this book, one may wonder whether Asia can inspire the West.

This chapter is just a preliminary step in this research program, as we shall try only to give a picture of Chinese businesses in Japan, in terms of numbers, industrial sectors, company size, as well as the nature of the subsidiaries they have established, whether as joint ventures with local partners or as wholly-owned subsidiaries (WOS). This contribution is based on three different and complementary sources: firstly, various press releases on the subject; secondly, the results of nine interviews conducted, in Japan, with Japanese and Chinese personnel directly involved in Chinese business circles there, including two Chinese entrepreneurs; and thirdly, data from Toyo Keizai (2007), which provides a listing of foreign businesses in Japan, including Chinese ones.

The structure of this chapter is as follows: Section 1 will estimate the extent of the phenomenon, namely the number of Chinese subsidiaries and enterprises in Japan, and their diversity in terms of industries; Section 2 will focus on the nature of the subsidiaries and enterprises, whether joint ventures or wholly-owned by Chinese interests.

1. Extent and Diversity of Chinese Businesses in Japan

The first major Chinese acquisition in Japan which drew attention in business circles occurred in January 2001 when Shanghai Electric (160,000 workers in China), together with the Hong Kong-based investment firm Morning Side, bought Akiyama Printing Machine, which ranked 6th worldwide in its sector, but had become bankrupt. In 2003, the Chinese Sanjiu Pharmaceutical group took over Toa of Japan, and renamed it Sankyu Seiyaku. In October 2004, Shanghai Electric bought the Japanese machine maker Ikegai which had gone into receivership in 2001. Other major transactions by Chinese companies in Japan were Haier (a Chinese manufacturer of household electrical appliances), which engaged in 2002 in a comprehensive strategic alliance with Sanyo Electric, for both the Japanese and Chinese markets; Lenovo acquiring Yamata Research laboratory as part of its acquisition of IBM PC in 2004; and Suntech Power taking over MSK, a Tokyo-based photovoltaic material producer, in 2006. Suntech Power had been established only in 2002, and its $US300 million purchase of MSK was the biggest acquisition so far by a Chinese company in Japan (Nakagawa, 2008). Between 2000 and May 2005, 17 Japanese companies either merged with or were bought by Chinese companies (*Yomiuri Shimbun* 2005). Most recently, in summer

2009, Suning Appliance Co., China's second-largest consumer electronics retailer, became the top shareholder in Laox with a 27.36 percent stake, which marked the first major Japanese consumer electronics discount chain to come under the umbrella of a Chinese firm (*Japan Times* 26 June 2009).

However, many other such cases have been reported, so drawing increased attention from more than only business circles. By 2006, over 320 Chinese enterprises had moved into Japan, according to the Xinhua Press Agency,[2] and the amount of Chinese investment in Japan stood at $US170 million at the end of 2006. These 320 cases do not, however, include firms set up by Chinese citizens who are residents in Japan, such as those who have studied and graduated there. In 2007, Chinese nationals numbered 606,889 in Japan, or 28.2 percent of all foreign residents, compared with 593,489 Koreans (27.6 percent) who had up to that point always represented the highest share of foreigners. Among the Chinese, 71,277 were Chinese students, 60 percent of all international students in Japan. A small number of them set up their own business in Japan, rather than returning to China, and some of them have become naturalized Japanese, and therefore are not even encompassed in those statistics.

Chinese investment in Japan remains, however, limited in relation to China`s overall investment abroad, as well as to the over $US200 billion annual trade flow between the two countries. In 2006, according to Xinhua Press Agency, Chinese investment in Japan amounted to US$ 18million, i.e. only about 1 percent of Chinese total outward FDI.

Among the 320 cases identified by Xinhua Press Agency, Toyo Keizai (2007) lists 68 subsidiaries or Chinese invested companies that replied to its questionnaire. Although limited in size, this sample may help to illustrate the nature of Chinese investments in Japan. As the 68 subsidiaries are rather diverse in terms of size, industries and business organization nature, we are confident of the sample's representativeness, although we lack some detailed information on the 320 cases identified by Chinese authorities to check it precisely. We may add that Toyo Keizai directories are widely used and regarded as highly reliable both by business circles and researchers. To the best of our knowledge, no other better source is available on Chinese investment in Japan.

Table 7.1, which is prepared on the basis of data from Toyo Keizai (2007), provides a breakdown of these 68 cases according to industry, and sheds light on their size.

Services dominate these investment cases, particularly for shipping and transportation between Japan, China and other destinations (11 cases), followed by banking and insurance (9 cases), possibly related to the trade between the two countries, software development (10 cases), and the textile trade (7 cases). Regarding other industries, such as food (5 cases), electronics (6 cases), or metal products and machinery parts (5 cases), investments are also trade related, that is to say they are mainly devoted to imports and exports between Japan and China.

2 http://news.xinhuanet.com/english/2007-04/06/content_5942480.htm.

Table 7.1 Chinese firms in Japan in 2006, industries and sizes

	Number of subsidiaries	Average number of employees (rounded)	Dispersion of number of employees (rounded)	Number of employees (smallest – highest)
Software development	10	44	45	2–130
Electronics	6	45	66	2–168
Food	5	11	6	7–15
Textile	7	6	24	4–11
Transport	11	35	43	8–110
Banking / Insurance	9	26	42	3–100
Raw materials and energy	2	9	9	2–15
Metal products, machinery parts	5	8	5	4–16
Chemicals	1	20	0	20
Pharmaceuticals	1	30	0	30
Others	11	13	15	3–49
Total	68	24	37	2–168

Source: Toyo Keizai (2007).

The very nature of the business in these subsidiaries (services and distribution) may explain why they remain limited in size. Among the 68 cases listed by Toyo Keizai (2007), only three carry out production activities (one in the pharmaceutical industry, and two machine makers), i.e. the three existing Japanese companies that have been bought out by the Chinese groups, Shanghai Electric, Sanjiu Pharmaceuticals and Suntech, as explained above.

New Chinese software development firms have opened subsidiaries in Japan since 2006, the year of data collection by Toyo Keizai (2007), as China becomes a growing centre for outsourcing in this field, and more broadly in Business Process Outsourcing (BPO).[3] For instance, a software park was opened in Tokyo, in 2008, by the Dalian Economic Zone, with 35 Chinese software companies having offices in it.[4]

3 Business Process Outsourcing (BPO) is the delegation of an information technology-intensive business process to an external provider. Multinational Companies (MNCs) developed a lot of BPO in India, and more recently in China, in various fields such as accounting, repetitive tasks with the help of computers, and more sophisticated tasks related to information management, data analysis (including health data analysis), software development, and so on.

4 For more on this the interested reader can refer to: http://www.bpovia.com/blog/china-outsourcing/dalian-enlarge-its-business-in-japan.html#more-1448, 'Dalian enlarges its business in Japan.'

One can expect, however, that Chinese investments in Japan will carry on diversifying in the near future, including more manufacturing activities. This has already happened through various mergers and acquisitions (M&A) as mentioned above with the examples of Shanghai Electric, Sanjiu Pharmaceuticals and Suntech. A more recent case is the Petrochina group which acquired, in 2008, 49 percent of refining capacities of Nippon Oil in Osaka, as a way of securing supply (*Japan Times* 08/05/2008).

2. Chinese Businesses in Japan, Joint Ventures or Wholly Foreign Owned?

Academic literature has investigated at length whether firms should enter a foreign market through a joint venture (JV) or through a wholly-owned subsidiary (WOS); more specifically, the emphasis has been placed on what circumstances would lead a firm to select between these two entry modes (Stopford and Wells 1972, Hennart 1988, Kogut 1988, Beamish 1993, among others). When the host country allows entry through WOS, as Japan currently does in almost all industries, the choice is based on both business environmental factors, such as the characteristics of competition in the industry, and firm-specific factors, such as whether or not a firm can bring crucial resources to the project, within the perspective of the Resource Based View approach.[5] The characteristics of competition may include strong existing relationships between suppliers and customers in a given industry, which set up entry barriers, as has been often mentioned in the Japanese case (Miyashita and Russel 1994). In such a situation, a strategic alliance with a local firm, particularly one which is regarded as a *keiretsu* member, may help to overcome such an entry barrier.

Chinese firms have been setting up businesses in Japan through both JVs and WOSs (Table 7.2). However, in most cases, they have set up WOSs (49 cases out of 68), which shows a strong inclination to secure total control over their operations in Japan. This willingness to keep control is also clearly apparent when they set up JVs, since in most cases they hold more than half of the shares (13 cases out of 19). This means that even when they look for resources that a Japanese partner may provide, including access to distributors, customers, or others, Chinese companies investing in Japan manage to keep a strong control over their businesses through share holding. In the case of joint ventures, since in most cases the major proportion of the capital is Chinese, the majority of positions on the board of Directors and

5 The Resource Based View (RBV), which finds its roots in the work of scholars such as Penrose (1959) and Barney (1991), emphasizes that the competitive advantage of a firm derives mainly from its ability to secure and develop resources which are difficult for other firm to get or to imitate, such as a talented and highly motivated work force, unique design ability, sophisticated technologies, and so on. In this perspective, the competitive advantage of a firm is not mainly derived from its positioning in an industry, as developed by Porter (1980) and his model of the five forces of competition.

of key management positions are also Chinese. These majority positions lead to a strong control over strategic decisions and operations, a phenomenon that has been well investigated in the literature (Killing 1982, Geringer and Hebert 1989). It should be noted that the desire to keep control over operations abroad is not specific to Chinese firms, nor to the host country, Japan. Beamish (1993), Jaussaud and Schaaper (2006a, 2006b), among others, find the same tendency among firms from different countries (the USA, Europe, Japan) in various environments, both developed and emerging markets.

From the academic literature (Pan 2009; Nakagawa 2008), and from the nine exploratory interviews carried out in Japan in 2008, it is clear that the main objectives of Chinese firms investing in Japan may be ranked as follows: (1) acquisition of technologies; (2) market access; (3) strengthening of position as an outsourcing partner of a Japanese company. These three objectives, including the second one when strong relationships between suppliers and buyers in Japan are taken into account, may explain why, in a significant proportion of cases (21 out of 68, that is to say 31 percent) Chinese companies resort in some cases to JVs rather than to WOSs, although the former reduces their level of control. According to the academic literature (Stopford and Wells 1972, Kogut 1988), those companies

Table 7.2 Entry mode of Chinese subsidiaries in Japan – JVs versus WOS

Industry	Joint ventures			WOS	Total
	Minority for Chinese stake	50/50	Majority for Chinese stake		
Software development	2	1	1	6	10
Electronics	0	1	2	3	6
Food	0	1	0	4	5
Textile	0	0	1	6	7
Transport	0	0	2	9	11
Banking / Insurance	0	0	1	7	8
Raw materials and energy	0	0	0	2	2
Metal products, machinery parts	0	0	2	4	6
Chemicals	0	0	0	1	1
Pharmaceuticals	0	0	1	0	1
Others	0	1	3	7	11
Total	2	4	13	49	68

Source: Toyo Keizai (2007).

who resort to JVs look for key competencies or resources from their partner, such as access to local business networks (distributors and suppliers), most often in an organizational learning perspective. However, this is made at the expense of independence in their strategic approach and control of their local operations.

Chinese companies in Japan, just as foreign companies from other countries, do not always succeed. Haier, for instance, failed in the promotion in Japan of cheap household appliances (the so-called 'white goods') with the help of Sanyo, which led the two partners to cease their cooperation on the Japanese market from 2007, although it is still active on the Chinese one. Haier, which had set up in Japan a WOS to market televisions and other 'brown products' on its own, also failed in that project, and now concentrates on mobile phones. In both cases, the reasons for failure appear to be both very strong competition in Japan, and Japanese consumers being highly sensitive to quality and brand image. In broader terms, Nakagawa (2008) mentions insufficient information collected by Chinese firms investing in Japan, bad financial planning, and, particularly in the case of M&A, weak regeneration plans when the target is a bankrupt company.

Conclusion

Chinese business development in Japan, although still an emerging phenomenon, appears to be a promising one, as various industries are involved, some units have grown to significant sizes, and Chinese firms usually succeed in keeping control over their businesses, including when they set up joint ventures with Japanese partners. Their strong desire to keep control over their activities in Japan leads them to set up mainly wholly-owned subsidiaries (WOS) rather than joint ventures. The current economic crisis does not seem to have dampened Chinese interests in expanding into Japan: Chinese companies are now cash-rich and eager to buy distressed companies at bargain prices. As reported in *Japan Times* (07/01/2009), foreign acquisitions of Japanese companies by firms in all countries declined overall in 2008. In the case of China and Korea, there was however an increase of 78 cases.

Competitive forces in Japan are very intense, however, and Japanese customers are very demanding, particularly in terms of quality. Chinese companies, as in the case of other foreign firms in Japan, face huge difficulties, and sometimes fail. From the diversity of cases that are listed in Toyo Keizai (2007) and mentioned from various sources in this chapter, it is clear that different Chinese companies may have varied advantages in competing on the Japanese market, and not only on cost.

However, additional research is needed to better identify these various competitive advantages, and to better assess related strategies by Chinese firms in Japan. More broadly, such research may increase our understanding of the difficulties and potential of firms from emerging countries on developed markets, not only in the case of China towards Japan, but also of other developing countries both towards Japan and Western countries. In some ways, the case investigated in this chapter, that of Chinese firms investing in Japan, might be seen both as a test case for Chinese investors, and as a prelude to what might become the new face of FDI in the future: systematic Chinese direct investments in Western countries, namely in the European Union and in the USA.

References

Barney, J. 1991. Firm resources and sustained competitive advantage. *Journal of Management,* 17 (1), 99–120.

Beamish, P.W. 1993. The characteristics of joint ventures in the People's Republic of China. *Journal of International Marketing*, 1(2), 29–48.

Calantone, R.J. and Zhao, Y.S. 2001. Joint ventures in China, a comparative study of Japanese, Korean, and US partners. *Journal of International Marketing*, 9(1),1–23.

Chittoor, R. and Ray, S. 2007. Internationalization paths of Indian pharmaceutical firms – a strategic group analysis. *Journal of International Management,* 13, 338–55.

Deng, P. 2009. Why do Chinese firms tend to acquire strategic assets in international expansion. *Journal of World Business,* 44, 74–84.

Ding, D.Z. 1997. Control, conflict, and performance: a study of US–Chinese joint ventures. *Journal of International Marketing*, 5 (3), 31–45.

Geringer, J.M. and Hebert, L. 1989. Control and performance of international joint ventures. *Journal of International Business Studies*, (Summer), 20, 235–54.

Hayashi, Y. 2007. Sustainable development of Japan-China economic relations and prospects for business alliance, Keynote Address. *The Symposium on Japan-China Business Alliance*, Beijing (7 June).

Hennart, J.-F. 1988. A transaction cost theory of equity joint ventures. *Strategic Management Journal,* 9(4), July–August, 361–74.

Isobe, T., Makino, S. and Montgomery, D.B. 2000. Resource commitment, entry timing and market performance of foreign direct investments in emerging economies: the case of Japanese international joint ventures in China. *Academy of Management Journal*, 43(3), 468–84.

Japan Times, daily newspapers, various issues: 08/05/2008, 07/01/2009, 26/06/2009.

Jaussaud, J. and Schaaper, J. 2006a. Control mechanisms of their subsidiaries by multinational firms: a multidimensional perspective. *Journal of International Management* 12(1), 23–45.

Jaussaud, J. and Schaaper, J. 2006b. Entre efficience, réactivité et apprentissage organisationnel: une étude qualitative sur le cas des filiales françaises en Chine. *Management International*, 11 (Automne), 1–13.

Khanna, T. and Palepu, K. 2006. Emerging giants: building world class companies in developing economies. *Harvard Business Review*, 84(10), 60–70.

Killing, J.P. 1982. How to make a global joint venture work. *Harvard Business Review*, (May–June), 60(3), 120–27.

Kogut, B. 1988. Joint ventures: theoretical and empirical perspectives. *Strategic Management Journal,* 9(4), (July–August), 319–32.

Lecraw, D. 1977. Direct investment by firms from less developed countries. *Oxford Economic Papers*, New Series, 29(3), 442–57.

Miyashita, K. and Russel, D. 1994. *Keiretsu, Inside the Hidden Japanese Conglomerates.* Maidenhead: McGraw Hill.

Nakagawa, R. 2008. Chugoku kigyo ni yoru kurosuboda M&A no hatten to sono igi/mondaiten (Meaning and problems of the development Chinese cross-border M&A) in *Heisei 19 Nendo, Chugoku kigyo no gurobaruka. Hokokusho,* (March). Tokyo: Kokusai Boeiki Toshi Kenkyusho (Institute for International Trade and Investment).

Pan, C. 2009. What is Chinese about Chinese businesses? Locating the rise of China in global production networks. *Journal of Contemporary China*, 18(58), 7–25.

Penrose, E. 1959. *The Theory of the Growth of the Firm*. Oxford: Blackwell.

Porter, M. 1980. *Competitive Strategy: Techniques for Analysing Industries and Competitors*. New York: The Free Press.

Rui, H. and Yip, G.S. 2008. Foreign acquisition by Chinese firms: a strategic intent perspective. *Journal of World Business,* 43, 213–26.

Stopford, J.M. and Wells, L. 1972. *Managing the Multinational Enterprise.* New York: Basic Books.

Toyo Keizai 2007. *Gashikei Kigyô Sôran* (Directory of Foreign invested firms in Japan). Tokyo: Toyo Keizai Shimpôsha.

Wang, M.Y. 2002. The motivation behind China's Government-Initiated industrial investment overseas. *Pacific Affairs,* 75(2), 187–206.

Yang, D. 2005. *China's Offshore Investments – A Network Approach.* Cheltenham and Northampton (MA): Edward Elgar.

Yomiuri Shimbun, Chugoku Shuzai Dan (eds), 2006. *Bocho Chugoku* (*Expanding China*). Tokyo: Chuo Koronsha.

Yomiuri Shimbun, daily newspapers: 23/05/2005.

Chapter 8
Indian Multinationals: Which Competitive Advantages?

Giovanni Balcet and Silvia Bruschieri[1]

Introduction

International investments and multinational strategies are at the core of the current status of the global economy, deeply affected by the current economic crisis. During the early 2000s, multinational companies (MNCs) from emerging countries (ECs), and especially from Asian countries, became new and very dynamic actors on the global scene (UNCTAD 2006). Indian corporations actively contributed to this trend, till the slowdown in 2008–09, due to the world economic crisis and the recession in most developed markets. After a deregulation period in the 1980s and since the liberalization process started in the 1990s, a growing number of firms have been able to acquire frontier technologies from Western MNCs, often through innovation-oriented joint ventures (JVs) and alliances, and in a subsequent stage to grow internationally, building multinational networks (Balcet and Bruschieri 2008). In particular, Indian outward FDI has been very dynamic, growing from a total of $0.1 billion in 1990 to $29 billion in 2007 (UNCTAD 2008). This trend represents a strong challenge to the conventional wisdom and to the consolidated theories of FDI and MNCs. The question arises of identifying the main drivers of this new trend, through traditional or alternative economic theories.

Starting from the late 1970s a strand of literature flourished on Third World multinationals (Lall 1983). More recently, the increasing expansion abroad by multinationals based in the emerging countries, also targeting OECD markets, has led scholars to take again an interest in the subject. This chapter discusses what competitive advantages new Indian multinationals possess, which strategies they have developed, what role their international partnerships have played, and what

1 The authors thank all the participants at the International Workshop on "Current Issues in the area of Integration" held in Venice, Università Ca' Foscari, on 30 January 30, 2009, for their precious comments on the subject of the present chapter. They also warmly thank Wladimir Andreff of Sorbonne University, Grazia Ietto-Gillies of London South Bank University, Vittorio Valli of Turin University, and the Editors of this book for their penetrating comments and creative suggestions.

motivations have been driving this process. The question is raised as to the main sources of international competitiveness of these industrial groups.

We first survey the relevant literature on EC multinationals, looking both to the traditional theories and to the specific explanations proposed for the new trends (Section 2). We then look at the internationalization process of four selected Indian companies operating in two sectors highly representative of the successful Indian entry onto the global market: the automotive and the pharmaceutical industry (Section 3). We then propose an alternative theoretical approach, stressing the role of skilled labor cost advantages and of institutional factors as key explanations for the multinational performance of Indian industrial groups, and discuss the relevance of this result for the wider theoretical issue of EC multinationals, and for the theory of the multi-national enterprise (MNE) itself (Section 4).

2. Explaining Emerging and Developing Country Multinationals

In this Section we will review and discuss the main theories explaining FDI and MNCs from emerging and developing countries. It is organized in two parts: the first one refers to traditional and consolidated theories and models that have been extended in order to include the EC MNCs; the second part refers to specific approaches proposed in recent years to interpret this new phenomenon.

2.1. The conventional wisdom: traditional theoretical approaches

Since the late 1970s, literature has been produced covering the issue of Third World, developing or less developed countries' (LDC) multinationals. In particular, we refer to three main theoretical approaches: a) the product life cycle model; b) the theory of localized technological change and of technological accumulation; and finally, c) the eclectic paradigm of international production, including the investment development cycle.

2.1.A. Third world multinationals and the product life cycle model Vernon (1966) first proposed the product life cycle theory (Vernon 1966) and considered the possibility of looking at LDC outward FDIs through his theoretical framework. At the end of the 1970s this scholar acknowledged that his model had lost part of its power in explaining FDI among industrialized countries (Vernon 1979). At the same time, however, Vernon maintained that the model could still be applied to the FDI undertaken by LDCs. In particular, referring to South-South FDIs, he pointed out that firms "in the more rapidly industrializing group [...] are demonstrating a considerable capability for producing innovations that respond to the special conditions of their own economies" (*ibidem*: 266).

Following the same approach, Wells (1981, 1983) argued that some LDC firms carry out foreign investments in other developing countries, mainly exploiting their skills in imitating and adapting to the local conditions both the product and the process innovations developed by industrialized countries' firms. Wells stresses in particular LDC firms' ability in adapting large scale technologies for small scale production. Wells' approach, however, does not seem adequate to explain the empirical evidence concerning today's flows of FDI from ECs, oriented to the most industrialized countries as well. EC MNCs and incumbent multinationals do not operate any longer in separate spheres – as regards both geographical markets and product segments – as it used to be for LDC and industrialized countries' MNCs when Vernon and Wells developed their theories.

2.1.B. Localized technological change and the technological accumulation theory Some shortcomings of Wells' approach were stressed in the 1980s by Lall (1983), who applied the localized technological change theory to interpret LDC firms' FDI. In Lall's contention, the range of firm specific technological advantages on which LDC firms' FDI is based is not necessarily confined to the imitation or adaptation of imported technology, but can originate in the same firms' own innovation. Technological innovation is not undertaken by a single firm in isolation, but it involves many other actors such as its suppliers, distributors and consumers. The technological edges of LDC firms consist in particular in productive techniques especially appropriate for the developing countries' factor price and quality conditions, in the efficiency of their production techniques at a smaller scale than the one used by industrialized country firms, and in their ability to develop products that match the local needs or tastes (Lall 1982). In this respect, Lall develops some ideas proposed in the wide and policy-oriented debate of the 1970s and 1980s on the 'intermediate technologies' or 'appropriate technologies' for developing countries (Balcet 1981). However, Lall points out that technological edges of LDC firms are not necessarily matured in small-scale, labor intensive technologies. Lall's empirical work about India proved that the FDI originating in this country is not confined to simple, low technology, small scale and labor intensive operations (Lall 1982).

The competitive advantages of LDC firms can evolve through a process of technology accumulation (Lall 1984), and these firms can develop 'genuinely unique and localized technological innovation' (Cantwell and Tolentino 1990: 16). As a result of this process, LDC firms' technological capabilities can put them in the position to be able to invest also in industrialized countries, a phenomenon about which Cantwell and Tolentino find empirical evidence.[2] These scholars offer an interpretation of Third World firms' internationalization that seems to better reflect some characteristics of today's emerging country MNCs. This is true as regards the variety of multinationalization experiences, a feature that is becoming frequent among contemporary emerging countries MNCs (Sauvant 2005, Tolentino 2008). This theoretical approach accommodates also the asset seeking FDI, and not only

2 Canwell and Tolentino (1990) in particular refer to FDI carried out in the industrialised countries by investors based in South Korea, Taiwan and Brazil.

the market-seeking one. For LDC companies that have already accumulated a certain level of technological advantages, asset-seeking FDIs represent a means to improve such levels by accessing technological resources in the industrialized countries.

2.1.C. The eclectic paradigm and the investment development path According to John Dunning's well-known eclectic FDI theory, also defined as the 'OLI (ownership, localization, internalization) paradigm', to engage in international production firms must possess ex-ante ownership advantages; there must be an incentive for them to internalize such advantages instead of exploiting them through external markets (internalization advantages), and there must exist some localization advantages in the host country (Dunning 1983). As their GNP per capita increases, countries pass through the different stages of what Dunning calls an investment development cycle or path (Dunning 1988), with their inward and outward foreign direct investment, and therefore the balance between the two linked to their stage of development. In particular, the existence of a positive correlation and of a J-shaped relation between the net outward investment and GNP per capita is assumed. He therefore argues that the emerging phenomenon of outward direct investment by developing countries can also be explained by the eclectic theory of international production.

The ownership advantages of LDC MNCs tend to reflect the structure of their countries' resource endowments, such as capital, labor, natural resources, individual entrepreneurship, and their ability to adapt imported know-how and technology (Dunning 1986). Other ownership advantages of LDC MNCs mentioned by Dunning are the better knowledge of the other LDC countries' demand and production factors' markets, the better mastering of technologies and skills that are particularly suitable for these countries and the shorter institutional distance with other such countries. These kinds of advantages can be exploited in other LDCs, in sectors requiring intermediate or mature technology and semiskilled labor, and where economies of scale are less relevant. Increasing EC MNCs' activity directed towards industrialized countries is explained by market-seeking FDIs needed to cover the growing costs of R&D activities in innovation-intensive sectors. Moreover, Third World multinationals may invest in more advanced countries to access or augment, rather than to exploit, their ownership advantages. Nevertheless, to do so they need to possess managerial, organizational, and institutional capabilities in order to effectively internalize the acquired assets (Dunning 2006, Dunning et al. 2006). Significantly, Dunning refers to these kinds of FDI as 'asset-augmenting' rather than 'asset seeking' investment.

Analyzing the 'alliance capitalism', Dunning extends his theoretical framework so as to include among the ownership advantages those that a firm gets from being part of alliances, including the management abilities in finding and leveraging resources and capabilities from abroad, and to coordinate them with the existing corporate assets (Dunning 1995; 2000).

2.2. Theories specific to the emerging country multinationals

More recently, other contributions have tried to propose specific explanations for the new phenomenon of multinationals from emerging countries. We discuss below three main approaches.

2.2.A. Asset-seeking motivations as a key explanation: the imbalance and the springboard approaches The theoretical approaches that we have previously outlined till now share the same fundamental assumption *à la* Hymer, i.e. that in order to expand and set up a subsidiary abroad firms must possess competitive edges over domestic firms strong enough to overcome the initial disadvantages that they will face in the host country. This assumption is questioned by some scholars with reference to the internationalization experience of the contemporary ECs, as the companies based in these host countries can be expected to lack monopolistic advantages in the strict sense, in particular as regards patents and strong brands.

Moon and Roehl advance the imbalance theory, to interpret what they call the "unconventional FDI", among which they include the investment undertaken by the LDC firms in the industrialized countries (Moon and Roehl 2001). They point out that there are cases in which a firm may go abroad to overcome its own disadvantages, such as the lack of technology or management know-how, or a limited market share. However, they admit that some ex-ante ownership advantages are needed also in the case of factor seeking FDI.

In the same direction of research, Luo and Tung (2007) argue that EC multinationals use outward investments "as a springboard" to acquire strategic assets. This is done through merger and acquisitions and strategic alliances in advanced markets, in particular to access sophisticated technology as well as brands, managerial skills and access to consumers. Moving from empirical evidence, these scholars highlight that the competitive advantages were not originally possessed by the companies in question but were mainly generated through their participation in international alliances, as well as through the spillover effects of inward FDIs. The linkages with foreign partners allow these companies to upgrade technological and management skills, to accumulate considerable financial assets, to develop learning experiences, and to be integrated into the internal network of their foreign partners, offering effective mechanisms for the transfer of tacit knowledge.

Luo and Tung (2007) point out that emerging country multinationals show a leapfrog attitude, because as latecomers they tend to internationalize rapidly, to catch up with incumbents. Therefore, they do not follow the incremental approach to internationalization (as described by Johanson and Vahlne 1977), as they frequently start their internationalization process simultaneously undertaking high-risk operations in different geographical markets, with a high commitment of resources, through acquisitions or greenfield investments.

2.2.B. Asset-seeking motivations as the key explanation: the linkage leverage and learning theory Moving from a resource-based view of internationalization,

Mathews' main claim is that the experience of some kind of MNCs does not fit with the OLI paradigm, because the internationalization process of such MNCs is not based on the possession of strong domestic assets to be exploited abroad (Mathews 2002 and 2006). In his contention, this is true for both newcomer MNCs and for "dragon multinationals".[3] In his view, the multinational growth represents the way through which latecomer multinationals acquire resources and improve their competitive position. While the OLI framework can be retained as fitting for the incumbent MNCs, Mathews (2002) proposes an alternative explanation for dragon multinationals. To interpret their internationalization process, the 'linkage, leverage, learning' framework (LLL) is advanced. Such companies are claimed to be skilled in establishing several kinds of *linkages* with incumbent firms: i.e. inter-firm relations. Latecomers adopt strategies to match those of the incumbents, for instance entering outsourcing networks, or via technology licensing contracts. Latecomers are not focused on their own advantages but on those which they can acquire externally, particularly as far as knowledge resources are involved. However, such outward orientation involves high risks and uncertainties. Thanks to their ability in weaving such linkages, latecomers can *leverage* resources 'from the strengths of others' (Mathews 2006: 14). With this concept, Mathews (2006) refers to the reach for resources beyond it by the firm, and to the process of absorption of new resources, in particular those most easily imitated, for instance, through reverse engineering, and the most transferable. As a result of the repeated application of linkage and leverage strategies, latecomers are very keen on *learning*, thereby enhancing their capabilities. Mathews (2002) too, as Luo and Tung (2007), points out that acceleration characterizes the internationalization process of EC MNCs, reaching in a few years a wide geographical coverage and a leadership position in some market segments.

2.2.C. Alliances and networks: a strategic instrument for catching-up Co-operative relationships of differing nature with foreign firms play indeed an important role in this context, where FDI represents only one of the means these companies resort to so as to grow abroad, and often not the most important one.

According to Castellani and Zanfei (2006), MNCs tend to develop external networks, with other firms and institutions, in order to increase the generation and diffusion of knowledge. The external network involves not only the multinational headquarters, regional and global, but also the foreign affiliates in each country. It includes cooperative relations not only with incumbent firms, but also with local specialized suppliers and clients, research institutions and universities. Ietto-Gillies (2005: chapter 15) stresses that the advantages of multinationality and the process of fragmentation of production lead MNCs to extend their external networks. These networks represent crucial instruments of learning and of technological catching-up.

---

3 With "dragon multinationals" Mathews refers to "successful latecomer" firms based in a country of "the Periphery" (Mathews 2002: 8).

On the contrary, the internal network of a MNC refers to the complex intra-group flows of goods, people, information and resources, connecting foreign affiliates and the regional and global headquarters; it represents a web of linkages among the internal units of the MNC, scattered in different geographical contexts. This approach suggests that the relations between these units are not only hierarchical, and a different mix of centralization or decentralization characterizes the stages of growth and the multinational expansion of the firm. Foreign affiliates are actively involved in the trade-off between autonomy and integration, while asset-seeking and market-seeking strategies co-exist. The need for local units to be autonomous to perform their task in the best way contrasts with the need to avoid centrifugal forces to disintegrate the MNC itself.

3. Empirical Evidence on Indian Multinationals

We now move to present some empirical evidence on the multinational growth of Indian enterprises in recent years, in order to assess and critically discuss the above theories.[4]

3.1. Competitive advantages[5]

The pharmaceutical and automotive sectors are particularly representative of the Indian successful entry into the global market, and for this reason, we select them for a study on Indian multinationals. Eight out of the 20 Indian companies that the Boston Consulting Group listed in 2006 among the 100 top enterprises from emerging markets (Boston Consulting Group 2006) were active in these industries. A number of operations in these fields have been undertaken overseas also in the industrialized countries, and in many instances through acquisitions. The pharmaceutical and the automotive industry respectively represent a high and a medium-high technology sector, as well as scale-intensive industries, which makes particularly interesting the case of the firms operating in these industries that successfully multinationalize from a developing – though emerging – country like India.

Table 8.1 maps the FDIs carried out by the four Indian companies active in the above mentioned sectors that we selected for our study. Their foreign investments turn out to be mostly oriented along the South-North direction, with developing and emerging countries being the destination of operations mainly engaged in marketing and distribution or sourcing rather than in manufacturing activities. FDIs carried out in the developed countries often show an asset seeking motivation, aiming at accessing resources such as technology, intellectual property

4 For a more thorough analysis of these issues, the interested reader can refer to Bruschieri (2009).

5 The present Section is based on Bruschieri (2009).

Table 8.1 The multinational growth of selected Indian corporations

Nicholas Piramal	Sun Pharmaceutical Industries	Mahindra and Mahindra (automotive business)	Bharat Forge
2004 – Establishment of NPIL Pharma Inc. in the US (Greenfield investment) – Marketing activity	1993 – Establishment of a 100% subsidiary in Russia (Greenfield investment) – Marketing activity	1969 – Establishment of a JV in Iran (closed about ten years later) – Manufacturing of auto parts	2003 – Acquisition of Carl Dan Peddinghaus GmbH & Co KG (Germany) – Manufacturing of forged parts mainly for passenger vehicles; R&D
2004 – Acquisition of the inhalation business of Rhodia Organique Fine Limited (UK) – Manufacturing of inhalation anaesthetics	1994 – Establishment of a representative office in Ukraine (Greenfield investment) – Marketing activity	1984 – Establishment of a JV in Greece (closed at mid 1990s) – Assembly unit for CKD utility vehicles	2004 – Acquisition of Aluminiumtechnik GmbH & Co KG (Germany) – Manufacturing of forged parts in aluminium for passenger and light commercial vehicles; R&D
2005 – Acquisition of Avecia Pharma (UK) (formerly part of AstraZeneca) – Custom manufacturing of active pharmaceutical ingredients; R&D	1995 – Establishment of representative office in Belarus (Greenfield investment) – Marketing activity	2004 – Establishment of a 51% JV in South Africa° – Import and distribution of fully built SUVs, pick ups and Logan cars, as well as their spare parts	2005 – Acquisition of Federal Forge (US) – Manufacturing of forged parts for passenger and light commercial vehicles
2005 – Acquisition of 100% of Torcan (Canada) through the acquisition of Avecia – Custom manufacturing of niche active pharmaceutical ingredients for biotechnology and mid-size pharmaceutical companies; R&D	1997 – Acquisition of 30% stake in Caraco Pharmaceutical Laboratories (US). Manufacturing and R&D*	2005 – Establishment of a 80% JV in Italy – Import and distribution of SUVs and pick ups	2005 – Acquisition of Imatra Kilsta AB (Sweden) and its wholly owned subsidiary Scottish Stampings – Manufacturing of forged parts for commercial and passenger vehicles; R&D
2006 – Acquisition of 25% of Reaxa Limited (UK) through the acquisition of Avecia – Custom manufacturing	2001 – Establishment of a 73% JV in Bangladesh – Manufacturing of formulations	2006 – Acquisition of 99% of the Stokes Group (Germany) – Production of forged components for the automotive industry	2005 – Establishment of a 52% Jv with FAW Group in China – Manufacturing of components for commercial and passenger vehicles
2006 – Acquisition of a Pfizer manufacturing unit in Morpeth (UK) – Active pharmaceutical ingredient and formulation contract manufacturing; R&D	2004 – Establishment of a 100% subsidiary in Brazil – Marketing activity	2006 – Acquisition of 68% of Jeco Holdings (Germany) – Production of forged components for the automotive industry	

2007 – Establishment of a sourcing office in Shanghai (China) (Greenfield investment) – Sourcing activity	2004 – Establishment of a 75% JV in Mexico – Marketing activity	2006 – Acquisition of 90.47% of Schöneweiss & Co (Germany) – Production of forged components for the automotive industry	
2008 – Acquisition of Tangent Data (Romania) – Contract research	2005 – Acquisition of the manufacturing operations of the US company Valeant Pharma in Hungary – Manufacturing of pharmaceutical ingredients and formulations; R&D activity	2008 – Acquisition of G.R.D Grafica Ricerca Design (Italy) – Design and engineering services for auto OEMs	
2009 – Acquisition of the inhalation anesthetic gas distribution business of RxElite Holdings Inc (US) – Distribution and sales	2005 – Acquisition of a plant in US from Valeant Pharma – Manufacturing of formulations	2008 – Acquisition of 100% of Engines Engineering srl (Italy) – Two wheels design and engineering services	
2009 – Acquisition of Minrad International (US) – Manufacturing of generic inhalation anesthetics	2005 – Greenfield investment – Establishment of a 99% subsidiary in Peru – Marketing activity	2008 – Acquisition of 100 percent of Metalcastello spa (Italy) – Manufacturing of gears and shafts for tractors and construction equipment	
	2005 – Acquisition of assets and intellectual property rights of Able Laboratories (US) – Manufacturing of formulations – R&D activity	2008 – Establishment of a 80 percent JV in Australia – Marketing, promotion and retail of utility vehicles and pick ups	
	2007 – Acquisition of Taro (Israel) (not yet finalized) – Manufacturing of formulations and active pharmaceutical ingredients – R&D activity		
	2008 – Acquisition of 100 percent of Chattem Chemicals Inc (US) – Manufacturing of active pharmaceutical ingredients		

Source: Bruschieri (2009).
**Furt*her shares of Caraco's capital bought in the course of time, so that in 2009 Caraco is a 74 percent subsidiary of SP.
° *In ea*rly 2009 M&M stake increased to 91 percent.

rights (IPRs) and management skills. Such motivation is nevertheless commonly accompanied by the attempt to exploit the competitive advantages possessed by the investing companies (see Table 8.2), so that a market seeking as well as an efficiency seeking motivation are also discernable in these operations. The acquisition and the JV respectively are the most frequent entry modes to which our focus companies resort to in the developed and in the developing or emerging countries.

Table 8.2 Competitive advantages of selected Indian corporations

	Firm specific competitive advantages	**Country specific competitive advantages**
Nicholas Piramal	Technological capabilities	Institutional context (before and after the economic liberalization) Trade and industrial policies Development of a National Innovation System Good level of some Indian educational institutions Education given in English Large pool of low-cost qualified labor Development of the Indian capital market
	Low cost of skilled and unskilled labor and of equipment	
	Managerial skills	
	Marketing skills	
	Financial resources	
	Being part of a family conglomerate	
Sun Pharmaceutical Industries	Technological capabilities	
	Low cost of skilled and unskilled labor and of equipment	
	Marketing skills	
	Strong financial resources	
Mahindra & Mahindra	Technological capabilities (vehicle/ auto ancillary sectors)	
	Low cost of skilled and unskilled labor	
	Marketing skills (vehicle business)	
	Managerial skills	
	Strong financial resources	
	Being part of a family conglomerate	
Bharat Forge	Technological capabilities	
	Low cost of skilled and unskilled labor	
	Financial resources	
	Being part of a family conglomerate	

Source: Drawn from Bruschieri (2009) and Balcet and Bruschieri (forthcoming), based also on direct interviews to top managers in February and April 2008.

The main sources of competitive advantages, both firm-specific and country-specific, that emerged in the case of our focus companies, are outlined in Table 8.2.

Country specific competitive advantages played an important role in shaping what seems to be the most important edges on which these companies built their international expansion. Firstly, though patent activity and research intensity are in general low, technological capabilities played a role in the internationalization process. Some circumstances signal such capabilities. As regards internationalization through exports, Sun Pharmaceutical Industries (SP) exported to other emerging and developing countries pharmaceutical products manufactured in India at low cost thanks to its strong basic innovative capabilities. Furthermore, it could acquire a US generic manufacturing company through a technology for equity agreement, and successfully apply for ANDAs (Abbreviated New Drug Application) in the USA. Nicholas Piramal could sell its products and services – through its contract research and manufacturing activity – to many global pharmaceutical companies, and Bharat Forge (BF) as well as Mahindra and Mahindra auto ancillary products were sold to global automotives companies. Besides, Mahindra & Mahindra brought to the market the Scorpio, the first multi-utility vehicle designed from scratch in India. The institutional change introduced with the economic liberalization process that started in the early 1990s – which led also to regulation reform that provides for patents on pharmaceutical products – forced Indian companies to increase their R&D effort, thereby fostering an increase in their technological and absorptive capacity (Cohen and Levinthal 1989).

The institutional context also played an important role in shaping the technological capabilities of today's Indian MNCs in the pre-liberalization era. Indeed, the former intellectual property rights regime allowed the local companies to develop basic innovative capabilities (Lall 1992) thanks to the learning by copying process (Kale and Little 2007). The restrictions on technology imports forced Indian industry to develop technical capabilities, which generated skills that made, for instance, the Indian casting and forging companies quite competitive (Forbes 1999). Secondly, unlike the old-style Third World multinationals (Wells 1983), to a certain extent marketing skills represent a competitive advantage for our focus companies. So, Mahindra & Mahindra's non-negligible capabilities in this field are attested to by the complex marketing activity developed for the Scorpio project. The good quality level of some Indian educational institutions, such as the Indian Institute of Technology and the Indian Institute of Management, is widely recognized, and the supply of skilled personnel contributes to the aforementioned competitive advantages of Indian companies. The fact that education is given in English represents a further quality element of the Indian education system. Furthermore, raising financial resources for their international expansion has not represented a problem for the companies in question. Their success on the Indian market allowed them to generate internal accruals, and their good business records gave them a reputation that allowed them to raise money through both the Indian stock market and the international financial market, thereby confirming the findings of Pradhan (2006). The level of development of the Indian capital market, and in particular of the stock market (Huang and Kanna 2003) played a role in this context.

Another institutional element to be stressed, as a strong source of competitive advantage for most Indian multinationals, is being part of a family controlled conglomerate group. It allows for the transfer of technology and cash flow within the group, to those sectors whose development is held as strategic (Richet and Ruet 2008). The presence inside the conglomerates of companies operating in the financial sector, as is the case for Mahindra & Mahindra, further enhances the possibilities to fuel strategic businesses.

Finally, access to a large pool of low-cost labor currently represents an important country-specific competitive advantage for the Indian firms. On the one hand, the low cost of unqualified manpower – as well as in many cases the low cost of other factors such as equipment and land – makes it profitable to carry out in India the mass production of, for instance, pharmaceutical ingredients and automotive components. On the other hand, local qualified human resources are also available and can be employed at a cost that remains far from that of the corresponding resources in Western countries (roughly amounting to one fifth of the remuneration of a corresponding US chemist employed in the pharmaceutical sector). This situation makes it possible to carry out some knowledge intensive phases of the production process in the country of origin. Therefore, the foreign investments of our focus companies often turn out to have both an asset seeking and an efficiency-seeking motivation. The former aims at complementing the Indian companies' resources – for instance as regards cutting edge technologies, IPRs and customer base. The latter allows integrating the productive process at the global level, thereby exploiting the competitive advantage offered by the low cost of both unqualified and skilled labor in India.

Some acquisitions carried out abroad, oriented to access otherwise unattainable resources, have been followed by the shift of production to India. This is, for instance, the case of the operation targeting Rhodia (UK) carried out by Nicholas Piramal in 2004.[6] Nevertheless, this is not a general trend. In other cases the Indian advantage of a low labor cost is successfully exploited through production abroad as in the case of the acquisitions carried out by Bharat Forge in Germany in the automotive component business. In this case technology was acquired as well as a customer base, and economies of scope were achieved. The supply of pieces from the Indian plants allows the MNC to exploit the Indian cost advantage globally.

3.2. External linkages

Looking to the Indian experience, both alliances and acquisitions, i.e. the external network and the internal multinational network, are key instruments in the process

6 The acquisition gave access to IPRs, to a customer base and a distribution network, and production was shifted from the UK to India in 2006.

of technological upgrading and catching up. Developing from Mathews (2002, 2006) and from the empirical evidence of our case studies, we can point out that learning and leveraging processes can be originated from both international alliances and acquisitions.

The decision to establish different kinds of alliances with foreign firms seems to emerge as a pattern of behavior among Indian MNCs,[7] while the acquisition of Indian units of foreign companies complements the above mentioned strategy.[8] The following sequences tend to characterize the growth trajectories of the multinational of Indian industrial enterprises and groups, following two main stages.

- In the *first stage*, alliances and JVs are located in India, creating a web of connections – whose width varies for the different companies – with Western and Japanese MNCs. Being part of this network – that in some cases also involves research institutions – in fact supports the companies in their growth on the domestic market. In particular, it gives them access to different kinds of resources, such as manufacturing expertise, basic scientific knowledge, high skilled human resources, advanced equipment, quality management techniques, managerial competencies, knowledge of foreign markets, and partners' distribution networks in foreign countries. Besides, some of these linkages offer the possibility of generating economies of

Table 8.3 Selected examples of partnerships established by case study companies

Nicholas Piramal	In-license agreements with Hoffman La Roche (1993) JVs with Allergan (1995) and Alliance Boots (1998) Collaboration agreements with research institutions since late 1990s
Mahindra and Mahindra (automotive business)	Technical collaborations with: - Willys Overland to assemble jeeps in India (1954) - Peugeot to manufacture diesel engines (1979) - a number of foreign companies for Scorpio project (late 1990s) JVs with a number of foreign companies since the 1960s
Bharat Forge	Technical collaborations, e.g. with SIFCO (1962) for hammer forging technology and design of the first forge JVs with Lemmerz (1996) and ArvinMeritor (1998)*

Source: Based on Bruschieri (2009).

* These JVs were not established by Bharat Forge itself, but by other entities of the Kalyani group, of which our case study is the flagship company.

7 This behavior is attested in three of the four MNCs case studies taken into consideration by Bruschieri (2009).

8 This is in particular the case of Nicholas Piramal.

scope. Table 8.3 above presents a sample of the relationships in question. In the same stage, foreign affiliates and multinational subsidiaries in the country are the target of acquisitions by Indian firms. Like partnerships, acquisitions also allow a rapid process of catching up, transfer and assimilation of foreign knowledge and technology.

- In a *second stage*, the international expansion takes place, *via* greenfield FDI in developing countries, or acquisitions in the most developed countries, thanks to the capabilities, resources and abilities accumulated during the domestic market-driven phase. It implies the establishment of an internal multinational network under the corporate control. Acquisitions again allow leveraging external resources – those of the target companies – represent the most common entry mode (Table 8.1), in particular as regards those FDI operations carried out in the developed countries, which represent the dominant destination. Another, alternative or complementary, way of multinational growth is still represented by alliances and JVs, usually established in order to overcome institutional barriers.[9] In this scheme, efficiency-seeking – in addition to market-seeking – and asset-seeking FDIs seem both to contribute to further enhancing the competitive advantage of the Indian MNCs and to make it possible for the latter to grow further.

These trajectories shape the new emerging multinational actors. As a consequence, Indian companies possess competitive advantages and firm-specific capabilities of a different nature, including the ability to obtain inputs on favorable terms, due to the importance or their monopsonistic influence, favored access to production inputs such as low-cost labor and raw materials, the supply of low-cost skilled labor and human capital – as in the case of Indian engineers and information communication technologies (ICT) scientists – the capacity for fast assimilation and creative recombination of transferred technologies and know-how, abundant financial resources (in the period of booming stock markets), marketing skills, and managerial abilities in finding and leveraging resources and capabilities from throughout the world, especially from foreign partners, and to coordinate them with the existing resources and capabilities.

9 This is for instance the case of a 52 percent stake in a joint venture set up by Bharat Forge in China with the major Chinese group FAW to manufacture automotive components; it is also the case of the majority JVs entered by Mahindra & Mahindra in the vehicle distribution in Italy and Australia, that allowed – among other things – accessing the partners' knowledge of the local market and institutional context.

4. Towards an Alternative Explanation of Indian and Emerging Country Multinationals

Confronting traditional and new theories on the one hand, and our empirical findings on the other hand, we can propose some new and complementary explanations on the key competitive advantages of Indian, and possibly other EC multinationals, and on the drivers of the process of their multinational expansion. Future research work could compare the Indian case within a comparative approach.

Both the traditional and the new and specific theories we presented in Section 2 suggest relevant drivers of the phenomenon we are discussing, providing useful insights and ideas, especially as far as technology transfer, adaptation and assimilation are concerned. However, they do not refer to labor costs differentials as major competitive advantages for EC MNCs. On the contrary labor cost differentials are considered the crucial factor explaining FDI flows from the OECD countries towards developing and emerging countries by a large volume of literature on north-south FDI, vertical international fragmentation of production and industrial re-location processes (Mouhoud 2008). Moreover, the reviewed approaches tend to neglect the historical and evolutionary perspective, as well as the crucial role of political, institutional and cultural factors, including corporate governance. Finally, the category of alliances may be deepened in its theoretical implications. Therefore, the existing theories and interpretations of EC MNCs tend to neglect or to under-evaluate some factors that we think can contribute to better understand this phenomenon, and on which we shed light in the case studies on Indian multinationals. We focus our attention in this section on three main factors.

4.1. Home country labor costs as a key competitive advantage

Surprisingly enough, the issue of labor costs is not discussed as a major factor by the theories of EC multinationals. Of course, a labor cost differential in favor of developing and emerging countries is typically considered as being one of the host country's major locational advantages for Western and Japanese multinationals, and for explaining their FDI *inflows*. It is therefore considered a major driver of the globalization of industry (Dunning 1983 and 1988, Andreff 2003, Ietto-Gillies 2005). This factor is in particular at the core of the theories of re-location processes (Mouhoud 2008), and it is consistent with the neo-classical notions of comparative advantages and factor-endowments. In this theoretical approach, developing and emerging countries are expected to attract foreign investment inflows in labor-intensive industries, mainly oriented to exports. But what about FDI *outflows* from emerging countries?

We must first integrate the consideration of the cost of labor with that of its quality, i.e. the availability and abundance of skilled and highly skilled labor costs. Our case studies, as well as other empirical evidence (Richet and Ruet 2008), show that the abundance and the relatively low cost of skilled labor *at home* are a major source of competitive advantages for Indian industrial groups becoming multinationals. It is the case, for example, of mechanical and electronic engineers, computer scientists and technicians, and researchers in the pharmaceutical area.

Low costs of skilled labor directly affect the costs and the duration of design and product development processes, and therefore the speed, direction and characteristics of the innovation processes (Figure 8.2). For instance, for five years Mahindra & Mahindra dedicated a team of 120 engineers to the development of the SUV Scorpio project, whose yearly remuneration was about $10,000, while it is estimated that a Western manufacturer would have carried out the work at a much higher individual annual remuneration (around $100,000) (Khanna et al. 2005). Likewise, product development costs at Tata Motors are estimated to be one third of the same costs for Western car-makers (Ruet 2007). The abundant supply of good quality, English-speaking and low-cost skilled and highly-skilled labor represents an ex-ante competitive advantage for Indian multinationals, explaining their capacity to afford the risk of investing and competing abroad, not only in developing and emerging markets, but also in the most developed countries, with market-oriented, efficiency-seeking and/or asset-seeking motivations. Also the abundant supply of low-cost unskilled labor emerges as a country-specific competitive advantage for Indian industrial groups, generating high profit rates at home.

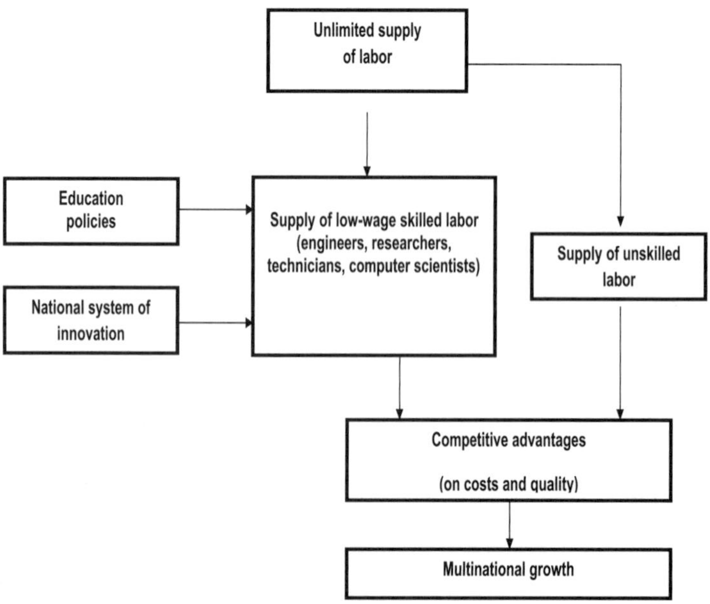

Figure 8.1 Indian multinationals: labor costs matter

Source: our elaboration.

Therefore, Indian multinationals are able to export low-cost components and intermediate goods to their foreign affiliates, improving in this way their profitability.

We can conclude that the cost and quality of labor act not only as an attractive factor for FDI inflows to India, but also, at the same time, as a competitive advantage for Indian multinationals, contributing to explain intense horizontal two-way FDI flows (Figure 8.1).

4.2. Institutions and policies matter: the role of conglomerate groups

The empirical evidence shows that the conglomerate nature of Indian private companies is a major source of competitive advantages in world markets, supporting their multinational growth. It allows intra-group technology transfers, dissemination of knowledge and managerial skills, including best practices, reallocation of financial resources, synergies from common brands and marketing structures, scale and scope economies, political and social recognition and flexibility. In particular, it must be noted that Indian conglomerate groups frequently control or are connected with banks and financial institutions: this feature provides them with significant advantages on the financial side.

Indian multinational groups are the beneficiaries of a peculiar institutional change that took place in the country in the last decades. Limiting private investments in the same industry, the regulatory framework imposed during the import-substitution era (from Independence to the late 1980s), also known as 'Licence Raj', provided a powerful incentive to Indian corporations to diversify into other sectors of activity. As a consequence, the Indian planning and mixed economy, highly regulated regime gave rise to a sort of 'conglomerate capitalism' and oligopolistic market structure, characterized by a family-owned corporate governance pattern (Ruet 2007).

When the slow and gradual de-regulation process started during the 1980s, followed since 1991 by a period of open liberalization, large and diversified private Indian groups were keen to react and to adapt to the policy change. They rapidly re-organized their structures and re-oriented their strategies, largely through strategic alliances with Western and Japanese multinationals (Balcet and Bruschieri 2008, Saripalle 2009).

This peculiar conglomerate feature of Indian multinationals contrasts with the industrial structure and corporate governance in the other emerging Asian economic power, China. On the one hand, Chinese private enterprises tend to be more specialized, frequently mono-product, and smaller in size (Richet and Ruet 2006). On the other hand, many Chinese multinationals are owned by public capital, i.e. by the central State administration, by Provinces or by Municipalities.

We must note that, in India, not only has state capitalism prepared in a first stage the emergence of private capitalism in the following stage, – in the context of a very slow and gradual liberalization process – but there has been a constant

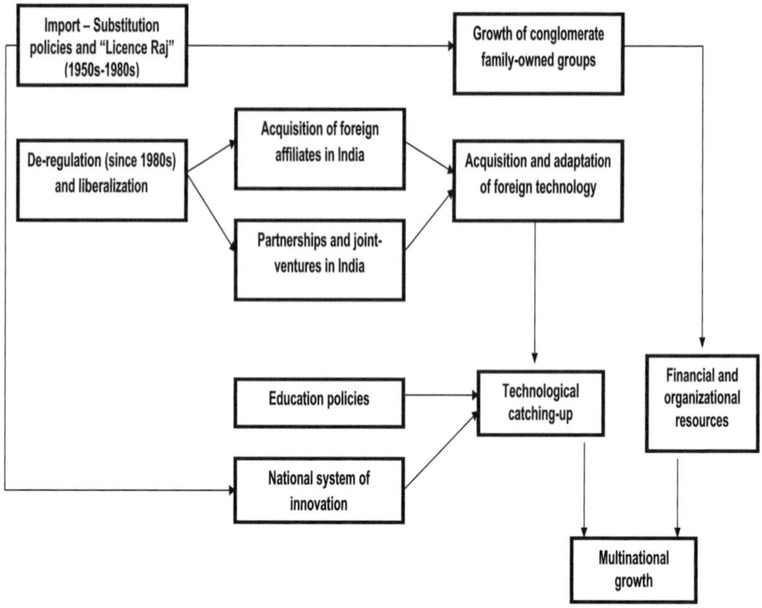

Figure 8.2 Indian multinationals: institutions and policies
Source: our elaboration.

connection and close cooperation between the state administration and the major family-owned conglomerates (Ruet 2007).

The empirical evidence on India we have presented in this Chapter leads us to the conclusion that both institutions and policies shaped the pattern of multinational growth of Indian industrial groups (Figure 8.2). This conclusion could be extended, as an hypothesis and a research question, to other emerging countries, to explain their different trajectories in the multinational growth process.

4.3. Leveraging resources through partnerships

Empirical evidence supports the idea that alliances, external networks and cooperative inter-firm behavior are at the core of any explanation of technological catching-up in India as well as in other ECs, including China. They represent crucial instruments to acquire assets from multinational partners, enhancing the capabilities and therefore the competitive advantages of Indian firms, especially in the field of the most advanced technologies. To understand them, some useful insights are provided by the theory of the joint venture, considered as representative of a wider range of alliances, aimed at strengthening cooperative ties between companies from different countries (Contractor and Lorange 2000).

Bridging the empirical evidence and the existing literature, we can point out that joint ventures, as a form of partnership, from a static point of view can be interpreted as a 'hostage', i.e. an institutional device created in order to protect each of the partners from the possible opportunistic behavior of the other partners. From a dynamic point of view, the joint ventures can be viewed as a "learning instrument" in a broad sense, with different and complementary motivations for each of the partners. Such motivations include the access to new technology and knowledge, learning of organizational and managerial skills, access to new markets, overcoming great distances, in a geographical, cultural and institutional sense (Balcet 2009). A dynamic approach helps to understand the evolutionary nature of joint ventures and alliances, that should always be related to their specific industrial, historical and geographical context.

Our results strongly support the hypothesis that alliances and partnerships are crucial instruments for catching-up, the transfer and creative assimilation of technology and knowledge, combined in different ways with the acquisitions of foreign affiliates in India and acquisitions abroad.

Conclusion

Integrating our observations and arguments on labor costs, institutional and political factors, and the nature of international partnerships can help to better understand the rapid evolution of India and other emerging countries from the role of host countries for multinational investments to the simultaneous role of the home country of fast-growing multinationals.

Our results may be viewed as opposed to conventional wisdom and the orthodox theoretical stream, i.e. the factor-endowment approach, consistent with the Heckscher-Ohlin and Nurkse tradition on the comparative advantages of nations. In this view, wage differentials and labor cost advantages are obviously considered as an attractive factor for relocation processes to developing and emerging host countries. But in no way are they considered as an explanatory factor for outward flows of capital, via direct investments, from emerging countries. They are used to explain the role of emerging countries as host, but not as home, countries of multinationals.

However, this competitive advantage, together with the ability to leverage resources through partnerships, and the peculiar institutional features, including corporate governance, as well as policies, can be considered, all together, as conditions allowing for multinational operations from Indian, as well as from Chinese and other EC corporations and industrial groups. We show that emerging countries can exploit skilled and unskilled labor cost advantages not only by exporting (as in the orthodox view) but also by investing and producing abroad. This view seems to us fully consistent with the explanatory framework of the oligopolistic theories *à la* Hymer, and in particular with the dynamic neo-schumpeterian explanations of the MNC based on innovation, imitation and assimilation of technological knowledge.

References

Andreff, W. 2003. *Les multinationales globales*. Paris: La Découverte.

Balcet, G. 1981. Industrializzazione, multinazionali e dipendenza tecnologica, Torino: Loescher.

Balcet, G. 2009. Economia delle joint venture. In Balcet, G. (ed.), *Economia dell'impresa multinazionale*. Torino: Giappichelli Editore.

Balcet, G. and Bruschieri, S. 2008. Technology Transfer, Joint Ventures and the Emergence of Indian Multinationals: The Case of the Automotive Industry. In Andreosso-O'Callaghan, B. and Zolin, M.B. (eds), *Asia and Europe: Connections and Contrasts*, Venezia: Libreria Editrice Cafoscarina, pp. 275–302.

Boston Consulting Group, 2006. *The New Global Challengers*. Boston: BCG.

Bruschieri, S. 2009. *Emerging Country Multinationals. A Case Study on Indian Multinationals in the Automotive and Pharmaceutical Sectors*. PhD dissertation, Università di Torino.

Buckley, P. and Casson, M. 1988. A theory of cooperation in international business, in Contractor F.J. and Lorange P. (eds), *Cooperative Strategies in International Business*. Lexington: Lexington Books.

Cantwell, J. and Tolentino, P.E. 1990. *Technological Accumulation and Third World Multinationals*, Reading University, University of Reading Discussion Paper in International Investment and Business Studies, No. 139.

Castellani, D. and Zanfei, A., 2006. *Multinational Firms, Innovation and Productivity*. Edward Elgar, Cheltenham.

Cohen, W.M. and Levinthal, D.A. 1989. Innovation and learning: the two faces of R&D. *The Economic Journal*, 99(397), 569–96.

Contractor, F.J. and Lorange, P. 2002. *Cooperative Strategies in International Business: Joint Ventures and Technology Partnerships Between Firms*. Amsterdam: Pergamon.

Dunning, J.H. 1983. Changes in the level and structure of international production: the last one hundred years. *The Growth of International Business*, Casson, M. (ed.), London: George Allen & Unwin.

Dunning, J.H. 1986. The investment development cycle and Third World multinationals, in Kahn, K.M. (ed.), *Multinationals of the South: New Actors in the International Economy*. London: Frances Printer.

Dunning, J.H. 1988. The eclectic paradigm of international production: a restatement and some possible extensions. *Journal of International Business Studies*, 19(1), 1–31.

Dunning, J.H. 1995. Reappraising the eclectic paradigm in an age of alliance capitalism. *Journal of International Business Studies,* 26(3), 461–91.

Dunning, J.H. 2006. Comment on dragon multinationals: new players in 21st century globalization. *Asia Pacific Journal of Management*, 23(2), 139–41.

Dunning, J.H., Kim, C. and Park, D. 2006. *Old Wine in New Bottles: A Comparison of Emerging Market TNCs and Developed Country TNCs*. Paper presented

at the International Conference "The rise of transnational corporations from emerging countries: threat or opportunity?", Columbia University, New York, 24–25 October.
Forbes, N. 1999. Technology and Indian industry: what is liberalization changing? *Technovation*, 19, 403–12.
Huang, Y. and Khanna, T. 2003. Can India overtake China? *Foreign Policy*, 137 (July/August), 74–81.
Ietto-Gillies G. 2005. *Transnational Corporations and International Production. Concepts, Theories and Effects*. Cheltenham: Edward Elgar.
Johanson, J. and Vahlne, J. 1977. The internationalization process of the firm – a model of knowledge development and increasing foreign market commitments. *Journal of International Business Studies*, 8(1), 23–32.
Kale, D. and Little, S. 2007. From imitation to innovation: the evolution of R&D capabilities and learning processes in the Indian pharmaceutical industry. *Technology Analysis & Strategic Management*, 19(5), 589–609.
Khanna, T., Lal, R. and Manocaran, M. 2005. *Mahindra & Mahindra: Creating Scorpio*. Boston: Harvard Business School.
Lall, S. 1982. The emergence of Third World multinationals: Indian joint ventures overseas. *World Development*, 10(2), 127–46.
Lall, S. 1983. The theoretical background. Lall, S. (ed.), *The New Multinationals. The Spread of Third World Enterprises*. Chichester: John Wiley & Sons.
Lall, S. 1984. India. *World Development*, 12(5–6), 535–65.
Lall, S. 1992. Technological capabilities and industrialization. *World Development*, 20(2), 165–86.
Lecraw, D. 1981. Technological activities of less-developed-country-based multinationals. *Annals of the American Academy of Political and Social Science*, 458, November, 163–74.
Luo, Y. and Tung, R.L. 2007. International expansion of emerging market enterprises: A springboard perspective. *Journal of International Business Studies*, 38, 481–98.
Mathews, J.A. 2002. *Dragon Multinationals. A New Model for Global Growth.* Oxford: Oxford University Press.
Mathews, J.A. 2006. Dragon multinationals: New players in 21st century globalization. *Asia Pacific Journal of Management*, 23, 5–27.
Moon, H. and Roehl, T.W. 2001. Unconventional foreign direct investment and the imbalance theory. *International Business Review*, 10(2), 197–215.
Mouhoud, E.M. 2008. *Mondialisation et délocalisation des enterprises*. Paris: La Découverte.
Pradhan, J.P. 2006. *Global Competitiveness of Indian Pharmaceutical Industry: Trends and Strategies*. ISID Working Paper 2006/05, New Delhi: ISID.
Richet, X. and Ruet, J. 2008. The Chinese and Indian automobile industry in perspective: technology appropriation, catching-up and development, *Transition Studies Review*, 15(3), 447–65.

Ruet, J. 2007. Emergence des firmes multinationals "du Sud" et lecture du capitalisme. *Annuaire Français de Relations Internationales*, VIII, 808–25.

Saripalle, M. 2009. *Learning Across Policy regimes: A Case Study of the Indian Automobile Industry*. Paris: GERPISA International Colloquium, June 17–19.

Sauvant, K.P. 2005. *New Sources of FDI: The BRICs. Outward FDI from Brazil, Russia, India and China*. Paper presented at the seminar on "Global Players from Emerging Markets: Brazil", São Paulo, 30 May.

Tolentino, P.E.E. 2008. Explaining the competitiveness of Multinational Companies from developing economies: a critical review of the academic literature. *International Journal of Technology and Globalization*, 4(1), 23–38.

UNCTAD, 2006. United Nations Conference on Trade and Development, *World Investment Report. FDI from Developing and Transition Economies: Implications for Development*. Geneva: United Nations.

UNCTAD, 2008. United Nations Conference on Trade and Development, *World Investment Report. Transnational Corporations and the Infrastructure Challenge*. Geneva: United Nations.

Vernon, R. 1966. International investment and international trade in the product cycle. *Quarterly Journal of Economics*, 80(2).

Vernon, R. 1979. The product life cycle hypothesis in the new international environment. *Oxford Bulletin of Economics and Statistics*, 41(4), 255–67.

Wells, L.T. Jr. 1981. Foreign Investors from the Third World. In Kumar, K.E. and McLeod, M. (eds), *Multinationals from Developing Countries*. Lexington: D.C. Heath and Company.

Wells, L.T. Jr. 1983. *Third World Multinationals: The Rise of Foreign Investment from Developing Countries*. Cambridge, Massachusetts: The MIT Press.

Chapter 9
Transnational Companies, Shareholder Value and the Chinese Innovation Policy

Michael von Wuntsch and Xiaojun Wei

Introduction

Non-economic institutions are important determinants of economic success. Economic coordination takes place within firms at a domestic and transnational level. Production and management systems[1] not only differ between countries and sectors, but are also influenced by variations in the social environment. Firms are embedded in complex political and cultural contexts which place constraints on their economic activities. Coordinating mechanisms at state and supranational levels determine economic behavior by providing a set of norms, rules and privileges. It is the State that regulates the various non-state coordinating mechanisms and that manipulates fiscal and monetary policy. In this sense, political institutions[2] can create economic conditions that attract technological progress and encourage foreign investment.

The power of states as coordinating actors tends to dissolve at the transnational level (Hollingsworth and Boyer 1997: 30). Moreover, collective forms of coordination, such as associations and unions, are rather weakly developed beyond the national level. At a low level of control, the market is the prominent form of transaction coordination among unrelated firms. At a higher level, economic coordination is carried out through hierarchies such as transnational corporations or collective forms such as international trade associations.

In this context, an often discussed question is whether globalization is necessarily heading towards the erosion of national barriers and the adoption

1 Neoclassical economic theory has tended to downplay the role of production and of firms (Hollingsworth and Boyer 1997: 19). A social system of production is a social configuration consisting of different levels such as industrial relations, the internal structure of firms, the connections between firms and their relationship to financial markets, the state and its policies as well as norms, rules and laws.

2 The competitiveness of a country's major social system also depends on international rules of the game. For example, the emergence of the World Trade Organization and of the European Union has influenced coordinating mechanisms at the nation-state level through new institutional arrangements. This raises concern that integration at a supranational level undermines national institutions and socio-economic-political forms of coordination.

of a uniform set of basic institutions worldwide (Miller 2008: 305). On the one hand, the expansion of Western values and standards as well as the dominance of capitalistic patterns of behavior on the world markets seem to confirm the view that, in the long run, globalization ends up in convergence. On the other hand, the remaining variety of political and cultural differences among countries resulting in different national institutions stand in opposition to a convergent path.

This raises the possibility that countries may derive comparative advantages from their institutional infrastructure (Hall and Soskice 2003). Within the global framework the selection of the most competitive site means scrutinizing and challenging the national set-up. It affects virtually all realms of politics. We will further analyze the reciprocal process of change at the corporate and institutional levels.

This chapter will examine global trends towards achieving standardization of management concepts and will look at the remaining national differences. In general, the various connections between the socioeconomic and political levels of market coordination are subject to our analysis. The aim is to survey the political and fiscal challenges resulting from the growing influence of value added concepts and shareholder value orientation in Europe and East Asia. In order to reduce complexity, we will focus on cross-border R&D investments and R&D policy in China. We will look at both:

- the role of transnational companies (TNCs) in off-shoring research and development activities, and
- the state of Research and Development (R&D) policy in China.

The rationale for choosing China lies in its increasing importance as an actor in the areas of production, finance and innovation. The country differs from the liberal market economy model of the UK and USA and from the German, Japanese and South Korean models.

Finally, the effects of fiscal instruments such as direct funding and tax incentives on R&D investments in China are an important concern of this chapter. Several studies indicate that a various mix of direct government's financing and tax incentives differ across OECD countries (Hall and Van Reenen 2000). While many manufacturing countries[3] offer both, other OECD countries have low direct and indirect funding and high private R&D expenditure. However, studies on the effectiveness of tax incentives in the context of developing countries are rare. Analyzing the effect of Chinese innovation policy will finally allow us to highlight some elements of coordination and modernization which can inspire and influence Western countries.

3 Recent proposals regarding the US tax plan also include the research tax credit that was to expire at the end of 2009. This US credit has been temporary for more than a decade and will now be made permanent.

The chapter is structured into four sections. Section 1 discusses basic business concepts and strategies of transnational companies. Section 2 describes recent developments in the role of transnational companies regarding cross-border R&D investments. Section 3 provides details on technology transfer to China and on Chinese R&D policy. Concluding remarks are contained in section 4.

1. The Impact of Shareholder Value Orientation on Transnational Corporate Operations – Comparing Models of the Market Economy

Although the institutional set differs from country to country, a strong trend towards economic convergence can be identified. Firms must respond to the pressure of the market. New challenges in the global market place are forcing corporations to re-evaluate traditional ways of doing business. Bartlett and Goshall (1990) discussed the trend towards transnational groups and integrated networks with respect to corporate governance. These models range from highly centralized to mostly decentralized conglomerates. The creation of global networks highlights their compatibility with the objectives of value management. Transnational corporations pool the resources of corporate headquarters and their foreign subsidiaries. Costs and proceeds are optimized to gain a competitive advantage.

With the new global economic crisis starting in the Autumn 2008, even president Obama vowed to pursue US American tax evaders and discourage offshore tax shelters. He announced a series of steps aiming at preventing US companies from sheltering foreign profits in tax havens like the Cayman Islands, where one single mailing address houses 18,857 corporations. Over a period of ten years his plan would generate US$210 billion in tax revenue, money needed to help reduce the swelling federal deficit. Under current law, US firms can write off domestic expenses for generating profits overseas.[4] The proposal focuses on headquarters` expenses regarding US foreign subsidiaries. While currently the costs used to generate offshore profits are deductable immediately, US tax payments can be deferred till those profits are repatriated to the American parent company.

The debate indicates that TNCs are taking advantage of low tax conditions overseas. The defense strategies of high-tax countries are not uniform. According to US tax law, foreign profits of domestic corporations are taxed in America. If a US firm invests in Ireland and earns Irish profits, it would have to pay up to 35 percent tax minus a credit for the foreign tax paid (12.5 percent). The total tax load would consist of both the domestic and foreign taxes and amount to 35 percent. In comparison to a German firm the result would be quite different because Germany would apply the exemption tax method on foreign profits. Paying no corporation tax on foreign income, the total tax load for a German corporation would only total 12.5 percent. Therefore, American firms tend to shelter their

4 Multinational corporations in the USA had an effective tax rate of 2.3 percent in 2004.

foreign profits in low-tax countries, while the repatriation of foreign profits is favorable for German firms.

The creation of multi-national production networks goes hand in hand with the formation of global financial markets. Since the 1980s financial globalization has accelerated. This is due to the deregulation of domestic securities and capital markets, the liberalization of borderless financial transactions and new technologies. Together, these have enabled economic activities to become global in that they can take place anywhere, anytime, and can span different time zones. Not only has this intensified inter-corporate competition, it has also increased competition between different types of capital investments. Hence corporate management increasingly relies on value management.

In line with a growing shareholder orientation in corporate management, creating shareholder value (Rappaport 1998) has become the prime responsibility of the market economy. This philosophy has gained widespread acceptance in the United States and Great Britain (Copeland et al. 2000: 3). In continental Europe and Japan, a broader view has long been more influential, ensuring participation and the continuity of the business rather than maximizing shareholder value. Reflecting upon the current financial and economic crisis, the question arises whether the shareholder value concept will more likely become the global standard for measuring business performance. After the recent financial shocks and the associated economic pain, there is a natural desire for a general reform of the regulatory system. After investors and financial institutions have simply outsourced their risk management it has become obvious that self-regulation has its limits.

Shareholders measure success in terms of increased dividend yield. Returns comprise dividend pay outs and added value of a particular stock. From a shareholder's perspective, added value consists of the difference between the purchase price and the realized sales price of a particular stock. The return thus represents interest on invested capital. In this model, sound financial management commences only when the interest yield of invested capital surpasses expectations, i.e. the opportunity costs of the investor.

In value based management, the yield expectation of shareholders is the decisive benchmark for investments. The yield entitlement, in a way, represents the calculated rate of return of the investor. The calculated rate of return is based on the weighed average cost of capital, which consists of the cost of equity and the cost of debt. The key term 'cost of equity' contains three components:[5] base yield (risk free yield), a general market risk premium and the systematic risk (beta factor).

A corporation's weighted average cost of capital represents the standard measure for corporate investment projects. Based on this corporate point of view, if operating cash flow exceeds the weighted average cost of capital, then the result

5 For a more detailed analysis see: Copeland, Koller and Murrin (2000: 201–232), or von Wuntsch, Knacke, and Neumann (2005: 31–34).

is an increase in the value of the corporation. The reverse scenario would lead to a decrease in the valuation of the corporation. This point of view assumes that value based management results in an efficient allocation of capital.

The emphasis on shareholder orientation is a response to heightened pressure of competition and the dominance of financial markets. In essence, we can highlight a new structure of investors. This development has also influenced businesses in Asian and continental European countries. Ownership of widely held stock has changed. Institutional investors such as investment funds, pension funds, banks or trusts and private shareholders own widely held stocks. Even in Germany, and particularly in Japan, there has been a significant increase in institutional investors. Next to domestic funds, American pension funds dominate with respect to international exposure. Siemens and Veba make an excellent case in point. Between 1993 and 1999, Siemens has registered an increase in institutional investors from 15 percent to 45 percent in its shares. At Veba, this increase has jumped from one percent in 1987 to 71 percent in 1999 (Streeck and Höpner 2003: 251).

Institutional investors are not tied to individual corporations when deciding on their investment options. Instead, their concern is purely financial, based on the rate of return and the degree of risk. According to a survey commissioned by the Deutsche Bundesbank[6] the average investment duration spans approximately one year. Competition between investment funds intensifies the pressure on corporate management. Sanctions or penalties range from under-allocation, the complete pull-out of capital all the way to rewards and incentives like over-allocation in portfolios.

The danger of a hostile takeover is minimized by focusing on a corporate policy, which is based on shareholder interests. Offers to acquire shares which are directed at shareholders of the target company directly represent the driving force of a capital market based corporate policy (Rappaport 1998: 1). Governance of widely held stocks by institutional investors with an international focus results in greater transparency with respect of selling to hostile takers.

In this perspective, the dominance of financial markets has led to an increased integration of operating and financial corporate functions. Players at the financial market level impact on corporate operations via friendly and hostile takeovers as well as through corporate acquisitions, which are financed with borrowed money. Corporate management on the other hand has to stand up to mergers and acquisitions, to stock buy-backs and restructuring of the financial markets while keeping an eye on the markets benchmarks.

A lot of managers in Germany and other continental European countries had to get used to the idea of making hostile takeovers part of their *modus operandi*. The late 1990s featured a steady stream of rumors pertaining to hostile takeovers of German corporations. This development came about as a result of the increased importance of institutional investors. With the new focus on value added management, performance based diversification was eliminated in favor

6 For a more detailed analysis cf. Deutsche Bundesbank (2001: 46 *et seq.*).

of concentrating on core business to improve earnings. In essence, diversified corporations deal with a proportionally greater danger of hostile takeover and of being sold below the value of all their parts. That is because the larger the corporation, the greater the possibilities of cross subsidization for unprofitable sub entities from profitable ones. The effective market value, thus, is assumed to be below the sum of the potential value of all the individual subsidiaries, i.e. the conglomerate discount.

These developments also give rise to important institutional changes in different countries. A perspective on institutional change can be outlined as it applied to Germany and Japan. We can view the German and Japanese models of capitalism as systems of incentives and constraints. In contrast to the UK and the US models, neither model is considered market based in the classic liberal sense. Both Germany and Japan are heading in that direction, i.e. approaching the model of shareholder value. The control that banks exert on corporations has diminished, especially in Germany within the last fifteen years. German corporations used to be highly dependent on their main banking institution. The bank would provide financing and at the same time would also hold a stake in the corporation itself. The highly lucrative investment banking system is progressively incompatible with the German main bank-based financial system. Corporations which are listed on the stock exchange have begun to be more dependent on equity investors (Vogel 2003: 317), who are more driven by the markets. That is why German banks have relinquished their industrial shares significantly since the late 1990s.

The restructuring of the bank-based financial system in Japan progressed along different lines. After World War II, administrative guidance developed into a system of informal relations between regulators and financial institutions. This involved a mix of formal restrictions and unwritten instructions on bank lending and branching policy. One was the practice of issuing new shares at par value rather than market value. Additionally, the state and leading financial institutions regulated access to capital markets through approval of the size and timing of new bonds. As a result of the 1997 Asian crisis, which brought weak Japanese banks to the brink of insolvency, the pressure to deregulate intensified and with it, the pressure to establish a politically independent central bank (Vitols 2003: 257).

Although Japanese corporations have eased their dependence on bank loans, new networks between banks and corporations have emerged. This holds true especially for small- and medium-sized companies. Banks continue to hold a large volume of industrial shares. The sale of these shares typically occurs with prior consultation with the companies involved. If a corporation incurred losses due to a financial crisis, it would be forced to shift back from equity financing to borrowing (Vogel 2003: 319).

In contrast to the liberal market economies such as North America and the UK, Germany, Japan and South Korea are generally viewed as coordinated market economies based on their institutional framework. Coordinated market economies can be further subdivided into industry-based coordination as in Northern Europe and group-based coordination (Hall and Soskice 2003: 34). In Germany, companies often cooperate within the same industry in the areas of training and technology transfer. Business associations and trade unions are organized along industry-specific skills and wage rates coordination. By contrast, business networks in Japan are built on families of companies (*keiretsu*) with interconnections across industries. Therefore, workers are encouraged to acquire firm or group specific skills. Workers are motivated to invest in skills acquisition because large firms offer life-time employment. While liberal market economies tend to concentrate their power in the political executive, coordinated market economies are rather governed by coalitional regimes. Fluid market settings can enhance investment in different kinds of assets or industries. By comparison, investment in specific industry assets or industries is more encouraged in coordinated market economies.

The inclusion of China in this assessment poses a challenge from the point of view of comparative institutional advantage.[7] This concept needs to be inclusive of all the varieties of market systems. Notwithstanding the idiosyncrasies of the Chinese way, it is clear that the Chinese focus has been on the economy. The Chinese emphasis on economic success as manifested since the late 1970s represents a shift towards an efficiency approach, very much in the sense of Max Weber. The new law of ownership enacted on October 1 2007 for the very first time, ever provides for equal protection of private, state and collective ownership.

In accordance with the World Trade Organization (WTO) protocol, China agreed, at the end of 2001, to put foreign banks on a par with Chinese domestic banks. Although China has yet to fully comply, China is increasingly opening up her financial sector. This policy of liberalization is evident at different levels (Von Wuntsch 2008: 246):

i. By the end of December 2006, the banking sector was gradually being made accessible to foreign competition. This was also true for purchasing shares in Chinese banks. For example, the majority shareholding of 20 percent in the Guangdong Development Bank was purchased by a Citigroup-led consortium. The complete liberalization of the banking sector will enable foreign banks to establish branch offices in China and also enable them to sell insurance products.
ii. State-owned investment banks are to change into a modern banking system with sufficient equity capital, strict internal controls and a high competitive edge. Banks will be allowed to establish investment funds as well. This will force valuation of investments in accordance with global value based management.
iii. The market for corporate bonds will be transferred to the more market based financial regulatory agency. The National Development and Reform

7 The approach to comparative political economy examines how national legal and political institutions reinforce specific patterns of economic coordination and generate distinctive forms of market economies (Hall and Soskice 2003).

Commission sets annual quotas and authorizes the issue of bonds on a case by case basis.

iv. China is a player in international stock markets and utilizes her steadily increasing reserves for strategic purchases. China Development Bank for instance strengthened the Barclays offer in the take-over spectacle for the Dutch ABN Amro bank by purchasing Barclays shares worth 13.4 billion Euro. This resulted in a higher offer on the part of Barclays for ABN Amro. In addition, China recently provided her state-owned investment company with 200 billion dollars to invest in foreign industry and financial products. This led to China buying into the US financial investor Blackstone.

China's increasing economic clout is evident in the valuation of Chinese companies. Already out of eighteen of the highest valuable companies in the world, based on market capitalization, six are Chinese. The expansion of the stock markets in China will inevitably further financial based value management with the primary assessment of cash flows and risk (market risk premium and systematic risk). Whether China can be categorized as more liberal or more group-oriented requires further investigation. China's remaining elements of state regulation seem to suggest that China's development represents a unique variety of the coordinated market economy model.[8]

We have pointed out that the shareholder value based way of doing business has gained more ground worldwide since the 1980s, although, this trend is still far more developed in the Anglo-Saxon countries. In so far as the financial dominance of markets has been questioned during the recent crisis, it will be interesting to find out whether businesses in Germany and Japan might tend to follow old paths again. This scenario can only be a result of turning back to former institutional standards. Currently, policy makers are considering regulatory actions to be taken to reflect the lessons learnt from this crisis. Although it should be clear that self-regulation has its limits, the political reaction on the extent of market regulation requirements differs from country to country.[9]

8 The regulatory framework is officially proclaimed as a 'socialist legal system'.

9 Hedge fund managers and policy makers in London and New York have already warned that excessive regulation would stifle the innovative qualities of the financial markets. They only voiced support for minimal requirements such as greater standardization regarding reporting, registration and disclosure. German policy makers rather believe that no institution, no market and no jurisdiction should be without proportionate regulation and supervision.

2. TNCs Role in Off-shoring[10] Research and Development

After we have pointed out the impact of corporate value management on the strategy and design of transnational companies, we will now describe how corporate R&D activities are embedded in their global value chain. The concentration on R&D investments and policy allows us to reduce complexity and to describe a specific area of economic and political coordination. The aims of this section are to:

- describe recent developments regarding cross-border R&D investments by TNCs,
- discuss opportunities and risks from the viewpoint of developing countries, and finally,
- survey the effect of R&D policy and fiscal instruments on R&D activities in China.

According to recent data provided by the United Nations, the current crisis has put an end to a growth cycle in international investment (UNCTAD 2009). Starting in 2004, foreign direct investment (FDI) flows reached a record of US$1.8 trillion in 2007. Global FDI declined by more than 20 percent in 2008 and a further decrease of nearly a third is expected for 2009. The fall in FDI results from a lower availability of capital, higher cost of capital, cuts in corporate profits since access to financial resources has been hit by a severe recession. While developed countries have been most affected in 2008, developing countries were still able to attract further FDI, but at a lower rate.

Although the visible precursor signs of the current financial crisis can be traced back to the second half of 2007 in the United States, sub-prime mortgage markets did not affect cross-border mergers and acquisitions (M&As) in that year. Due to relatively favorable financing conditions for debt-financed M&As and despite a changing lending behavior since mid-2007, large deals were completed in that year. The mega-acquisition of ABN-AMRO Holding NV by the consortium of Royal Bank of Scotland, Fortis and Santander through RFS Holding BV took place. The liquidity crisis in money and debt markets began to depress M&As in 2008. In so far as buyout activities by private equity investors have slowed down rapidly, the sustainability of private equity funds gives rise to doubts. Risks related to the high leverage of firms, the increasing cost of debt and possible regulation may weaken private equity activity. Although economic growth in emerging countries could compensate for weaker growth in developed countries, a further slowdown during and after 2009 is a reasonable scenario.

10 Off-shoring is defined as the transfer of activities abroad. It can be done internally and/or externally. Internally, it involves moving services from a parent company to its foreign subsidiaries or affiliates (captive off-shoring). However, the involvement of a third party provider abroad refers to the external concept.

However, the current crisis does not alter the fact that the development of international production indicated by exports of foreign affiliates, value-added activities, employment and other factors has increased during recent years. TNCs aim to benefit from market liberalization and deregulation in host economies. The 2008 World Investment Report mentions that 79,000 TNCs control an estimated 790,000 affiliates worldwide. Gross product of foreign affiliates is still growing by a rate of 19.4 percent and accounted for 11 percent of global GDP in 2007. One fifth of their sales were exports and the number of employees amounted to 82 million.

FDI inflows to developing countries reached a new record level of $500 billion in 2007. South Asia, East Asia and South-East Asia accounted for half of this FDI, with China (and Hong Kong) remaining the largest FDI destination in the region, followed by India (OECD 2008a: 8). Progress towards regional integration and policy developments contributed to this performance (see chapters 4 and 5 in this volume). Rising costs of production are, however, increasing competition with South and South-East Asian regions. The 2008 World Investment Report points out that some foreign firms are turning to areas with lower wages in Bangladesh, Vietnam or inland China (OECD 2008a: 51). On the other hand, it is interesting to see that South Asia, East Asia and South-East Asia have also become a significant source of FDI for other developing countries. FDI outflows from South, East, and South-East Asia reached a level of about $150 billion in 2007.

A broad trend towards the off-shoring of research and development can be detected. In so far as the global environment is characterized by shorter product life cycles, rapidly developing technologies and increasing costs for R&D, firms aim to access the skills of foreign locations and adapt products to local markets. TNCs are playing a major role in offshoring R&D through FDI and technology alliances (UNCTAD 2006: 2). Although the expansion of R&D across borders has already been indicated in the past, the rising scale of offshoring R&D and the selection of developing countries as destinations is remarkable and can be seen as a part of the broader process of offshoring services (Table 9.1).

Between 1993 and 2002, R&D expenditure of foreign affiliates worldwide rose from 10 percent to 16 percent of global business R&D (or from $30 to $60 billion). Compared with developed host countries the increase was significant in developing host countries, where the share rose from 2 percent to 18 percent between 1996 and 2002 (UNCTAD 2005: 125). The geographical distribution of foreign affiliates involved in R&D worldwide in 2004 stresses the share of developing Asia. While more than 10 percent of foreign affiliates worldwide engaged in R&D are located in developing countries, 207 out of 264 foreign affiliates in developing countries are registered in South, East and South-East Asia. Other data on recent greenfield R&D projects also indicate that the majority of new R&D jobs have been created in developing countries, mainly in China and India and in the information and communication sector (UNCTAD 2006: 7). The off-shoring of R&D in developing countries involves internationally well known firms such as IBM, Intel, Microsoft, Nokia, Oracle and SAP.

Table 9.1 Geographical distribution of R&D foreign affiliates*, 2004

Region/Economy	**Number of Affiliates**
Total World	2,584
Developed Countries	2,185
of which:	
Western Europe	1,387
United States	552
Japan	29
Developing Countries	264
of which:	
Asia	216
South, East and South-East Asia	207
Latin America and the Caribbean	40
Africa	4

Source: UNCTAD 2006, p. 7.
* On the basis of 2,284 majority-owned foreign affiliates identified in the Who Owns Whom database that are engaged in commercial, physical and educational research, commercial economics and biological research, non-commercial research and testing laboratories.

On the other hand, keeping up with new technologies is a major challenge for developing countries. By introducing a favorable set of economic conditions and fiscal incentives for attracting international R&D investments, these countries are aiming at accelerating their economic development. There is a broad consensus among economists that R&D and human capital are two of the most influential drivers of productivity (Romer 1990). The rationale is that technological knowledge, created through R&D activity, enhances the production and diffusion of innovations and promotes productivity growth. According to theoretical growth models (Coe and Helpman 1995) total factor productivity depends on both the stock of R&D accumulated in a country and in other countries, hypothesizing that knowledge spills over from the other countries proportionally to aggregate import flows. This correlation between cross-border spillovers and productivity seems questionable. Only a small amount of imports are able to expand productivity across countries. A plausible approach to productivity spillovers must consider the possibility that only imports of capital goods will be effective in transferring technical knowledge across countries (Xu and Wang 1999).

While TNCs are taking advantage from the offshoring of R&D, the associated opportunities and risks must be discussed additionally from the viewpoint of the developing countries. The participation of developing countries in the globalization of R&D has so far been rather uneven regarding growth and value creation (UNCTAD 2006: 2). Their policies should therefore focus on achieving technology spillovers from TNCs R&D. Spillover effects can be generated by:

- encouraging scientists and engineers to focus on patentable research and to form start-ups,
- building up an indigenous R&D and innovation culture among local companies,
- commercializing R&D results at the same location and,
- expanding R&D activities globally in order to access world knowledge.[11]

The benefits of R&D for host countries depend on the level of technology transfer. Indigenous technology units are closely linked to manufacturing units and are established to adapt a parent's product and process to local conditions in host countries. Also, regional technology units are established to serve regional markets and to develop links with local innovation actors. However, global and corporate technology units are far more centralized in order to serve the interests of the parent company and to protect the competitiveness of the firm (UNCTAD 2006:11). The greater the degree of control by a TNC, the lower the scope for host countries to access key knowledge and new technology.

In this sense, benefits from R&D investments within transnational company groups depend on many factors and are not automatic. The productivity potential will be rather low if R&D activities are an integral part of a merger and acquisition. These kinds of transactions focus on a simple change of ownership. Takeovers especially can create a negative effect on local capacities by scaling down R&D investments in the acquired firms (UNCTAD 1999). In other cases, TNCs may mainly be interested in transferring the results of innovation undertaken in the developed countries than developing the innovatory capacity in a developing country itself. The comparison and the evaluation of opportunities and risks in respect of R&D investments by TNCs in developing countries is therefore a necessary step for policy makers.

3. Technology Transfer to China, Chinese R&D Policy and Tax Considerations

3.1. Technology transfer to China – a critical insight into the Chinese R&D policy

Although FDI has been regarded as a prominent means of technology transfer by the Chinese authorities, studies on it have tended to remain very much at the macroeconomic level, given the difficulty of obtaining appropriate and reliable data at the regional level (Andreosso-O'Callaghan and Qian 1999). Some recent

11 The Chinese company Huawei has set up five research institutes in the United States, India, Sweden and Russia (OECD 2008b: 146). In addition, Beijing Automotive Industry Corporation is currently trying to take over the German Opel AG. The idea is to transfer worthy technology and know how from the German developed automotive industry to China.

research based on the case study approach is also notable. Chen et al. (1995) argued that the transfer of low and intermediate technology is dominating because China relied primarily on Hong Kong and Taiwan FDI. Based on a case study of 84 Hong Kong garment firms in China, Thompson (2002) disclosed that there is technology transfer and inter- and intra-industry spillover from Hong Kong to China. However, both Li and Yeung (1999) and Andreosso-O'Callaghan and Qian (1999) found that firms from the European Union (EU) have tended to play an important role in transferring technology in some high-tech industries such as the automotive and telecommunication industries in China.

The EU has traditionally been the largest source of technology for China (Andreosso-O'Callaghan et al. 2005). In contrast, US firms have been more cautious than their EU counterparts when they transfer technology to China. European IT & Telecom companies are the main couriers of technology transfer in the telecommunication industry. R&D investment in this sector reached €2.5 billion by 2007. The important role played by EU firms in transferring technology to China has also been stressed in empirical studies (Benett et al. 2001). The analysis of EU Technology Transfer in the automotive industry (Zhang and Taylor 2001) has provided evidence indicating that transfers of low and intermediate technologies to Chinese indigenous companies are found in the context of learning-by-doing. By focusing on the case of Shanghai Volkswagen Automotive Company and Shanghai Bell Telephone Equipment Manufacturing Company, Li and Yeung (1999) found inter-firm technology transfer and knowledge spillovers in both cases.

According to the European Chamber of Commerce in China, more than 20 of the largest EU companies such as BP, BASF and Bayer, in the petrochemical, chemical, oil and gas sectors are actively involved in oil and gas exploration and production, oil products retail and downstream development, gas infrastructure and Liquefied Natural Gas (LNG) import into the Chinese market.

Young and Lan (1997) examined the problems facing FDI-linked technology transfer to China. By conducting a case study of Dalian, a city within one of China's economic and technological development zones, the authors conclude that, based on the level of technological and economic development in China, FDI-linked technology transfer was at the expected level but that there was a greater potential for the utilization of FDI as an instrument of technological development than theory would suggest. Zhang and Taylor (2001) examined China's economic growth over the twenty year period following Deng Xiaoping's 1978 policy of open-door economic reform. This period is marked by China's transition from labor-intensive to capital and technological-intensive production. Their research focused on the First Automobile Works in Changchun, Jilin Province. The authors suggested that in order to successfully compete in a global market and sustain FDI-linked technology transfer, the Chinese government must continue to implement state-owned enterprises (SOE) policy reforms and that by maintaining an open-door policy that facilitates technology transfer, both Chinese and foreign enterprises would benefit and, thus, so would the consumer. Liu (2002) investigated the effects of FDI on technology transfer experienced by firms and sectors. Empirical data was gathered from twenty-nine manufacturing industries among six ownership sectors located in the Shenzhen Special Economic Zone of China over a five year period from 1993 to 1998. Based on empirical results, the study found that FDI generates technology transfer and raises the level and growth rate of productivity of recipient manufacturing industries, the benefits of which are felt most significantly by state-owned and joint-owned domestic sectors.

A recent article by Marcotte and Niosi (2005) studies the influences of enterprise size on the effectiveness of technology transfer and learning by recipient Chinese partners. The authors surveyed twenty-eight Canadian manufacturing firms involved in technology transfer to China and carried out seven case studies to serve as a complement to their empirical data. The authors' study sample revealed that effective technology transfer and learning in recipient partner firms was not significantly associated with Canadian transferor's size. The authors also point out that the predominance of state-owned recipient firms in China may yield different results than other developing countries where most recipient firms are private.

With regard to spillover effects associated with technology transfer, Liu et al. (2001) and Wei and Liu (2001) also showed that foreign presence is associated with higher labor productivity in the Chinese electronics industry. Wu (2000) and Zhao (2001) both noted that FDI can raise wages of skilled labor in China. Singh (2004) argued that investment expenditure on innovation projects is likely to be low if it is left in the hands of private economic agents as they have a tendency to under-invest due to the 'public good' nature of the outcomes of R&D. Based on empirical research, Xue (2001) analyzed the factors that influenced TNCs to set up independent R&D institutions from the point view of demand, efficiency and environment. The increasing competition in the market and the access to specialized staff were considered important factors.

Although, thanks in large parts to technology transfer, the Chinese innovation system is increasingly dynamic, R&D investments by Chinese firms have not reached an advanced level in terms of funding and personnel. According to the OECD review of China's innovation policy (OECD 2008b) the innovation capacity of the Chinese business sector is still weak regarding the level of technological development. However, Chinese firms are also aiming at strengthening their technology capacity by developing international alliances. This is not only favorable for foreign companies. Some leading Chinese companies have already acquired technology-based foreign companies or their divisions. For example, Huawei has formed joint laboratories with Motorola, Intel, Agere, Altera, Sun and Microsoft. The Chinese company is also expanding globally by setting up research institutes in Silicon Valley and Dallas in the United States, in Bengalore in India, in Sweden and in Russia. IBM's PC division has been acquired by the Chinese Lenovo company for US$1.75 billion, representing the largest deal for a Chinese company so far. The objective is to become a high-end global PC maker by acquiring core technology and a brand name (OECD 2008b: 146).

Companies in countries all over the world deal with a set of institutional requirements over which they do not have complete control. Hence, in analyzing comparative institutional advantages, public policy making must be addressed. While specific legal regulations influence the economic arena in which stakeholders compete in the market, multinational companies apply this legal framework in order to improve their performance and to increase their value.

Globally active corporations take advantage of the respective cost conditions and incentives in different countries. Capital-market based pressure to increase corporate value brings about a rigorous emphasis on cost efficiency. The importance of site selection based on local cost conditions and the exploitation of international taxation differences is vital to value management. Corporations more than ever base their investment and site decisions on fiscal incentives (Wei et al. 2007: 164). In the same vain, R&D related FDI depends on the policy environment in the host countries. Important factors for such TNCs are therefore:

- macro-economic progress and political stability (including protection of affiliates),
- protection of intellectual property rights,
- skilled labor and a well developed innovation system (clustering of firms and research institutions), and
- incentives (direct funding and tax reductions).

According to the OECD (2008b), academics and policymakers have criticized the fact that foreign firms are charging unduly high license fees for their patents. They are crowding out domestic firms, monopolizing technology standards and thwarting technology transfer as well as knowledge spillovers. As a result, the Chinese government is aiming at promoting domestic companies to develop indigenous innovation. After China's entry into the WTO, R&D capacities of TNCs swarmed into China and became a vital part of China's technological innovation system. In order to attract TNCs to set up R&D institutions in China, the government has taken appropriate measures such as:

1. Improving the intellectual property protection system. Xue (2001) has shown that inadequate protection of intellectual property rights in China is the main obstacle to the development of R&D institutions. China's weak protection of intellectual property rights is regarded as a major factor blocking R&D development. The state of intellectual property rights of TNCs in China has an important impact on the establishment of R&D institutions.

2. Strengthening the information infrastructure, since it affects significantly the efficiency of R&D institutions. With continuously shortened product cycles, performance depends on technical development, first-mover advantage and on expanding global markets. At present, the establishment

of R&D institutions regarding TNCs in China are concentrated in Beijing and Shanghai due to better infrastructure. This tends to widen the gap between the developed Eastern part of the country and the rest.

3. Establishing a multi-level financial system in order to leverage firms' investment in R&D. New policies enforce policy-related finance and commercial finance. Besides implementing new financial funds, high-technology enterprises are encouraged to list on the Chinese stock market (OECD 2008b).

3.2. R&D-based investments and tax considerations

Apart from the importance of locational factors such as public infrastructure or labor costs, tax considerations are gaining significance in the selection of location and investment. The statutory tariff burden and the effective marginal tax rates are highly relevant. Statutory tax rates on corporate profits are applicable over time and across countries. They represent a simple but incomplete measure of the real tax conditions faced by multinational companies. In addition to the pure statutory rate, the effective marginal tax rate also includes special tax credits, accelerated depreciation schemes and other tax incentives. This leads to a lower taxable income on which firms are actually charged under the tax code in a country.

Discussions on the rationale for FDI may therefore be undergoing a shift. While some ten years ago Markusen's survey on the motives for FDI (Markusen 1995) concluded that there is little support for the idea that tax avoidance is important, a substantial body of empirical work has since provided evidence indicating that high taxes have a significantly negative effect on the ability of a country to attract FDI (Gorter and Parik 2001, Haufler and Stöwhase 2003). According to Devereux (1992), a distinction between competition for physical capital and competition for (paper) profits must be drawn. Transnational companies tend to follow a two-step strategy.

As a first step, location advantages, including a good infrastructure and incentives such as write-off methods, are highly relevant for attracting physical capital and hence production activities. In this sense, investment undertaken for production purposes primarily reacts to the measure of the effective tax rate. In a second step, the TNC may shift taxable profits to a country offering a low statutory tax rate. In this setting the amount of production capacity can be very low in the country to which profits are shifted. Both types of capital competition allow TNCs to take advantage of the best of two worlds, benefiting from non-tax factors and tax incentives on the one hand and, transferring the economic rent of the investment to a tax haven on the other hand.

Investments in different sectors respond to tax incentives with different elasticities. Haufler and Stöwhase (2003) found[12] that especially service-related FDI depends on the level of the statutory tax rate. Service-related FDI tends to be more independent of the real variables of a host economy. In this sector, traditional location advantages are less influential and, the selection of a location is therefore more determined by the goal of minimizing the worldwide tax load of a TNC. But, tax incentives seem also to influence investment undertaken for production purposes. A reason for this is that write-off methods can only be fully applied and developed in the presence of relevant industrial capacities.

A traditional instrument of profit shifting among countries is transfer pricing for intermediate goods traded between the parent and subsidiary. Transfer pricing for purchasing and selling products within the firm conglomerate is a major instrument of achieving cost advantages. Corporate fixing of transfer pricing for miscellaneous sales offers tremendous potential for full exploitation. The corporate strategy is clear. The value added chain is structured in such a way so as to allow companies set up in low-cost and low-taxation regions that earn high yields. Intra-company transfer-pricing accompanies and further augments this effect.

Transfer pricing affects the transfer of services as well. Profit shifting seems to be increasingly related to internal trade in services, including payments for overhead services, royalties and interest paid on intra-firm loans (Mintz 2001). In general, intangibles are witnessing a strong growth, leading to an expansion of special rights such as licensing rights and patents. Firms in low tax countries have an incentive to overprice services and goods sold internally to high tax countries. The high tax importing country takes a loss and thus reduces taxable earnings and local tax liability. Proceeds accumulate in the low tax country, thus providing a great tax advantage for the conglomerates. Some 84 percent of all developing countries believe that profit transfers are solely intended for the purpose of reducing company tax loads (UNCTAD 1999: 31).

The off-shoring of R&D is linked to the transfer of patents, licenses and other rights regarding the usage of intellectual property.[13] To determine the fair market

12 The survey conducted by Haufler and Stöwhase (2001) covered foreign activities of German TNCs in eight European countries (Austria, Belgium, France, Ireland, Italy, the Netherlands, Spain and the UK).

13 Issues related to FDI in R&D are also addressed in Double Taxation Conventions (DTCs). The majority of these agreements regarding the avoidance of international double taxation provide protection to TNCs' intellectual property and to tax revenues regarding royalties derived from the ownership of a patent, trademark or other right. The contracting state where the owner of a patent or other right is resident has the exclusive right to tax royalties. Since the owners of these kinds of payments are mostly resident in developed countries, article 12 of the OECD-Model (OECD 2003) discriminates against developing countries. However, some divergent DTCs favor the position of developing countries by allowing a parallel tax on royalties in the state in which they arise. An example is the DTC between China and Germany. China as the source state may tax royalties at a rate of a

price for these kinds of intangibles is a difficult task. So far, tax authorities of developed and emerging countries have been adopting the OECD Transfer Pricing Guidelines (OECD 1995). This especially applies to the 'dealing at arm's length' principle, which emphasizes external comparison. The principle states that prices set on transactions between related parties should be determined as though these parties were independent.

Examples for the relevance of tax considerations in respect of investment decisions and FDI can also be found in China. Until the end of 2007, the Chinese tax policy aimed at attracting FDI by adopting a dual corporation tax system. While Chinese funded companies were subject to a statutory tax of 33 percent, foreign funded firms enjoyed a preferential tax of only 15 percent. Although foreign firms experienced a strong growth in their share of total tax revenues in China from 1995 to 2005, their share in gross industrial output exceeded their tax contribution by nearly 10 percentage points. On the one hand, this policy encouraged the inflow of foreign capital. On the other hand, it provoked tax avoidance and tax evasion of Chinese companies. These companies tended to transfer their capital to foreign countries and to reinvest it in China. Most of these investments came from off-shore financial centers like Hong Kong. In trying to equalize the tax treatment of domestic and foreign firms, China has been applying a new unified tax rate of 25 percent since 2008. The effective corporation tax rate on foreign companies will be increased gradually over a period of five years till the new standard is reached. However, specific high-tech industries will continue to be taxed at a preferential 15 percent rate in order to encourage innovation (Kong et al. 2007).

According to the National Plan for Science and Technology Development (2006–2020) and China's National Science and Technology Development Plan (2006–2010) a number of tax incentives have been proposed such as a 150 percent tax credit on R&D expenditure by enterprises, and tax exemptions for low value equipment and for qualifying firm laboratories and university parks (OECD 2008b: 614).

Most studies on R&D incentives have analyzed the impact of direct government funding and tax credits in developed countries. However, there is only little empirical evidence from industrial sectors in China. The first empirical studies conducted in Shanghai show interesting results. On the one hand, government direct funding has positive effects on industrial R&D investments. Government direct funding can stimulate firms' own investments and minimize technical and market risks by promoting inter-company R&D cooperation. The expenditure on R&D in China has grown rapidly from 0.6 percent of GDP in 1996 to 1.1 percent in 2002. With expenditure of nearly US$60 billion in 2001 it already ranked third in the world. The industrial sectors' own funding is the most important source of R&D investment in the Shanghai area. Firms account for 72 percent of the funding

maximum of 10 percent according to art. 12 sect. 2 DTC China-Germany. This DTC rather follows the UN model.

for science and technology activities (Zhu et al. 2006: 55). This might already demonstrate the regional strength of the industrial sector regarding innovation.

On the other hand, tax incentives affect the composition of R&D.[14] In so far as firms tend to reduce their cost levels, fiscal incentives favor projects generating high profits in the short run. A substitute effect between two kinds of innovation activities has become evident. Expenditure has been shifted from research to development activities. During the period 1993 to 2002 investments in applied research decreased from 8.3 percent to 5 percent, while investments in development increased from 91.7 percent to 95 percent (Zhu et al. 2006: 56). The trend towards experimental development instead of research seems to be in line with firms' costs and market strategies. Developing applications for existing technologies rather than creating new technologies is less cost intensive and reduces market risks. From this point of view, the adoption of foreign technology is an appropriate innovation strategy.

This section has illustrated how a country relying solely on foreign technology in the early decades of its modern economic take-off has started to develop its own innovation and technology policy so as to develop indigenous technology-based industries. In line with the discussion in the earlier sections, tax considerations are given a key role in stimulating R&D based Chinese TNCs. The next stage, which has already commenced as seen here, involves the off-shoring of Chinese research entities.

4. Concluding Remarks

The corporate strategies of transnational companies tend to converge on a global scale and TNCs take advantage of their conglomerate structure. The international set-up enables them to transfer profits to foreign subsidiaries with lower tax rates and to achieve value added results. The strategic objectives of value management are thus in perfect agreement with this concept. On the one hand, political and fiscal challenges are resulting from the growing influence of value added concepts and shareholder value orientation. On the other hand, coordinating mechanisms at state and supranational level determine economic behavior by providing a set of norms, rules and privileges. This raises the possibility that countries may derive comparative advantages from their institutional infrastructure.

In this chapter, the specific emphasis on Chinese R&D investment and policy allowed us to describe a specific area of economic and political coordination and

---

14 Tax cuts are not appropriate for adjusting the composition of industry R&D, but they can increase the amount of such investment. Tax incentives rather affect applied or short term research while direct funding affects basic or long-term research more. Tax cuts favor firms with a high profit potential. A consistent innovation strategy calls for an integrated long-term policy framework applying various types of support for big, small and middle-sized companies.

to survey the effect of fiscal instruments on R&D activities in China. Under strong global market competition, firms aim to access the skills of foreign locations in order to cut their R&D costs and to adapt products to local markets. A broad trend towards the off-shoring of research and development can be detected and we have pointed out that TNCs are playing a major role in off-shoring R&D through FDI and technology alliances.

The general finding is that the Chinese government's funding as well as the industrial sectors' own funding in science and technology activities have positive effects on industrial R&D investment. The effect of tax incentives, however, is not straightforward. The reason is that R&D activities have focused on development more than on basic research. As firms in China are mainly driven by market demand, the adoption of existing technology created elsewhere turned out to be a low-risk strategy.

China's economic policy has undergone a major transition over a period of more than 25 years. While the government withdraws from micromanagement of economic activities step by step, there has been a gradual move from governing by executive order towards the rule of law. Parallel to economic reforms, China is following a modernization strategy which emphasizes science and technology. This is seen as the cornerstone of modernization and a new development model directed towards greater social, ecological and environmental sustainability. China faces the challenge of making the transition from sustained to sustainable growth. Therefore, the country is seeking better access to global knowledge and technologies, especially, information and communication technology and biotechnology. As a result, market based funds for financing innovation have increased significantly.

China's spending on R&D is still heavily focused on experimental development. Only 11 percent of patents by Chinese firms are considered inventive, compared to 74 percent of patents by foreign firms patenting in China. Therefore, the planning process during the last years involved debates on the importance of indigenous innovation. The aim is to improve R&D in Chinese companies. Long-term planning over the past decades helped China to develop the economic environment and direct the allocation of resources (OECD 2008b: 432).

Policy recommendations based on an empirical survey conducted in Shanghai (Zhu et al. 2006) suggest three steps:

i. The government's direct funding should be continued in order to stimulate innovation investments at industry-level.
ii. The investment environment and the access to further financial resources, such as bank loans and foreign investments, should be improved.
iii. Low-tech investments should be discouraged by allocating tax incentives onto high-tech activities.

So far, market orientation and long-term oriented innovation policy have resulted in greater productivity of the Chinese economy. Compared with the rapid privatization and liberalization in Eastern Europe, in East Germany and in the former Soviet Union during the 1990s, which can be described as a shock therapy, China is following a gradual strategy characterized by a mixture of planned and market elements of governance. While globalization is putting pressures on the role of governments and policy worldwide, the Chinese model may represent a successful way of directing regional resources towards sustainable development. Due to the worldwide financial and economic crisis, Western countries may face the challenge of creating a new coordination mechanism in order to compensate for the reduced impact of political institutions. Stronger political governance in China is heading towards a flexible consensus in terms of balancing the various interests; the more innovation-driven Chinese strategy might become a point of reference for some European countries.

References

Andreosso-O'Callaghan, B., Nicolas, F. and Wei, X. 2005. *The Sustainability of EU-China Economic Relations in the 21st Century – Between Complementarity and Rivalry*. Conference on EU, China and the quest for a multilateral world, 4 July, European Economic and Social Committee Building, Brussels.

Andreosso-O'Callaghan, B. and Qian, W. 1999. Technology transfer: a mode of collaboration between the EU and China. *Europe-Asia Studies,* 51(1), 123–42.

Bartlett, C.A. and Goshall, S. 1990. *Internationale Unternehmensführung, Innovation, globale Effizienz, differenziertes Marketing*. Frankfurt/New York: Campus.

Bennett, D., Liu X., Parker, D., Steward, F. and Vaidya, K. 2001. Technology transfer to China: a study of strategy in 20 EU industrial companies. *International Journal of Technology Management,* 21(1/2), 151–82.

Chen, C., Chang, L. and Zhang, Y. 1995. The role of foreign direct investment in China's post-1978 economic development. *World Development,* 23(4), 691–703.

Coe, D.T. and Helpman, E. 1995. International R&D spillovers. *European Economic Review,* 39, 859–887.

Copeland, T., Koller, T. and Murrin, J. 2000. *Valuation – Measuring and Managing the Value of Companies*. New York: John Wiley & Sons.

Gorter, I. and Parik, A. 2001. A quantitative study on the relationship between foreign direct investment (FDI) and effective tax rates in the European Union. *CPB Working Paper,* The Hague.

Hall, P.A. and Soskice, D. 2003. *Varieties of Capitalism – The Institutional Foundations of Comparative Advantage*. Oxford/New York: Oxford University Press.

Hall, B. and Van Reenen, J. 2000. How effective are fiscal incentives for R&D? A review of the evidence. *Research Policy,* 29 (4–5), April, 449–69.

Haufler, A. and Stöwhase, S. 2003. Taxes as a determinant for foreign direct investment in Europe. *DICE Report. Journal for Institutional Comparisons,* 1 (2), 45–51.

Hollingsworth, J.R. and Boyer, R. 1997. *Contemporary Capitalism, The Embeddedness of Institutions*. Cambridge: Cambridge University Press.

Li, X. and Yeung, Y. 1999. Inter-firm linkages and regional impact of transnational corporations: Company Case Studies from Shanghai, China. *Geografiska Annaler,* Series B, Human Geography, Blackwell Publishing, 81(3), October, 61–72(12).

Liu, X., Parker, D., Vaidya, K. and Wei, Y. 2001. Impact of foreign direct investment on labour productivity in the Chinese electronic industry. *International Business Review,* 10 (4), 421–39.

Liu, Z. 2002. Foreign direct investment and technology spillover: evidence from China. *Journal of Comparative Economics*, 30 (3), 579–602.

Marcotte, C. and Niosi, J. 2005. Small and medium-sized enterprises involved in technology transfer to China: what do their partners learn? *International Small Business Journal*, 23 (1), 27–47.

Markusen, J.R. 1995. The boundaries multinational enterprises and the theory of international trade. *Journal of Economic Perspectives* 9, 169–89.

Miller, D. 2008. *Grundsätze sozialer Gerechtigkeit.* Frankfurt/New York: Campus.

Mintz, J. 2001. Taxation of investment and finance in an international setting: implications for tax competition. *CoFE Discussion paper,* 00–33, Constance.

OECD 1995. *Transfer Pricing Guidelines.* Paris.

OECD 2006. *Globalization of R&D and Developing Countries*. New York and Geneva.

OECD 2008a. *World Investment Report 2008*. New York and Geneva.

OECD 2008b. *OECD Reviews on Innovation Policy China*. New York and Geneva.

Rappaport, A. 1998. *Creating Shareholder Value – A Guide for Managers and Investors*. Revised and updated edition. New York: The Free Press.

Romer, P.M. 1990. Endogenous technological change. *Journal of Political Economy*, 98 (5), 71–102.

Schüller, M. 2007. Arbeitskonferenz zum Finanzsektor: Neue Weichenstellungen, in *China aktuell*, No. 1/2007, 127–34.

Singh, L. 2004. Globalization, national innovation systems and response of public policy. *International Journal of Technology Management and Sustainable Development,* 3(3), 215–30.

Shen, Y.H. 1994. *Foreign Direct Investment from Western Europe.* Beijing: Shishi Publishing House.

Thompson, E.R. 2002. Clustering of foreign direct investment and enhanced technology transfer: evidence from Hong Kong garment firms in China. *World Development*, 30(5), 873–90.

UNCTAD 1999. Transfer pricing. *UNCTAD Series on Issues in International Investment Agreements,* UN, New York and Geneva.

Vitols 2003. From banks to markets: the political economy of liberalization of the German and Japanese financial systems, in *The End of Diversity? Prospects for German and Japanese Capitalism,* edited by K. Yamamura and W. Streeck, Ithaca/London, 240–260.

Vogel 2003. The re-organization of organized capitalism: how the German and Japanese models are shaping their own transformations, in *The End of Diversity? Prospects for German and Japanese Capitalism,* edited by K. Yamamura and W. Streeck, Ithaca/London, 306–33.

Von Wuntsch, M. 2008. Value management and transfer pricing in an integrating world – a trend towards convergence and diversity, in *Asia and Europe: Connections and Contrasts*, edited by B. Andreosso-O'Callaghan, B. Zolin and B. Venezia, Cafoscarina, 239–56.

Von Wuntsch, M., Bach, S. and Trabold, H. 2006. *Wertmanagement und Steuerplanung in der globalen Wirtschaft.* München: Vahlen.

Von Wuntsch, M., Knacke, G. and Neumann, G. 2005. Financing and valuation problems of the East German real estate market. *Real Estate Review.* New York University, 34 (1), 17–39.

Wei, X., Andreosso-O'Callaghan, B. and Von Wuntsch, M. 2007. German investment in Ireland and in the Central and East European countries. *Intereconomics, Review of European Economic Policy,* 42(3), 156–66.

Wei, Y. and Liu, X. 2001. *Foreign Direct Investment in China: Determinants and Impact.* Camberley: Edward Elgar.

Wu, X. 2000. Foreign direct investment, intellectual property rights, and wage inequality in China. *China Economic Review*, 11 (4), 361–84.

Xu, B. and Wang, J. 1999. Capital goods trade and R&D spillovers in the OECD. *Canadian Journal of Economics*, 32 (5), 1258–74.

Xue, L. 2001. Analysis on effective factors of multinational firms R&D establishment in China. *Scientific Management Journal*, 22(4), 132–43 (in Chinese).

Young, S. and Lan, P. 1997. Technology transfer to China through foreign direct investment. *Regional Studies*, 31(7), 669–79.

Zhang, W. and Taylor, R. 2001. EU technology transfer to China: the automotive industry as a case study. *Journal of the Asia Pacific Economy*, 6(2), 261–74.

Zhao, Y. 2001. Foreign direct investment and relative wages: the case of China. *China Economic Review*, 12 (1), 40–57.

Zhu, P., Xu, W. and Lundin, N. 2006. The impact of government's fundings and tax incentives on industrial R&D investment – Empirical evidences from industrial Shanghai. *China Economic Review*, 17, 51–69.

Chapter 10
'Equipment Hypothesis' and Skills: The Case of Die and Mould-making – Japan and Ireland

Tomoko Oikawa

Introduction

This chapter examines the importance of skills in relation to the 'equipment hypothesis' as put forward by De Long (1992) and De Long and Summers (1991, 1992) and applies it to a specific industry in a Asia-Europe comparative perspective. According to the 'equipment hypothesis', there is a strong and causal relationship between equipment investment and economic growth. De Long (1992) and De Long and Summers (1991, 1992) attempted to find a correlation between equipment investment and growth not only in the post-World War II period, but also in the longer run. While not supportive of the findings of De Long and Summers (1991, 1992), Field (2007) provided a valuable contribution to the equipment hypothesis by exploring eight decades of 20th century US economic growth. Our focus here is on a meso-economic level, as we look at the relationship between economic growth and technological knowledge in a sub-set of the machinery industry.

The primary objective of this chapter is to provide an extension to the equipment hypothesis by showing the equal importance of skills as equipment investment, to economic growth. We will examine the concept of skills in relation to technology, which relate and contribute profoundly to process or product improvement and innovation. In this context, we explore the die and mould-making industry in both Japan and Ireland, so as to verify the importance of skills to machinery and equipment for economic growth. These issues are viewed in a long waves approach, so as to connect them with the possible occurrence of crises. The comparative analysis should ultimately help detect whether either economy, one mature Asian economy and the other a recently emerged European economy, could be used as a benchmark for future economic growth.

The first section will examine the issues connected with the 'equipment hypothesis'. Next, the concept of skills will be explored in relation to the concept of technolgy. We will analyze the importance of skills in relation to improvement and innovation. Finally, we will examine and contrast the die and mould-making industry in Japan and Ireland as an example of an industry where skills, in relation to machinery and equipment, are essential for economic performance.

1. The 'Equipment Hypothesis' Issue

The 'equipment hypothesis' (De Long 1992, De Long and Summers 1991, 1992) sees a correlation between the rate of machinery and equipment investment with the rate of economic growth. These authors argue that investment in machinery and equipment has a higher propensity to generate externalities in using industries, resulting in a systematic and substantial divergence between its social and private return. This hypothesis is linked to the assumption of Robert M. Solow (1957) and Denison (1967) that most of the increase in economic growth is due, not to differences in measured investments, but to a 'residual', encompassed in total factor productivity (henceforth TFP).

In their attempt at analyzing the correlation between equipment investment and economic growth not only in post-World War II period but also in the longer run, De Long (1992) and De Long and Summers (1991, 1992) chose seven countries (Argentina, Canada, Germany, Italy, Japan, the United Kingdom and the United States) over roughly eight periods from 1870 to 1980. Their analysis revealed a close association between output per capita growth and a net concept of equipment investment from 1870 to 1980. De Long and Summers (1991, 1992) also discussed the results of cross country regressions on data from 61 countries over the years 1960–1985. They maintained that these results suggest a strong and causal relationship between equipment investment and economic growth. Further, they indicated that large external benefits can arise from equipment investment 'if learning-by-doing helps to create a workforce experienced and competent at handling modern technologies, and helps organizations to develop rules-of-thumb and standard operating procedures necessary to produce efficiently, which other firms can imitate' (De Long and Summers 1992: 194).

A summary of their various studies can be provided as follows:

1. Growth-measured by labor or by TFP is tied to equipment investment; this is as much the case for rich countries as for newly industrializing countries. Countries with high equipment investment grew rapidly, even controlling for a number of other factors. This suggests a causal relationship as follows: rapid growth went with high equipment investment, no matter whether high investment was a consequence of high savings or of a low relative equipment price.
2. Variations in equipment investment, arising from different sources, have a similar impact on growth. In the case of Argentina and Japan differences in government policies towards equipment are linked with poor performance in Argentina and with impressive performance in Japan over the few decades under analysis (De Long and Summers 1992: 178–184).

3. Any government that wishes to have its economy grow rapidly must make sure that investors in equipment see the economy as a hospitable environment, with ample provision of infrastructure, a skilled, trained, and motivated workforce, and low taxes on new capital.
4. Equipment investment and growth are strongly associated through channels that would make social returns higher than private ones. One such important channel is 'hands-on experience', the key role of which is visible through experience and feedback; this allows the economies to produce efficiently by using new technologies. Such 'hands-on experience' presupposes investment in equipment from which to learn.

In a recent study, Madsen (2005) provides strong support for the hypothesis of De Long and Summers (1991, 1992) by examining the nexus between economic growth and investment in equipment and structures using data for 11 OECD countries which covered the period 1960 to 1999. The study points out that policies which aim to enhance investment in equipment, i.e. in particular the removal of taxes on equipment, more generous depreciation rules for tax purposes and subsidies, should be given top priority in these OECD countries.

In line with De Long (1992; De Long and Summers 1991, 1992) Field (2007) took a long-term view between 1919 and 2000, with a particular focus on the interwar period in the United States. He explored the lessons to be learned from the natural experiments provided in different time periods in the 20th century in the United States.

He contrasted equipment and structures,[1] and argued that the claimed asymmetry between the ability of equipment as opposed to structures investment to generate TFP growth is not supported by the historical record. First of all, for the last 80 years of the 20th century, TFP growth rates in the United States trended generally downward. In Field's own words, 'the lowest ratio of equipment to structures occurs during the period of highest TFP growth (1929–1941). The highest ratio of equipment to structures (1989–2000) is associated with the second lowest TFP growth rate' (Field 2007: 55). He contrasted the effects of the boom in street and highway and other infrastructure construction during the 1930s with the rather different government financed capital formation boom – a large part of it was for equipment, particularly machine tools. Field (2007) concluded that the equipment hypothesis, as applied to the case of the USA, is in doubt. 'Taking a broad overview of eight decades of 20th century US economic growth, there is absence of evidence of a systematic positive relationship between rates of equipment investment and TFP growth' (Field 2007: 56). He concluded by stating that the importance of the equipment hypothesis must vary across particular sectors and particular epochs, or else that it might be swamped by the effect of other influences.

---

1 According to Field (2007), factory buildings and infrastructure (streets, highways and so on) are classified as 'structures'.

With reference to Japan, De Long and Summers (1992) explain that the rapid growth of the Japanese economy since the 1970s is attributed to the low prices of producer goods (e.g. machine tools) and high quantities of equipment, compared with the poorer performance in the United States which has had low equipment investment since World War II. In the case of the South Asian economies, some studies claim that there is no single explanation for their growth performance (Grosskof and Self 2006), and also that it is not just one single factor of machinery equipment investment, but many factors – for example, human capital investment and unspecified investment – that have positive effects on economic growth (Jalilian and Odedokun 2000). It is also argued that while machinery equipment investment implies very high returns, in terms of economic growth in developing countries, some expansion is necessary allowing for externalities to equipment investment in poor countries (Temple 1998).

A study on the sources of Japanese economic growth over the period 1975–2003 by Jorgenson and Nomura (2005) shows that the share of GDP devoted to information technology products (henceforth IT) such as computers and telecomm equipment increased sharply after 1995, and that the revival of TFP growth from the IT sector in Japan has accounted for the modest resurgence of the Japanese economy since 1995. Another study (Jorgenson and Motohashi 2005) compares the sources of economic growth in both Japan and the United States from 1975 to 2003. It claims that after 1995, the contribution of TFP growth from the IT industry in Japan increased in parallel to the sharp rise of investment in computers, telecommunications equipment and software, while the contributions of labor input and productivity growth from the non-IT sector lagged behind that of the United States.

While these arguments above suggest an extension to the equipment hypothesis, they demonstrate the macro economic aspect of the equipment hypothesis. Interestingly, De Long (1992: 320–323) remarked the relationship of this macroeconomic aspect with machinery investment and innovation as follows: 'The macro pattern is of strong association between machinery investment and economic growth. This macro pattern is consistent with a picture of the micro structure of innovation ... The fit between such micro narratives and the macro patterns should lead them to place more confidence in their narratives of machinery investment and innovation'. However, it seems that he left the matter of innovation to the historians of technology and thus in his discussion above, no indication of mediation between equipment investment and innovation was suggested.

As mentioned above, De Long and Summers (1991, 1992) described the importance of some 'channels', through which equipment investment and growth are strongly associated. One such channel, 'hands-on experience' or technological knowledge, implies something which is hard to summarize and difficult to transmit through education, and that is played by experience and feedback. This channel ultimately enhances efficiency by using new technologies. Such channel is close to the notion of skills.

We are particularly interested in such channel. Sections 2 and 3 will provide an indication that the equipment hypothesis can be supplemented by additional evidence which shows the equal importance of skills to equipment investment for economic growth. At first, the clarification of the concept of skills is necessary.

2. Equipment, Technology, Skills and Business Cycles

2.1. Issues surrounding the concept of technology in relation to skills

Definitions of and relationships between skills, knowledge and technology are hardly clear, as shown in the following quotes:

> Although organizational scholars have generated extensive literature on technology and knowledge in organizations, they rarely recognize the symbiotic relationship between material technology and the knowledge these tools support (Thurk and Fine 2003: 107).

> There is little agreement on the definition and measurement of technology (Orlikowski, W.J. 1992: 398).

While technology has more systematically been the object of explanations, skills have been given lesser chances to be focused on in relation to technology. Skills tend generally to be treated together with other elements such as education, training, knowledge and so on (e.g. 'social capability' as coined by Abramovitz 1986, 1995). Abramovitz (1986: 386) refers to the level of technology 'which is embodied in a country's capital stock', and suggests that, the 'technology embodied in each vintage of its stock was at the very frontier of technology at the time of investment' and thus 'new capital can embody the frontier of knowledge'. In fact, skills are not linked to his definition of technology.

De Long and Summers (1992) stressed the importance of channels, through which equipment investment and growth are strongly associated and which are responsible for the most important outcome relating to what the experience of installing and using capital teaches workers and organizations about how to use modern technologies efficiently. Further they assumed equipment as a catalyst for learning-by-doing and upgrading skills. They claimed that such hands-on experience presupposes investments in the equipment upon which to learn. Here, equipment is distinguished from technology and technology from learning-by-doing upgrading skills. Also, a type of interaction between them is suggested.

Orlikowski (1992) argues that these views as seen in De Long and Summers (1992) or Abramovitz (1986) above were partially correct, but also one sided. This is because he sees that both aspects as such deal with technology, as an objective and external force on the one hand, and as the strategic choice and social action on the other. Orlikowski (1992: 423) instead proposed 'an alternative theoretical conceptualization of technology which underscores its socio-historical context and its dual nature as objective reality and as socially constructed products.' Focusing on the differences of skills supplied in the less developed countries (LDCs) and the OECD economies, Acenmoglu and Zilibottti (2001) argued that such skill differences create a mismatch between the requirements of many technologies and the skills of LDCs' workers, and lead to sizable differences in total factor productivity and output per worker in the LDCs from the OECD economies. In other words, richer countries will benefit more from the more skill-biased technologies than the relatively skill-scarce LDCs. Here the importance of skills for economic growth are described in relation to the particular term of 'skill-biased' technologies. Also, this may suggest a similar definition to Orlikowski's (1992), that technologies have a dual nature as stated above.

These varied aspects of technology and skills could be epitomized by relying on Orlikowski (1992: 403): 'While technology may appear to have objective forms and functions at one point, these can and do vary by different users, by different contexts of use, and by the same users over time.' This statement may imply that technology presents interactive relationships with skills, and further, this may allow us to extend technology as such to connect it with skills in terms of conceptualization.

2.2. Concept of skills

With reference to the concept of skills, Koike (1999) stresses the importance of intellectual skills rather than manual ones. Intellectual skills are the ability to deal skilfully with such problems and changes that are called 'unusual operations' (Koike 1999). It is the ability to predict the problems or changes, which can take place during the process, at the very beginning in the design stage. Dosi (1988) includes skills in technology and describes technology as follows:

> Technology has elements of tacit and specific knowledge that are not and cannot be written down in a "blue print" form, and cannot, therefore, be entirely diffused either in the form of public or proprietary information (Dosi 1988: 1131).

He uses the term 'knowledge base', which is made up of different technologies and which are characterized by the degree of publicness and universality versus tacitness and specificity of their knowledge. Following Michael Polanyi (1961), Dosi (1988) refers to tacitness as being those elements of knowledge, insight and so on, that individuals have, which are ill defined, uncodified, unpublished, which they themselves cannot fully express and which differ from person to person, but which may, to some significant degree, be shared by collaborators and colleagues who have a common experience.

Dosi (1988) subsumed skills under technology, which is subsumed under the term 'knowledge base' which is made up of different technologies and which are characterized by the degree of publicness and universality versus tacitness and specificity of their knowledge. It is this 'knowledge base' that is central in the context of technological innovation. While Dosi (1988) distinguished tacit knowledge from public and universal technology as knowledge, it is not clear how such skills as tacit knowledge are linked organically or structurally with the 'knowledge base'. It seems that skills as tacit knowledge are not given much weight in his discussion of the 'knowledge base'.

Skills have also another aspect. They are always found within the dynamics of change and advance, which are affected by advanced technology or new market trends. They are eventually substituted for engineering technology, or some skills will have to be maintained improved or advanced and others may become obsolete (Asai 1996).

Based on this discussion, we can summarize the main thrust of the argument in Figure 10.1. This suggests a developing process of interactive relationship between skills and technology, and skills and improvement or innovation as time goes by. Improvement and/or innovation could be achieved by means of imagination and inference based on intellectual and working skills as tacit knowledge.

2.3. Equipment hypothesis, skills, and long waves

An important question is to analyze how growth and skills can be positioned in a context of business cycles, represented by short-run and/or long-run cyclical variations, such as long waves. This is of particular importance in today's world

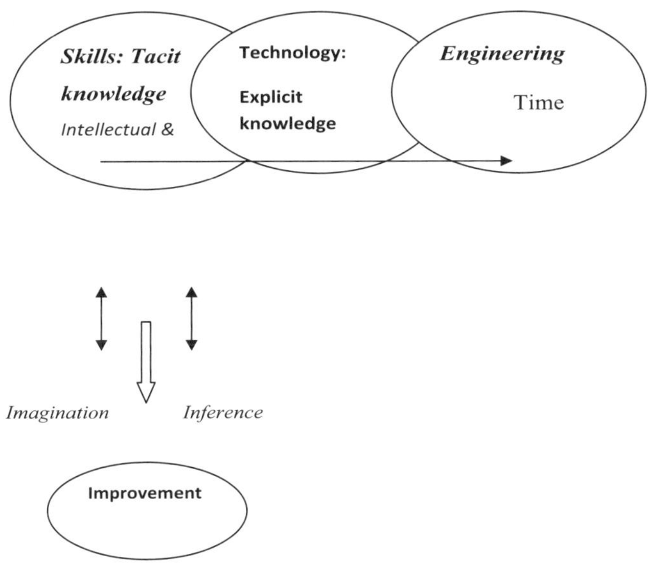

Figure 10.1 Relations between skills, knowledge, and technology
Source: Author's diagram based on Miyoshi (1998), Asai (1996), Koike (1999), Koshiro (1999).

economy where a global crisis seems to have sanctioned the inability to derive profit opportunities from equipment growth and skills improvements, but rather from more intangible financial markets.

De Long (1992: 309) observes 'long run shifts in growth rates instead of short-run cyclical fluctuations'. This view of business cycle may accord with the long waves view in one way. Long waves refer to long-term economic growth cyclical fluctuations. Joseph Schumpeter (1934, 1939) pointed out that innovation is the only factor to raise the value-added of the economy and tried to reconstruct his theory of economic development with reference to the concept of Kondratiev cycle. He attributed the cause of the business cycles to technological innovation and suggested that innovation takes place intermittently to form clusters and to stimulate the economy. As reiterated subsequently by Freeman: 'There is here the germ of a theory which could link the diffusion of new technologies to the movement of the long wave ... The basic justification for attempting to relate the long waves to technical change is that the process of diffusion of any major new technology is a matter of decades and not months or years' (Freeman 1984: 107). In fact, inputs from long wave theory may provide the equipment hypothesis with a proof of long-term economic growth in terms of the relationship between skills and innovation, which is shown in Figure 10.1. Technological innovation develops within a definite time span reaching maturity (Hirooka 2003). In other words, improvement and innovation need a certain time span of skills and technology accumulation for breakthrough, which could be followed by diffusion of improvement and/or innovation again after a definite time span. Such a relationship is shown in Figure 10.2.

This view may also be associated with the *foundations* (author's emphasis) aspect of Field (2007), according to which the remarkable TFP performance

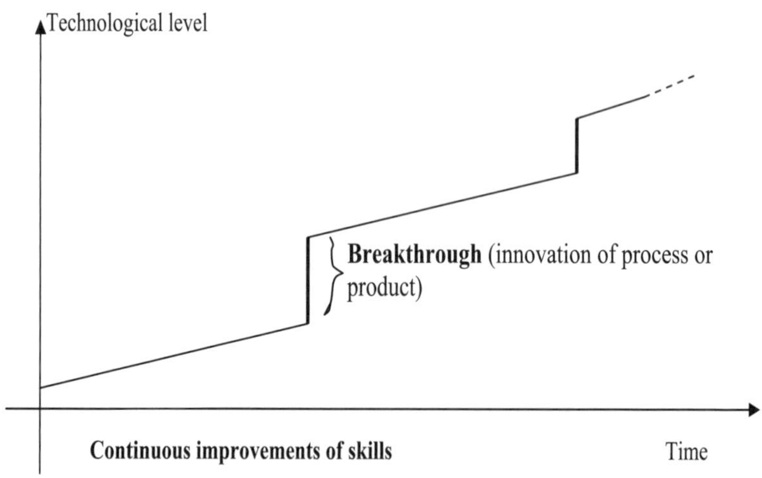

Figure 10.2 Relationship between innovation, skills and technology

Source: Author's diagram based on Björm Hedlund, Innovation step by step, VDMA, 13.06.2003.

over the period 1929–1948 has almost uniformly been credited to innovation and learning-by-doing during the Second World War and most of the *foundations* for postwar prosperity were already in place by 1941.

We could claim therefore that a theory of long waves may provide a profound and vivid aspect for the equipment hypothesis in terms of equal importance of skills linked to innovation in equipment investment (technology) in long-term economic growth with intermittent innovation.

3. Importance of Skills: *Kanagata* (die and mould-making) in Japan and Toolmaking in Ireland

3.1. The kanagata (die and mould-making) industry in Japan

The *kanagata* industry is outstanding in its heavy reliance on both skills and machinery equipment. It is a major supporting industry of the machinery industry in Japan. It is the *kanagata* industry that is a major source of the strength of machinery manufacturing industry. Die and mould are indispensable for mass production, particularly in the machinery manufacturing industry, where most products are assembled with parts formed by mould and die. One die or mould consists of tens to hundreds of parts and they are used repeatedly thousands to millions of times. Therefore both accuracy and durability are essential for *kanagata*.

In order to fulfil this requirement, both skills and equipment are substantial. In the West, dies and moulds are mostly made-in-house in the principal firms, and only a minority are made by toolmakers as special tooling (Taguchi 2001, Nishino 1998). For example, dies for pressing for the body parts of cars, were 70–80 percent made in house in the West, in contrast with 20–30 percent in Japan, where the rest, including most crucial parts, are made by specialized enterprises, i.e. *kanagata* makers (Nishino 1998). It could be said that the principal firms are just assemblers (Taguchi 2001). This is the chief reason why this industry is referred to a source of competitive strength for the machinery manufacturing sector in the international market. It links up skills, technology, and equipment utilization, which comprise the core of *kanagata* making. In spite of such importance attached to the machinery manufacturing industry, there have been few economic studies on this industry until recently. The first comprehensive study on the Japanese *kanagata* industry was published in 2001 (Taguchi 2001).

Table 10.1 shows the ratio of skills and machinery equipment in the *kanagata* industry compared with other machinery and manufacturing industries, in terms of production costs in Japan in the mid-1990s. The production cost of direct labor as well as the equipment rate of IT and precision processing machinery in the *kanagata* industry is more than double that in the other machinery and manufacturing industries. Also, whereas in both machinery and other manufacturing industries the ratio of direct material costs in total production costs greatly exceeds the one of direct labor, this is not the case in the *kanagata* industry but quite the reverse.

Table 10.1 Comparison of manufacturing costs (Japan, 1995, in percent)

			***Kanagata* (die and mould)**	**Machinery Industry**	**Other manufacturing industries**
Production Cost	Direct cost	**Direct materials**	**18.1**	**40.9**	47.1
		Purchased parts	5.2	7.5	4.2
		Put-out works	23.8	23.2	13.6
		Direct labor	**29.9**	**14.3**	15.2
		Other direct costs	2.3	0.7	1.8
		Subtotal	79.3	86.6	81.9
	Indirect costs	Indirect materials	1.4	0.6	1.4
		Indirect labor	2.1	2.6	2.7
		Welfare	3.6	1.7	2.0
		Depreciation	**5.7**	**2.5**	3.8
		Rent	1.3	0.8	1.1
		Insurance	0.3	0.0	0.1
		Maintenance	0.9	0.5	1.1
		Supplies (lighting, water, heating)	0.6	0.5	1.0
		Fuel	0.3	0.2	0.7
		Other manufacturing costs	4.7	4.0	4.2
		Subtotal	20.7	13.4	18.1
		Total	100.0	100.0	100.0

Source: Small & Medium Enterprise Agency, quoted in Nishino, K. (1998, p. 43, Author's translation and emphasis), reprinted with permission.

Depreciation costs in the *kanagata* industry are more than double compared with the machinery industry. These facts suggest the substantial importance of both skills and equipment in the *kanagata* industry compared with the other industries.

Given the basic importance of the *kanagata* industry for the Japanese machinery industry, and by extension, for the economy as a whole, the discussion above indicates typically that both skills and equipment investment are critical to economic growth. In terms of the relationship between skills and technology in the *kanagata* (die and mould) industry in Japan, the *kanagata* industry is heavily dependent on both technology and skills compared with other manufacturing industries. Further skills in die and mould making are more crucial than machinery or equipment, depending on the phase of production process, where technology functions depend on the degree of skills needed in terms of its capability.

The grinding operation in *kanagata* production accounts for 30 percent of the total operation volume in the whole *kanagata* making process (Miyoshi 1998). Miyoshi and his research group spent seven years analyzing the data input. Based on this experiment, they formulate the distinction and also the interface between skills and technology as follows:

> Skills are working capability and knowledge that cannot be put into words nor digit, and cannot be automated. This is tacit knowledge. Technology is working capability and knowledge, which can be put into words, digit and computer program. Thus it can be automated. That is explicit knowledge. Both skills and technology may partly overlap. It is the overlapped part that can be replaced by technology (Miyoshi 1998: 13).

Skills are continuously found at the cutting edge of technology in the *kanagata* industry (Asai 1996, Koshiro 1999). This is the main reason why skills as tacit knowledge relate to improvement or innovation.

3.2. The case of the die and mould-making industry in Ireland

Examining the die and mould-making industry in a Western country, one that best approaches the definition of the Japanese *kanagata* industry, is done in order to see whether the conclusions of the previous section are transposable to the Western case.

The die and mould-making industry in Ireland is subsumed under the toolmaking industry, and is classified as part of it. 'The toolmaking industry is part of the engineering sector involving the supply of injection moulds, press tools and dies for the manufacture of products containing plastic injection appliances, consumer electronics, toys and medical devices manufacturers' (WDC 2004: 33). In fact, the distinction between toolmaking and precision engineering is often ambiguous. Both of them produce die and mould, and their products often overlap. In addition, toolmaking subsumes foundries and castings.

Technologically, toolmaking is subsumed 'under mechanical engineering', conventionally classed as low-to-medium technology, and 'die and mould-making classed as medium-high technology' (Cogan and MacDevitt 2001: 3). It is of vital significance as an indigenous industry for the Irish economy in terms of employment, ubiquity and solidity. The die and mould-making industry in Ireland has its own particular characteristics. The economic location of the die and mould-making industry in Ireland is distinguished from that in Japan. Foreign-owned companies have overwhelmingly captured large parts of manufacturing as a whole and have contributed greatly to economic growth in Ireland.

With regard to the Irish die and mould-making, mechnical engineering grew by over 6 percent per annum in the first half of the 1990s, and 'this is taken as evidence that, rather than simply building on traditional strength, indigenous industry has shown signs of developing new areas of competence' (Cogan and MacDevitt 2001: 3). However, 'the mould-making industry in Ireland has peaked in the mid-1990s without achieving its growth potential' (Cogan and MacDevitt 2001: 7). The study explains that 'mould-making itself is viewed as a strategic industry in many countries, and the volume of toolmaking orders is used as an indicator of industrial strength' (Cogan and MacDevitt 2001: 2). This statement may underpin the basic importance of the die and mould-making industry to economic performance in Ireland.

In this section therefore we will focus rather on whether both skills and equipment investment have an equal importance to economic performance of four individual toolmaking enterprises. We focus on four indigenous toolmaking companies in Ireland. The survey was carried out during 2005–2006, when all the Managing Directors in all these four companies were interviewed. The following are the findings of our interviews and observations.

Companies A, and E (henceforth A, E) have focused on mould-making products related to the medical devices industry. Companies B and C (henceforth B, C) are engaged in precision engineering and precision tooling respectively, but not in die and mould-making.

A is distinctive from E in the following points: (1) Profitability is steady and upward; (2) While the ratio of direct labor to production cost is decreasing, that of depreciation costs is increasing; (3) As part of new technology, two robotics are used, only by this company in this case studies. The Managing Director (henceforth MD) is confident in the company's marketing and expanding exports to Britain. This confidence is based on the company's capability of innovation, which is derived from its technology and skills. The MD stressed the importance of continuous reinvestment and personnel. E is the oldest among the interviewed companies and has been involved in precision engineering. It is outstanding that the ratio of direct materials to direct labor stands at 8:37, and that depreciation costs have not changed over 2001 to 2005, while profitability has decreased.

B and C are engaged in precision engineering and precision tooling respectively, but not in die and mould-making. B has targeted the medical device industry and makes precision components (plastic, aluminium, metal and stainless). B has been 'always growing beyond expectation' since its establishment. The MD said that 'technology – machinery and training – is the foundation of innovation'. B has acquired 18 CNC machines and is procuring new machines every year. Further, he said that to be competitive in an international market, the rate of labor costs must be reduced and the company must rely more on machinery. Direct labor costs are increasing as well as depreciation costs. The MD stressed repeatedly the importance of training – particularly focused on 'getting skills for manipulating new technology (new machinery)' – during the interview. C has targeted a niche market in the medical device industry. Equipment investment in C has decreased though turnover is increasing.

Either company A or company B can be a good model for toolmakers (die and mould-makers). They have had a clear view of the fundamental importance as regards both continuous adaptation of advanced machinery and training. They have not failed to realize the importance of training to acquire skills for new machine tools. They have been looking for new markets, A through new innovative products, and B by using challenging new difficult materials for components. Both have invested more in improving technology – machinery and skills – than the others.

4. Concluding Remarks

Starting with the equipment hypothesis, which proposes a strong and causal relationship between equipment investment and economic growth over the course of history, this Chapter particularly focused on one of the 'channels' through which equipment investment and economic growth are associated. It is found that one such channel, described as tacit technological knowledge, is equivalent to skills, which are explored in relation to improvement and/or innovation and technology in terms of concept. The importance of skills is demontrated, which has led us to explore the concept of skills as applied to the case of the die and mould-making industry in Japan and Ireland. It is therefore suggested that the equipment hypothesis could be supplemented by taking into consideration the equal importance of skills as equipment investment for economic growth.

Skills and technology which is described as the mobile factor of equipment need to be interactive to be efficient in use. Further skills may be a source of improvement and/ innovation of process and/or product. We have seen that a long waves approach (business cycle) is also useful. The case studies of the die and mould-making industry in Japan and in Ireland showed the equal importance of skills as equipment investment for successful performance. Through exploring the *kanagata* industry, we have learned: 1. The *kanagata* industry has basically underpinned the machinery manufacturing industry in particular and has thus contributed to economic growth in Japan; 2. The strength of the *kanagata* industry is derived substantially and equally from both skills and equipment investment. In the case of Ireland, the contribution of the die and mould-making industry to economic growth is not clear in terms of its degree. However, the case studies may have shown how crucial continuous investment in both equipment and training for skills is for successful performance.

References

Abramovitz, M. 1986. Catching up, forging ahead, and failing behind. *The Journal of Economic History,* 46 (June), 385–406.

Abramovitz, M. 1995. The elements of social capability. *Social Capability and Long-term Economic Growth* edited by Bon Ho Koo and Dwight H. Perkins. New York: St Martin's Press.

Acemoglu, D. and Zilibotti, F. 2001. Productivity differences. *The Quarterly Journal of Economics*, May.

Asai, K. 1996. Gijutsukakushin jidai no gino keisei-*kanagata* sangyo wo chusinni (Skill formation in the era of technology innovation-focusing on die & mould industry-). *Shoko kin'yu*, 46 (10), 20–37.

Cogan, D.J. and McDevitt, J. 2001. *Mould-making in Ireland: Case-studies Report*. The Converge Project supported by the TSER Programme, the European Commission.

Denison, E.F. 1967. *Why Growth Rates Differ: Postwar Experience in Nine Western Countries*. Washington, DC: Brookings Institution.

De Long, J.B. 1992. Productivity growth and machinery investment: A long term look, 1870–1980. *Journal of Economic History*, 52 (2), 307–24.

De Long, J.B. and Summers, L.H. 1991. Equipment investment and economic growth. *The Quarterly Journal of Economics*, 106 (May), 445–502.

De Long, J.B. and Summers, L.H. 1992. Equipment investment and economic growth: How strong is the nexus? *Brookings Papers on Economic Activity*, 157–99.

Dosi, G. 1988. Sources, procedures, and microeconomic effects of innovation. *Journal of Economic Literature*, 26 (3), 1120–71.

Field, A.J. 2007. The equipment hypothesis and US economic growth. *Explorations in Economic History*, 44, 43–58.

Freeman, C. 1984. Keynes or Kondratiev? How can we get back to full employment? In Marstrand, P. (ed.) *New Technology and the Future of Work and Skills*. London: Frances Pinter.

Grosskopf, S. and Self, S. 2006. Factor accumulation or TFP? A reassessment of growth in Southeast Asia. *Pacific Economic Review*, 11 (1), 39–58.

Hirooka, M. 2003. Nonlinear dynamism of innovation and business cycle. *Journal of Evolutionary Economics*, 13, 549–76.

Jalilian, H. and Odedokun, M.O. 2000. Equipment and non-equipment private investment: a generalized Solow model. *Applied Economics*, 32, 289–96.

Jorgenson, D.W. and Motohashi, K. 2005. Information technology and the Japanese economy. *Journal of the Japanese & International Economies*, 19 (4), 460–81.

Jorgenson, D.W. and Nomura, K. 2005. The industry origin of Japanese economic growth. *Journal of the Japanese & International Economies*, 19 (4), 482–542.

Koike, K. 1999. Manual dexterity vs. Intellectual skills. *Nihon Rōdō Kenkyū Zasshi (The Monthly Journal of the Japan Institute of Labour)*, 41 (7), July.

Koshiro, K. 1999. The technological structure of skill and the hollowing-out of the manufacturing industry. *The Monthly Journal of The Japan Institute of Labour*, 41 (7), 11–21.

Madsen, J.B. 2005. A century of economic growth: The social returns to investment in equipment and structures. *The Manchester School*, 73 (1), 101–22.

Miyoshi, T. 1998. Jukurenn ginou no gijutuka, konpyūta-ka (Technologisation and computerisation of skills), *Keisoku to Seigyo* (Measurement and Control), 37(7), 1–15.

Nishino, K. 1998. *Nihon no kanagata sangyo wo yomu* (Reading the Japanese Die & Mould industry). Tokyo: Kogyo chosakai.

Orlikowski, W.J. 1992. The duality of technology: Rethinking the concept of technology in organizations. *Organization Science* 3 (August), 398–424.

Schumpeter, J.A. 1934. *The Theory of Economic Growth*. Cambridge, MA: Harvard University Press.

Schumpeter, J.A. 1939. *Business Cycles*. New York: McGraw-Hill.

Solow, R.M. 1957. Technical change and the aggregate production function. *Review of Economics and Statistics*, 39 (3), 312–20.

Taguchi, N. 2001. *Nihon kanagata sangyo no dokuritsusei no kiban* (The foundation of the independence of the Japanese die & mould industry). Kanazawa: Dept of Economics, Kanazawa University.

Temple, J. 1998. Equipment investment and the Solow model. *Oxford Economic Paper*, 50 (39), 39–62.

Thurk, J. and Fine, G.A. 2003. The problem of tools: Technology and the sharing of knowledge. *Acta Sociologica* 46, 107–17.

Western Development Commission 2004. *Enterprise and Employment in the Western Region: Issues, Challenges and Recommendations*. Statement to Enterprise Strategy Group (National Development Plan), March.

Chapter 11
Policy Support for SMEs – China and Europe

Esmeralda Gassie and Ju Hu[1]

Introduction

Small- and medium-sized enterprises (SMEs) are increasingly considered as the backbone of economic growth and economic integration. Sustained competitiveness for small firms in an internationalized economic and financial environment is primordial for European as well as Asian countries. Following the era of multinational corporations' boom, a corollary to deregulation, policy makers are giving increasing importance to locally based companies. The recent financial and economic crisis proved the extent of the international interdependence of economic structures. If studies are still being undertaken on the factors leading to the depth and immediacy of the crisis spread, our analysis will focus on the role of smaller sized firms as a potential economic recovery instrument in the coming years. SMEs could be responsible for a reorganization of the economic canvas at the national and international levels. Fostering competitiveness amongst SMEs is a theoretically based idea. In microeconomic theory, firms reach economic efficiency by increasing size and decreasing production costs to ensure competitiveness at the level of the industry.

In policy making terms, firms' growth goes in tandem with an increase in employment and turnover. EU policy documents recognize the importance of SMEs for employment and growth as well as innovation. In fact, there seems to be agreement at supranational organizations level on the channels economic development has to go through (*cf.* Washington Consensus). SME development was also mentioned as an important element of the World Bank policies at the end of the nineties (Bartlett and Bukvic 2002). The conditions and the targets of an SME policy encompass access to the banking system, flexible labor markets, limited administration procedures. Rarely are the organizational features of firms, as a function of the cultural background where the firm operates, considered as fundamental.

The aim of this chapter is to find a common ground in order to compare SME policies in Europe and China. The focus is on the mechanisms of SME development

1 The authors would like to thank both editors, Bernadette Andreosso-O'Callaghan and Bruna Zolin for their support and comments.

in China and their comparison with channels of SME development in Europe. Interestingly, in spite of the divergence in the degree of government involvement in economic issues, smaller productive units seem to be unanimously recognized as the future of business development. Nevertheless, the channels of development are different; European firms are not export-oriented (EUROSTAT 2008) while Chinese firms do follow a more export-oriented path of growth (Hamilton 1996). This chapter will explore the causes of such differences and their consequences for policy makers and researchers of economic development. Could Europe draw lessons from the Chinese structural dissimilarities in terms of growth strategies? Or will China have to follow the example of the EU countries' SME policy as one deriving from mature market economic conditions towards which each country should converge? It will be shown that social networks are a phenomenon at play in the economic sphere in Europe and in China. Their effect needs to be taken into account in empirically based business growth policies, through business or through personal networks used for business purposes. The strict differentiation between formal and informal networks is not sufficient in understanding the complexity of interdependent economic activities.

This chapter is organized in three sections. The first introduces the empirical characteristics of SMEs in China and in Europe as well as the efforts aimed at correcting obstacles to developing SMEs. The second section analyzes the emergence and features of SME policies in both regions as well as the theoretical canvas underlying SME policy design. The third section enlarges the debate on the criteria appropriate in the area of SME development policy, by questioning the transferability of economic policies to geographical areas with different cultural dimensions. The accuracy of the issue of transferability becomes prominent when going beyond the strict area of economics and enriching the study by including anthropological features. Economists have not attempted to ally these two very complementary fields of study while still respecting their main area of research. The current crisis's consequences on restructuring the ideological embeddedness of economic policies might also involve a reconsideration of the economic principles taught and researched on so far.

1. Characteristics of SMEs in China and Europe

Based on EU legislation (EC 2003), EUROSTAT (2008) defines SMEs as enterprises employing up to 249 workers and realizing an annual turnover of less than EUR50 million and/or an annual balance sheet (assets) total not exceeding EUR43 million. Enterprises above the designated size fall under the large enterprise category. SMEs are central to employment in the EU27. They represent 99 percent of all enterprises in both the EU and China and 58 percent of the GDP in China and 56 percent of the value added in the EU in 2006. But productivity is still an issue. Filling this productivity gap is the main objective of SME development policies in the EU and in China. Before proceeding to the analysis of SME policy, a few elements have to be mentioned on the features of SMEs in the EU and in China. As will be seen, the economic characteristics, obstacles to their development and policy targets are identified in a similar fashion.

Unlike multinational firms, SMEs are locally based. In the case of the EU, the figures mirror the *glo-calization* of SMEs: 89 percent of EU-27 SMEs hired locally in 2007 (EUROSTAT 2008). In 2007, only 5 percent of European SMEs reported that they had subsidiaries or joint ventures abroad and about one in ten SME in the EU, or 8 percent of all SMEs, reported some export figures (Gallup 2008). SMEs are the most numerous, in terms of employment, in the construction, trade and hotels and restaurants, real estate and renting sectors. Value added figures follow the same order (EUROSTAT 2008: 83). Figure 11.1 gives a better view on the situation of the EU27 SMEs in 2006.

The figure shows that SMEs in the EU are more numerous than large enterprises. They employ twice as many employees as large enterprises. The SMEs' contribution to value added is 20 percentage points above that of the large enterprises. Nevertheless, a question arises on the productivity of those two categories of enterprises. Figure 11.2 shows productivity of labor data for a selected number of industries in the EU for 2005 as published by Eurostat Structural Business Statistics.

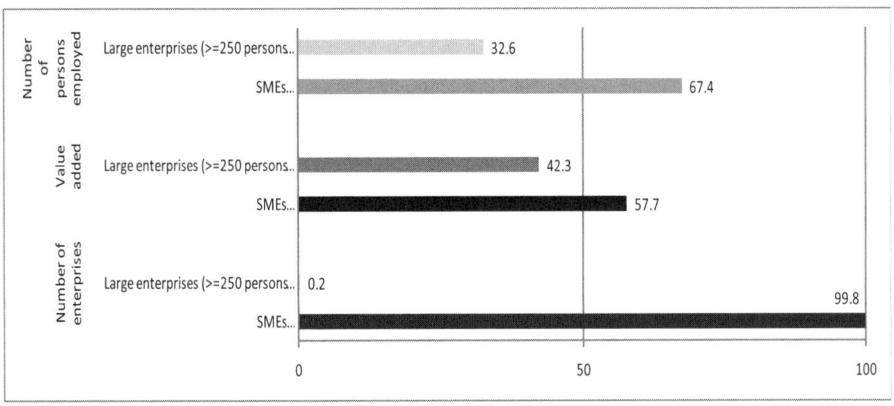

Figure 11.1 Main indicators broken down by size class, non-financial business economy, 2006 (% share of total)

Source: Eurostat Structural Business Statistics, Luxembourg.

Figure 11.2 clearly demonstrates the productivity gap between large enterprises and SMEs. The gap is higher for the construction and non financial sectors than for textile, hotels and restaurants and manufacturing sectors. The reasons for such a gap are related to insufficient benefits of economies of scale available to smaller firms and the increased competition of multinational corporations. Most importantly, the cost of labor and research and development are two areas that need particular

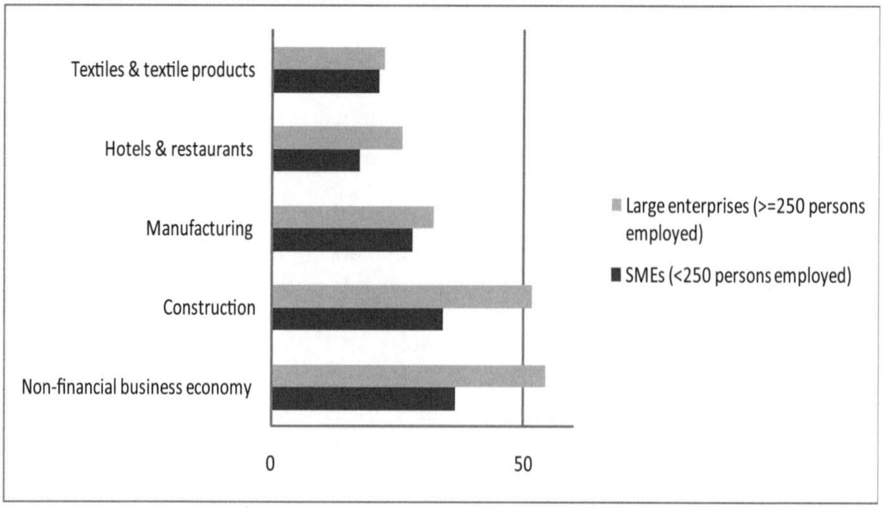

Figure 11.2 Apparent labor productivity by enterprise size class, EU-27, 2005 (EUR thousand per person employed)

Source: Eurostat SBS, Luxembourg.

attention when analyzing SMEs. Wage rates, taxes and employer contributions do represent a major inhibitor for European SMEs. Therefore a better ratio employee costs/output value needs to be reached by SMEs in comparison to large firms.

Unlike European firms, whose classification is based on size, turnover and balance sheet total (assets), Chinese firms are primarily classified by ownership. A first group encompasses individual businesses operated by an individual or a family. They are the equivalent of micro enterprises in the EU context. The second category refers to private enterprises, which are limited liability companies owned by two or more individuals. This category corresponds to the small enterprise EU version. A third group is made up of collectively-owned enterprises owned publicly and privately. The shareholders could be village committees or urban communities. Fourthly, township and village enterprises (TVEs) which were created during the 1960s and 1970s and evolved into modern companies are another category. TVEs have mixed ownership between private entities and public ones. The final category comprises state-owned enterprises, which during the past decade have already been reconfigured into joint equity enterprises or private enterprises. In relation to SMEs, the 2003 Law of the People's Republic of China on the Promotion of Medium and Small Enterprises similarly defines the standards for medium and small enterprises according to the number of employees, turnover, total amount of assets of the enterprise etc. The difference with the EU resides in the scales used for these standards. It actually varies depending on the industry considered (Table 11.1). The criteria for turnover and assets are the same across industries, but the number of employees varies depending on the industry. Consequently, with the

Table 11.1 Chinese SME definition

Industry	Size (number of employees)		Turnover (in million Yuan)		Assets (in million Yuan)	
	Small	Medium	Small	Medium	Small	Medium
Manufacturing	<300	300–2,000	<30	30–300	<40	40–400
Construction	<600	600–3,000	<30	30–300	<40	40–400
Transportation	<500	500–3,000	<30	30–300	n.a.	n.a.
Postage	<400	400–1,000	<30	30–300	n.a.	n.a.
Wholesale and retail	<100	100–500	<10	10–150	n.a.	n.a.
Food and lodging	<400	400–800	<30	30–150	n.a.	n.a.

Source: Chinese National Bureau of Statistics, Beijing.

same turnover criterion, the manufacturing industry and the wholesale and retail sector are considered as more productive (productivity is measured here as the ratio between turnover and the number of employees), followed by restaurants and hotels, services in general, transportation and construction sectors.

Chinese SMEs account for 58 percent of GDP, 50.2 percent of tax receipts, 68 percent of exports and 75 percent urban employment opportunities. They have an important role in employment and technology innovation. They represent 65 percent of the invention patents, 75 percent of technology innovation and 80 percent of new product development. SMEs have shifted from labor intensive industries such as light-industry, textiles, machinery and construction into capital intensive industries and technology intensive industries. Finally, the governance system has developed from individual or kinship dominated governance (Siu-lun 1985) into cooperation amongst shareholders (Gold et al. 2002).

The situation of SMEs in the EU and China shows similar signs of a productivity gap in relation to large firms, in parallel with the development of the private sector, a corollary to the progressive withdrawal of government from ownership of business.

Table 11.2 illustrates the productivity issue with Chinese SMEs. Most SMEs are still uncompetitive. The economic environment is not very favorable to SME growth as large enterprises use their market power and government support (Fan et al. 2007, Li et al. 2008) to gain a competitive edge. Although the Law of the People's Republic of China against unfair competition entered into force in 1993, it has never been seriously implemented. A second issue is the access to funds. The overall quality of SME services is low, SME management is out of date, and there is a lack of innovation ability and human capital. Less than 10 percent of staff have a higher education background and 60 percent have only junior middle school education. The development of these firms mainly relies on pricing strategies, cheap labor and natural resource consumption. When analyzing their product structure, one finds low value-added simple processed products. Only 17 percent of SMEs have a website, and less than 10 percent of Chinese SMEs have Enterprise Resource Planning and Customer Relationship Management systems.

Table 11.2 Labor productivity measures (1) in 2005 USD by enterprise size

Country	Small enterprise	Medium Enterprise	Large Enterprise
Taipei (2)	22,227	30,649	78,732
People's Rep. of China	15,073	16,795	31,130

Note: (1) Small: 5–49 workers for all countries except People's Republic of China (9–49 workers); Medium: 50–199 workers; Large: 200 or more workers (2) Used output per worker.
Source: Asian Development Bank 2009.

If SME policy is identified with the neo-classical theory of firms' growth in a perfectly competitive market, the recent crisis contagion does push for the requirement of additional public action. Not only, on the one hand, do small firms need specific favorable operating conditions to be targeted intentionally, but on the other hand, multinational firms can hardly manage the consequences of permanent cost cutting strategies due to a structural transformation of economic activities, such as the ones currently adopted worldwide. Those consequences can be socially and politically destabilizing. Although SMEs in both the EU and China have tended to be an economic and political stabilizing force by providing employment, they also tend to be labor intensive and less productive than large firms. SME policies in both economies try to tackle these issues based on established fields of neo-classical economics where competitiveness, cost efficiency and market orientation predominate. The next question to be answered is the one on the elements pushing for public action in the EU and China in an international crisis context: is action to be determined by internal forces (employment issues, privatization, etc.) or by external to the region factors (competitiveness, integration in the global market, global economic and financial crisis, etc.), and to what extent do they converge or diverge? The next section deepens this analysis.

2. Stimulating Firms' Growth: An *ad hoc* or a Structural Policy Making?

Articles 157 and 163 of the Consolidated Treaty of the European Union insist on the importance of the competitiveness of the Community's industry and on encouraging SME development. The Treaty of the European Union (EU 1992), recognizes the importance of building a stimulating environment for 'small and medium undertakings' (art. 130). In article 1 of the protocol on Social Policy, the emphasis is put on limiting 'administrative, financial and legal constraints in a way which would hold back the creation and development of small and medium undertakings' (EU 1992: 91). Six years earlier, for the first time, the Council recognized the important role of SMEs for employment, with the development of SMEs being an essential part of the Community's policies (Council 1986). So policy design in favor of SME development has been oriented towards the minimization of 'red tape', i.e. administrative bureaucracy. The recent crisis has nevertheless pushed for the requirement of strong government intervention (stimulus plans quasi uniformly adopted worldwide).

Policy design was to be monitored by the European Commission, to act only as a complement and to coordinate the existing national policies. The resolutions of 1994 (Council) and 1995 (Council) highlight what was previously acknowledged, and insist on the necessity to foster research and development amongst SMEs. Technological innovation quickly became the most important element in SME policy making and more broadly the main factor to increase productivity and competitiveness. The third multi-annual program for SMEs in the EU (1997–2000) was launched (Commission 1997). It established the Joint European Venture program, involving the EU financially in SME policy making (50 percent of the ensuing expenses and 10 percent of the investment would be undertaken by the EU budget). In 2000, the Lisbon European Council set a multi-annual program for Enterprises and Entrepreneurship, and in particular for small- and medium-sized enterprises, running until 2005. The focus of SME development policies is to help small- and medium-sized companies to grow, in terms of staff employed or turnover/balance sheet total. In accordance with this policy, the Directorate General Enterprise and Industry acts as a facilitator. During 2006, the DG allocated grants and funding facilities to European SMEs, to allow them to organize conferences and seminars on entrepreneurship and innovation (Commission 2003). SME policy is standardized EU-wide through the *European Charter for SME Development*[2] now integrated in the Lisbon agenda reports as part and parcel of the 'Growth and Jobs' objective the European Council agreed to in 2000. To some extent the Charter is exported outside of the EU (O' Brennan and Gassie 2009) while bearing many similarities to the World Bank's *Doing Business* indicators[3] and the US Small Business Act.[4] The new SME policy communication

2 The assessment on the implementation of the Charter in each country is based on progress in the eleven following areas: education and training for entrepreneurship; cheaper and faster start-up; better legislation and regulation; availability of skills; improving online access; getting more out of the Single Market; taxation and financial matters; strengthening the technological capacities; making use of successful e-business models and developing top class small business support; developing stronger, more effective representation of small business' interests at Union and national level.

3 The first Doing Business report was published in 2003. The SMEs' business environment is measured in 181 countries based on the following indicators: regulations for starting a business, dealing with construction permits, employing workers, registering property, getting credit, protecting investors, paying taxes, trading across borders, enforcing contracts and closing a business.

4 The Small Business Act endorsed by the US Department of Commerce makes the development of small businesses a priority through: enhancing their ability to export; facilitating technology transfer; enhancing their ability to compete effectively and efficiently against imports; increasing the access of small businesses to long-term capital; disseminating information concerning State, Federal, and private programs and initiatives;

was adopted in 2005, after a report of the European Parliament (Vlasto 2005). In a clear common direction with the Lisbon agenda, the objectives of the policy are: 'promoting entrepreneurship, improving access to markets, cutting red tape, improving SMEs growth potential and strengthening dialogue and consultation' (EC 2005: 2). A resolution on the Small Business Act for Europe was adopted by the European Parliament in December 2008 following the conclusions of the Competitiveness Council. In the end, the EU SME policy is integrated in a long term larger growth and employment economic strategy that aims at inserting EU SMEs in the global market. The role of the European Commission is more of a coordinator than a supporter, except for allocating some of the structural funding dedicated to strengthening the SMEs in the EU.

Chinese SME policy was built around five pillars that bear similarities with the basic elements of the EU policy but is not motivated by the same factors. Firstly taxation policy has been fundamental in fostering SME development. The value-added tax rate was of only 4 percent for small businesses while the normal rate was 17 percent. Former employees of state-owned enterprises may be exempted from turnover tax, income tax and local tax; the special non-profit credit guarantee organization and re-guarantee organizations for SME are exempted from sales tax for three years. The necessity of managing the transformation of the Chinese economy is clearly here the primary motivation. The transformation has a double path: on the one hand, the transition from state to private owned enterprises and on the other, the shift of the Chinese population from rural to urban areas. Nearly 80 percent of former employees of stated-owned enterprises get, most of them peasant laborers, reemployed in SMEs. Second, public support has also stimulated the creation of SMEs. According to the Law of the People's Republic of China on the Promotion of Small and Medium-sized Enterprises issued in 2003, the state provides substantial funds to SMEs, in stark contrast with the EU SME policy, where structural funding for SMEs has been quite modest. The purpose is to support the SME Institute to serve SMEs by provision of training, helping create new businesses, helping SMEs access credit loans, providing business consulting services etc. In 2007, the National Development and Reform Commission created a fund to support the establishment of SMEs clusters and a public service platform for SME.

Third, legislation clearly states the importance of SME development. SMEs were recognized as 'supplementary to the socialist market economy' in 1978 but became an 'important component of market based socialist economy' in 1999 (Lin and Zhu 2007). Fourth, the government has concerns related to SMEs' access to funding. Generally, the most pressing and prominent problem that SMEs encounter is the difficulty to access funds. Table 11.3 reflects the financial situation for China and the neighboring East-Asian Pacific region, as well as Ireland and Germany as examples of the situation in the EU. The case of Chinese

---

ensuring that the interests of small businesses are adequately represented in bilateral and multilateral trade negotiations.

Table 11.3 Enterprise survey (figures are in percentage)

Finance	China (1)	East Asia and Pacific (2)	Ireland (3)	Germany (4)	All countries (5)
Firms using banks to finance investments	28.76	32.1	37.41	44.95	24.3
Other financing for investment	50.98	20	21.28	13.28	7.1
Firms using banks to finance expenses	38.34	35.4	46.12	42.21	27.55
Value of collateral needed for a loan (percentage of the loan amount)	88.45	100.3	143.86	125.99	129.6
Firms identifying access to finance as a major constraint	22.8	20.5	7.4	15	30.8

(1) 3,948 firms surveyed in 2003; (2) China, Cambodia, Indonesia, Lao PDR, Malaysia, Mongolia, Philippines, Thailand, Vietnam; (3) 501 firms surveyed in 2005; (4) 1,196 firms surveyed in 2005; (5) 114 countries worldwide.

Source: International Finance Corporation/World Bank.

firms' access to the banking system is more problematic compared to the regional and EU situation, even though the value of collateral needed for a loan is lower in China compared to the East-Asian Pacific region or the rest of the world. Only a third of the surveyed firms use banks to finance investments, but half of them use other external resources to finance investment. The correlated existence of a cash economy and heavy subsidies from the government is not coincidental.

The Chinese SME International Cooperation Association, the SME Foreign Cooperation Coordination Centre of National Development and Reform Commission and Nakai University Corporate Governance Research Centre conducted a national survey of 309 SMEs from January 2003 to June 2004. The objective of the survey was to measure a composite SME index of economic development (SMEI). The index is compounded out of four areas of interest in firms' growth: institutional environment (favorable public policy and legal system etc.), market organization (competition, distribution channels, etc.), financial capacity (asset management, profitability etc.) and corporate governance (shareholder meetings, presence of a board of directors etc.). Table 11.4 shows some of the results obtained in five industries. The closer the index is to 100, the better the quality of the SME development environment in the industry.

The results of the manufacturing industry are more significant as the number of observations is higher. The indices are all above average, which shows that Chinese businessmen think of the business environment as being a relatively satisfactory one. Given the partnership behind this research project, between an

Table 11.4 SMEs in China – descriptive statistics, 2005

Industry / Statistical results	Construction	IT	Manufacturing	Transportation Storage and Postage	Wholesale and retail
Mean	63.52	67.30	61.70	57.30	60.27
Std. Deviation	7.24	8.68	8.29	8.28	7.63
Number of Observations	32	6	234	4	10

Source: Nakai University.

academic research structure and policy implementing organisms, such results would have been expected. Nevertheless, the table above gives an idea about the criteria used to measure SME development as well as the relative achievements in the industry, as declared by the businessmen themselves. The criteria retained are very similar to the ones used in the EU SME Charter. The alignment efforts of Chinese policy makers with international standards of SME development criteria and policy performance criteria, once again appear clearly. EU SME policy does not aim to support financially European SMEs given the differences in fiscal policies amongst member countries. So EU SMEs cannot access finance given the high cost of bank loans, whereas in China the results are the same but the reason is related to the use of other financing sources. The Chinese National Development and Reform Commission cooperated with other ministries to promote a credit guarantee system for SMEs. By the end of 2000, China had established 3,366 credit guarantee structures for SMEs, which can cover up to 805 billion Yuan. Finally, an important component of the recent development of SMEs in China has been the government administrative reorganization in support of the implementation of the SME policy. The SME promotion leading group was created in 2000. The group consists of representatives of 14 ministries. Twenty provinces have set up special SME administrations.

Thus, policy making in terms of SME development relates back to issues of competitiveness (adaptation to the global market) in the European case and structural transformation of the national economy (domestic phenomenon) in the Chinese case. Besides these dissimilarities, differences also exist in terms of types of intervention by public operators and the speed of policy reform. Notwithstanding the divergence in public governance between the EU and the PRC, there is convergence in timing and objectives of SME policy. The next section will specify the extent to which both policies are comparable and the conclusions that can be drawn on firms' growth based on their cultural dissimilarities. Hence the next section is founded on the assumption of the existence of cultural dissimilarities affecting SMEs and public governance convergence at the international level.

3. Transferability of Economic Policies and Lessons to be Drawn

Transferability of economic policies from one culturally different area to another is not intentional but a consequence of policy making. For this reason, the fairness of the comparison viewed under the light of strict economic policy design might be questioned. Nevertheless, the consequences of such an exercise are interesting for researchers in economic policy making processes and their theoretical foundations. In fact, when testing policy efficiency with regard to its empirical results, which is not common amongst policy evaluators (Potter and Storey 2008), such an exercise becomes even intriguing. How to effectively explain the persistence of an influential social network within the business sphere (*guanxi*) despite the various measures taken by the Chinese government? How can one account for the cumbersome obstacle mostly mentioned by EU owners of SMEs (EC 2008, Gallup 2008), i.e. access to funding, despite the deregulation of the banking system and the consequent inexpensive capital? In the latter case, increased regulation is to be implemented after the consequences of the current crisis are absorbed. It could therefore be more difficult for those businessmen to access funding. They might resort increasingly to family and friends for funding as they already do to some extent (Corbetta and Montemerlo 1999). Other ways of envisaging social phenomena from an economic perspective have to be considered in order to use the existing customs appropriately as has started to be done already (Schuerkens 2008).

From the arguments and facts elaborated above, European and Chinese approaches to SME policy making are similar in their perception of firms' growth. Even though progress on the matter of adoption of the market economy system in the People's Republic of China (PRC) is undeniable, there seems to be consensus on the efforts needed to be made by the Chinese government in order to fight the existing clan system or the widespread nepotism amongst business agents. Policy makers seem to fight the same phenomena on one side and the other of the world based on a neoclassical view of microeconomics. The policy makers' concern is the increase in the size of the firm and economies of scale. But Chinese firms grow through exports and networking. This strategy is based on the cultural concept of fluidity and social harmony common in China: the most important matter is that resources are in the network, and ownership and size are not important. Such *network* strategy of development cannot happen without the support of a strong social canvas. Despite the People's Republic of China centralization of policy making, it somehow tolerates the existence of *guanxi* probably because it is a permanent feature of Chinese culture. The persistence of cultural traditions crowds out institutionalist arguments, which blame the lack of functioning market institutions for the persistence of, what would be in the institutionalist vocabulary, informality or prominent social capital (Durlauf 2002). Building market economy institutions does not have to mean evicting existing socio-cultural patterns.

The same phenomenon happens in Europe, although to a lesser degree. The EU could consider the mounting voices on the efficiency of Diaspora (ethnic) networks in stimulating foreign direct investment (FDI) (Héricourt and Poncet 2009) and private sector development. For example, the family network can act as a collateral for small businesses, whenever tangible or intangible assets are not available (Biggart and Castanias 2001, Chua et al. 2007). Network capitalism, i.e. firms' cooperation with business and social networks, can be particularly useful in socially dense countries such as the new member states of the EU or in the future member countries (Bartlett et al. 2002, Smallbone and Welter 2009). These suggestions are to be implemented at the empirical level. At the theoretical level the phenomenon of homophily has pushed for a reconsideration of the theories of socio-economic interactions as they were developed so far. Homophily is the tendency people have to choose friends based on familiar criteria and not completely randomly. The individualization of social life in western societies, together with the development of competitive market structures was thought to be a permanent feature of modernity. In fact, people still refer to their family background when choosing with whom they are going to socialize. This pre-determination of the choice of one's social networks undermines the idea of rationalization of their formation (Jackson and Rogers 2007, McPherson et al. 2001) and invites one to consider their embeddedness in long-term cultural traditions. Concretely, this might mean that the Chinese model of firms' growth, by relying on business and social networks are not alien to a progressive construction of the market economy. Social network formation in Europe shows signs of homophily as well. Therefore denying the impact of social networks on economic activity is not a realistic standpoint. The current period of rethinking of economic mechanisms is favorable to the adoption of a bottom-up approach in policy making, integrating the importance of social networks. The efficiency of policy making, as a function of firms' growth through networking and not ownership and governance might increase. Further research is necessary to show that a change of paradigm in economics, closer to the empirical socio-cultural features of human activities, can grasp additional aspects of economic reality.

Contrary to the common idea of the centralization of the Chinese economy and decentralization of the EU economies, the aforementioned factors lead to consider the multipolarity of Chinese firms into micro (social networks) and macro (Diaspora networks) levels of industrial organization (Schuerkens 2008).[5] On the other hand, there is centralization of EU SME policy through national governments and the geographical limitation of EU firms. In order to fully understand the stakes underlying the question of policy transfer, there is a need for a specification of the factors pushing for the adoption of converging economic policies worldwide.

---

5 According to the Chinese authorities, globalization can only be multipolar, but this Chinese world is global insofar as the Chinese diasporas are spread over the five continents and try to increase Chinese transnational solidarities. The Chinese authorities have pursued a policy directed to the Chinese diasporas, asking them to develop China through investment and industrial relocations, and by the promotion of Chinese products and Chinese cultural heritage (Schuerkens 2008: 6).

A compromising answer to the aforementioned question would affirm that there is a synthetically determined globalization process. Internal and external factors are important in both the Chinese and European cases. In other words, the type of economic system adopted is (or has to be considered) as fundamental as the specific socio-cultural and political foundations on which it rests. SME policy in the EU, even if adopted more as a response to the requirements of the current economic period,[6] still follows mainstream microeconomic theories. To put things into a theoretical context, SME development represents firms' growth (microeconomics) coupled with economic development (macroeconomics). The policy objectives are designed to foster the implementation of the market economy and the adoption, or consolidation, of new rules for economic operators. The corollary objective is to strengthen the single market by implementing uniform economic policies across the EU, as well as in future member countries. Following the consolidation of the single market, national policies across the EU are quite homogenous in the aims and forms they take.

According to international trade theories, the increased competitiveness of small- and medium-sized firms facilitates their integration in the world market. The growth constraint on small firms has often been explained by market failure, particularly by the difficulty to access funding (Beck and Demirguc-Kunt 2006, Beck et al. 2008). The inclusion of social networks in business activities, for example family and friends providing start up capital or investment financing, is considered as being a market failure in the worst case, and in the best, as a malfunctioning of economic institutions. Another method of development for a firm in the neo-classical perspective of firms' growth is to build partnerships and raise capital through joint ventures. In that regard other studies have focused on foreign investment legislation, land rights, free trade agreements and other taxation issues. They have shown the lack of functional economic institutions in China, as an explanatory factor for the existence of obstacles to firms' growth. Meanwhile, rarely has the influence of social networks on economic activity been considered. Meanwhile social networks are a typical long-term feature of human life, even though they adopt different characteristics from one culture to the other. But in economics, the cultural background is seen as a limitation to the integration in the global market. Table 11.5 below illustrates the arguments developed so far.

Social embeddedness of economic activities in China requires a particular coordination of the state, the community and the kinship network (Boisot 1996). Be it because of their locality or flexibility, small and medium firms are the perfect antidote to the current economic mayhem. Chinese policy makers would gain in favoring socio-cultural based networks by orienting their public expenditure and infrastructure by including them in the economic system. For example, family and

6 According to an internal evaluation of the European Commission's project with regard to Entrepreneurship and the SME Charter from the DG Budget, this recognition has come more as an *ad hoc* than as a clearly thought strategy Commission 2006.

Table 11.5 Chinese and European SME policy making compared

Policy/Theory/Business	China	Europe
SME policy making	Centralized	Decentralized
Policy objectives	Social stability, employment, privatization	Firm competitiveness, employment
Theoretical underpinnings of SME policies	Firm growth model, Neo-liberal microeconomics	Firm growth model, Neo-liberal microeconomics
Real life business	Network-based SME (decentralized)	Locally based SME (centralized)
Issues/Obstacles	Access to funding, informality/corruption	Access to funding, cumbersome regulation
Lessons for policy making	Adopt a bottom up approach enriched by socio-cultural features	Adopt a bottom up approach enriched by socio-cultural features
Rectifications to SME policy	Change perspective on firm growth and ownership: heterogeneous vs. uniform Use the existing cultural traditions to implement hybrid forms of economic structures	Change perspective on firm growth and ownership: heterogeneous vs. uniform Develop network based economic structures

Source: Authors' table.

kinship networks can be collateralized when material assets are difficult to find (Chua et al. 2007, Hamilton 2006). Kinship networks can be mobilized in rural areas and they have already proven to be effective for increasing employment (Yusheng Peng 2004). When combining family and transnational business networks the effect on firms' growth can be very valuable (Yeung 2000). *Guanxi* envisaged within market economy rules should not be harmful to firms' competitiveness (Chung-Leung et al. 2008, Zhou et al. 2008). The European social model would also gain in including the social networks already at work while the market is taking time to recover. Market oriented economies are more affected by the crisis than developing countries, most of which are export-dependent. Consequently, in addition to more regulation, recognition of the human features at play during this crisis is healthier than rejecting them (Akerlof and Shiller 2009), which would mean risking recidivism.

Conclusion

The achievement of the inclusion of the socio-cultural structure in economic models transformation has to undergo the enlargement of mainstream theoretical models followed by a reform of policy making. SME policy is a good example of a much needed reformulation of priorities and accountability. The latter has to be directed not only towards the public sphere, as the tendency seems to be nowadays, but also towards the understanding of the combination between the socio-cultural characteristics of economic structures and their interaction with top to bottom approaches of policy makers. Situations where human behavior will not follow market rules will repeat. Therefore, reflection must continue on how to best compromise between the requirements of economic development and the respect of human nature.

This chapter shows that SME policies in both the EU and China present similarities in terms of policy design and the chronological emergence of the policy. The latter came more as an *ad hoc* strategy for the national and regional public authorities, given the persisting importance of SMEs for employment and their contribution to GDP. So, on the one hand there is currently an increased concern for the development of the private sector (SME, FDI) and on the other hand the involvement of public finances through stimulus plans is heavier. Efficiency through cost cutting and economies of scale might have been appropriate during the post World War II mass production and consumption period, but it is reaching its limits at a time when labor costs develop hand in hand with the service economy. The objective of convergence to a knowledge-based economy, which is one major item on the Lisbon agenda, could be reached through empowering the existing socio-cultural environment of the individual. More precisely, the main argument of this chapter is that the inclusion of social networks in economic models, public policy and economic decision making worldwide is not to be considered as a divergence from building a market economy but a requirement for more sustainable foundations of the economy.

In addition, this chapter tried to make the point that a policy making process that complements national governments, i.e. in the EU case, is aimed at being decentralized but is *de facto* limited given the restrictions national governments have on public spending. At the other end of the governance spectrum, the most centralized economy, i.e. China, develops policy making expansively, not only based on public strategy but also on ethnic and cultural networks. The EU could adopt a network based perspective and the Chinese government can gain from disengaging from regulating economic activity. But both economies will progress by enlarging their perception of market functioning from strictly economic to socio-economic frameworks. Political economy, long vanished, can be reborn as economics of cultural networks.[7] Future empirical research will show the extent to which a contextualized socio-cultural economics field of study can be sustainable.

Today's concerns about the consequences of the financial and banking system crisis on a country's unemployment, inflation and public finances are important

7 Chung-Leung et al. (2008) call the Chinese system currently in place 'network capitalism' to emphasize the role of personal networks in business. They consider the influence of political networks on business development and find a positive impact of networking with government officials on administrative innovativeness.

and will persist over time. Economic and financial recovery needs concerted public efforts. The point was made that on the one hand EU and Chinese policy makers have to take into account the cultural characteristics of their respective private small and medium firms. On the other hand, the neo-liberal theoretical background of SME policy design is to be reviewed under the light of culturally and socially based paths of economic development. The longevity of such practices, despite the implementation of market based institutions, has yet to be researched and proven empirically. But it was shown that, at this stage, it can be an interesting field of analysis.

References

Akerlof, G.A. and Shiller, R.J. 2009. *Animal Spirits: How Human Psychology Drives the Economy, and Why It Matters for Global Capitalism.* Princeton; Oxford, Princeton University Press.

Bartlett, W., Bateman, M. and Vehovec, M. 2002. *Small Enterprise Development in South-East Europe: Policies for Sustainable Growth*, Boston, Mass., London, Kluwer Academic Publishers.

Bartlett, W. and Bukvic, V. 2002. What are the main barriers to SME growth and development in South-East Europe. In Bartlett, W., Bateman, M. and Vehovec, M. (eds), *Small Enterprise Development in South-East Europe: Policies for Sustainable Growth.* Boston, Mass., London, Kluwer Academic Publishers.

Beck, T. and Demirguc-Kunt, A. 2006. Small and medium-size enterprises: access to finance as a growth constraint. *Journal of Banking & Finance,* 30, 2931–43.

Beck, T., Demirguc-Kunt, A., Laeven, L.U.C. and Levine, R. 2008. Finance, firm size, and growth. *Journal of Money, Credit & Banking (Blackwell),* 40, 1379–1405.

Biggart, N.W. and Castanias, R.P. 2001. Collateralized social relations: the social in economic calculation. *American Journal of Economics and Sociology,* 60, 471–500.

Chua, J.H., Kellermanns, F.W., Chrisman, J.J. and Wu, Z. 2007. Family involvement as social capital in debt financing of new ventures.

Chung-Leung, L., Yau, O.H.M., Sin, L.Y.M., Tse, A.C.B., Chow, R.P.M. and Lee, J.S.Y. 2008. The effects of social capital and organizational innovativeness in different institutional contexts. *Journal of International Business Studies,* 39, 589–612.

Commission, E. 1997. *Commission Decision of 5 November 1997 Approving a Support Mechanism for the Creation of Transnational Joint Ventures for SMEs in the Community.*

Commission, E. 2003. *Annual Activity Report of the Directorate General Enterprise and Industry.*

Commission, E. 2006. Evaluation of the Commission: reporting on results. DG Budget.

Corbetta, G. and Montemerlo, D. 1999. Ownership, governance, and management issues in small and medium-size family businesses: a comparison of Italy and the United States. *Family Business Review*, 12, 361–74.

Council, E. 1986. Council Resolution of 3 November 1986 Concerning the Action Programme for Small and Medium Sized Enterprises.

Council, E. 1994. Council Resolution of 10 October 1994 on Giving Full Scope to the Dynamism and Innovatory Potential of Small and Medium-Sized Enterprises, Including the Craft Sector and Micro-Enterprises, in a Competitive Economy.

Council, E. 1995.Council Resolution of 27 November 1995 on Small and Medium-Sized Industrial Enterprises (SMEs) and Technological Innovation.

Durlauf, S.N. 2002. On the Empirics of Social Capital. *Economic Journal,* 112, 459–479.

E.C. 2003. Commission Recommandation of 6 May 2003 Concerning the Definition of Micro, Small and Medium-Sized Enterprises. In E.C. (ed.) Brussels, Belgium, Official Journal of the European Union.

E.C. 2005. Annual Activity Report of the Directorate General Enterprise and Industry.

EU 1992. Treaty on the European Union. In EU (Ed.), Official Journal 92/C 191/01.

EUROSTAT 2008. Key Figures on European Businesses. In Statistics, U.G.S.B. (Ed.) Luxembourg.

Fan, J.P.H., Wong, T.J. and Zhang, T. 2007. Politically connected CEOs, corporate governance, and Post-IPO performance of China's newly partially privatized firms. *Journal of Financial Economics*, 84, 330–57.

Gallup 2008. Observatory of European SMEs. In Eurobarometer (ed.) *Enterprise Observatory Survey.*

Gold, T.B., Guthrie, D. and Wank, D.L. 2002. *Social Connections in China: Institutions, Culture, and the Changing Nature of Guanxi.* Cambridge, Cambridge University Press.

Hamilton, G.G. 2006. *Commerce and Capitalism in Chinese Societies*. New York, London, Routledge.

Hamilton, G.G.E. 1996. *Asian Business Networks.* New York, Walter de Gruyter.

Héricourt, J. and Poncet, S. (2009) FDI and credit constraints: firm-level evidence from China. *Economic Systems,* 33, 1–21.

Jackson, M.O. and Rogers, B.W. 2007. Meeting strangers and friends of friends: how random are social networks? *American Economic Review*, 97, 890–915.

Li, H., Meng, L., Wang, Q. and Zhou, L.-A. 2008. Political connections, financing and firm performance: evidence from Chinese private firms. *Journal of Development Economics*, 87, 283–299.

Lin, S. and Zhu, X. 2007. *Private Enterprises and China's Economic Development.* London, Routledge.

McPherson, M., Smith-Lovin, L. and Cook, J.M. 2001. Birds of a feather: Homophily in social networks. *Annual Review of Sociology*, 27, 415.

O'Brennan, J. and Gassie, E. 2009. From stabilization to consolidation: Albanian state capacity and adaptation to European Union rules. *Journal of Balkan & Near Eastern Studies* 11, 22.

Potter, J. and Storey, D. 2008. *Framework for the Evaluation of SME and Entrepreneurship Policies and Programmes*. O.E.C.D.

Schuerkens, U. 2008. *Globalisation and Transformations of Local Socio-Economic Practices*. New York, Routledge.

Siu-Lun, W. 1985. The Chinese family firm: a model. *British Journal of Sociology,* 36, 58.

Smallbone, D. and Welter, F. 2009. *Entrepreneurship and Small Business Development in Post-Socialist Economies*. London, Routledge.

Vlasto, D. 2005. Report on implementing the European charter for small enterprises. European Parliament.

Yeung, H.W.-C. 2000. Limits to the growth of family-owned business? The case of Chinese transnational corporations from Hong Kong. *Family Business Review,* 13, 55–70.

Yusheng Peng, D.R. 2004. Kinship networks and entrepreneurs in China's transitional economy. *American Journal of Sociology*, 109, 1045–1074.

Zhou, K.Z., Poppo, L. and Yang, Z. 2008. Relational ties or customized contracts? An examination of alternative governance choices in China. *Journal of International Business Studies,* 39, 8.

Chapter 12
The Impact of High-Speed Rail on Accessibility and House-Price Variability: The Case of Two Taiwanese Regions

David Emanuel Andersson and Oliver F. Shyr

Introduction

High-speed rail (HSR) is a new type of transportation infrastructure that until recently was confined to Japan and some of the more developed regions in the European Union, primarily France, Germany, and Spain. The most substantial investments in this technology after 2000 have however occurred in Asia outside of Japan, particularly in China, Korea, and Taiwan. It is in Taiwan that the longest high-speed track is being used at the time of writing; Taiwan's HSR traverses the 345 kilometers between Taipei and Kaohsiung in about 90 minutes.

The East Asian enthusiasm for HSR investments should not come as a surprise. The area is home not only to some of the world's highest economic growth rates, but also to extraordinarily high population densities. Taiwan, for example, has the second greatest population density in the world after Bangladesh (if we exclude city states such as Hong Kong and Singapore); the economic viability of railroad and transit investments reflects wealth per unit of land area rather than its per capita counterpart.

One of the more interesting questions concerns the extent to which we should expect HSR to impact future land uses. The actions of participants in various land and real estate markets provide information about their plans and expectations. If such actors perceive HSR transportation as offering new and valuable economic opportunities, we should expect HSR accessibility to affect their willingness to pay. The integration of previously separated labor and land markets may also occur, since HSR investments result in drastic reductions in travel times. A smaller number of individually larger functional urban regions is thus also a possible HSR effect. Such urban enlargement processes may have substantial economy-wide consequences in the form of emergent agglomeration economies.

Not all regions are equally propitious for HSR investments. Generally speaking, rail-based infrastructure benefits from agglomerations of wealth, high population densities, and high nodal densities. Central Honshu in Japan – which hosts two of the world's largest and richest metropolitan regions – is perhaps the most suitable region. But Taiwan may be a more interesting example from a

European perspective, since per capita wealth and income is slightly lower than the Western European average, whereas nodal and overall population densities are higher. The overall suitability of HSR for various European corridors may be an interesting research area, since several regions within the north-south corridor from the Netherlands to northern Italy approach Taiwanese densities on key economic – rather than on population-based – measures. Amidst increasing concerns about rising oil prices and the environmental and economic sustainability of a society centered on the use of automobiles for personal transportation, it seems likely that rail-based infrastructure and high-density real estate investments will both become increasingly attractive policy options in the coming years.

This chapter takes a closer look at the economic effects of Taiwan's HSR by estimating the influence on land prices of relative HSR accessibility in two medium-sized Taiwanese regions (Hsinchu and Tainan). The selected method is hedonic estimation of implicit prices for housing. The first section provides some background regarding the impact of HSR and other investments in rail transportation on land-use patterns and the urban economy. Section 2 discusses hedonic price estimation, while section 3 gives an overview of the observations that are used for estimating hedonic price functions. The penultimate section describes and discusses the empirical results. It is followed by some tentative conclusions about what lessons the Taiwanese HSR experience offers for regions in the West.

1. High-Speed Rail, Land-Use Patterns, and the Urban Economy

High-speed rail is usually defined as those rail systems that operate at maximum speeds of at least 300 kilometers per hour. Until the 1990s, there were only three HSR systems in existence in Japan, France, and Germany (Sands 1993). Over the past 15 years, the European network has been extended to Spain and Belgium. There have been no hedonic price studies undertaken that deal explicitly with high-speed rail effects in these countries, but studies of population and employment growth have shown a significant association between HSR connectivity and such growth in Japan, particularly employment growth in business services such as advertising and consulting (Nakamura and Ueda 1989). The evidence from Europe has largely been inconclusive, perhaps a reflection of less flexible land-use regulations; (note, however, that there are many countervailing factors that may confound simple correlations between regional growth rates and HSR presence). The only comparable hedonic study from Europe analyzed accessibility to the regular-speed rail network in the Netherlands, and found a substantial and statistically significant 25 percent price premium for housing near stations (Debrezion et al. 2006a). The lack of hedonic price studies of HSR effects reflects the convention of analyzing long-established metropolitan areas, even though one of the aims of HSR investments is to enlarge functional labor and housing markets. The present study thus aims to fill a gap in the empirical hedonic literature.

Asia is where the most ambitious HSR plans have been formulated or implemented in the years after 2000. In China, the first phase of its new network consists of the new line between Beijing and Tianjin that was opened shortly before the Beijing Olympics, and which is currently being extended to Shanghai. Another line will connect the central city of Wuhan with Guangzhou in southern China. In Korea, the rail connection between the two main cities of Seoul and Busan uses high-speed tracks for the section between Seoul and Daegu.

Taiwan's high-speed rail was inaugurated in early 2007, and consists of eight stations in seven metropolitan regions. It runs parallel with the pre-existing west-coast railroad line. The old line encompasses many more stations as well as a few more peripheral stations in the extreme north and south of the island. The new trains and tracks have led to a dramatic shrinkage of the time distance between Taiwan's cities: the scheduled time for the fastest Taipei-Kaohsiung connections has been cut from four and a half hours to just over 90 minutes.

The increased interregional accessibility of Taiwan's cities has been achieved at a substantial cost, however. The investment cost of the HSR amounted to US$15 billion, which is equivalent to about five percent of the annual gross domestic product. To put this figure into perspective, we note that it was the world's most expensive build-operate-transfer infrastructural investment and that a proportionate cost to the American economy would amount to about US$700 billion – almost the size of the 2009 US stimulus package.

When the Japanese colonial government constructed Taiwan's west coast railroad in the first half of the twentieth century, it resulted in the relocation of traditional city centers to areas adjacent to the new train stations. Over the past 30 years, Taiwan's downtown areas have moved anew, this time in the direction of new business developments. The later relocation away from railroad stations reflects both the growing importance of road and air transportation as well as the low and deteriorating quality of the buildings in old city centers. This "downtown drift" has been particularly obvious in the three largest cities; the eastward drift of central Taipei has been accompanied by similar westward and southward movements in Taichung and Kaohsiung, respectively.

While the HSR station in Taipei is co-located with the old railroad station and the main transit interchange, all other stations are located on suburban greenfield or brownfield land. There has, therefore, been a reshuffling of the relative regional accessibility of urban neighborhoods, with the possible exception of Taipei City. While intraregional accessibility is usually considered to be the main factor accounting for land price variability within metropolitan regions, this is not necessarily the case in Taiwan. The new time distances between several of the metropolitan regions are in many cases short enough to enable the integration of previously separated housing and labor markets. Table 12.1 provides an overview of time distances by rail before and after the completion of the HSR (road travel times are usually longer than time distances by conventional rail).

Empirical studies from Western Europe have shown that commuting frequencies drop dramatically once a one-way time distance of 50 minutes is exceeded

Table 12.1 Examples of time distances by high-speed rail and conventional rail, minutes

Origin – destination	High-speed rail (HSR)	Conventional rail (TRA)
Taipei – Kaohsiung	96	280
Taipei – Hsinchu	34	65
Taoyuan – Hsinchu	22	36
Hsinchu – Taichung	26	65
Taichung – Tainan	43	115
Chiayi – Tainan	19	42
Tainan – Kaohsiung (Zuoying)	17	33

Sources: Taiwan High Speed Rail and Taiwan Railway Administration schedules (2009).

(Andersson and Andersson 2008). It is thus clear that the Taipei metropolitan area – as conventionally defined – is now within the reach of the Taoyuan and Hsinchu areas, while Kaohsiung is within the reach of Tainan. Taiwan's third largest metropolitan area, Taichung, has for the same reason become a feasible choice for daily commuters from Hsinchu, Chiayi, and Tainan. Figure 12.1 shows the location of HSR stations and also shows the extent of the relevant metropolitan areas according to official government statistics. Table 12.2 gives population figures for these metropolitan areas as well as the time distance from the central business district (CBD) to the HSR station by means of public and private transportation. The relative time distance of public as compared with private transportation both reflects local investments in public transportation services and road congestion levels.

Official government delimitations of metropolitan areas – both in Taiwan and elsewhere – tend to be based on historical observations of actual commuter flows between outlying areas and the core of a region. An outlying area is usually considered an integrated part of the metropolitan region if the proportion of its residents commuting to the core exceeds a certain threshold; in Taiwan's case this threshold is set at 1.5 percent (National Statistics, People's Republic of China 2008). But there are also other ways of defining a metropolitan region. A more future-oriented way is to measure whether relative accessibility to the core has a significant impact on house prices – and by implication on land values – in a location. If it does, this implies that market participants expect center accessibility to be a valued attribute among participants in various property markets, which would be tantamount to functional economic integration.

The question thus becomes if – and to what extent – accessibility to HSR stations impacts land prices. If it does, this would indicate both a positive evaluation of HSR accessibility and an ongoing integration with the land and labor markets of newly accessible downtown areas in other Taiwanese cities. With urban land prices being subject to various neighborhood effects such as zoning regulations or socio-economic characteristics, HSR effects can only be approximated if one

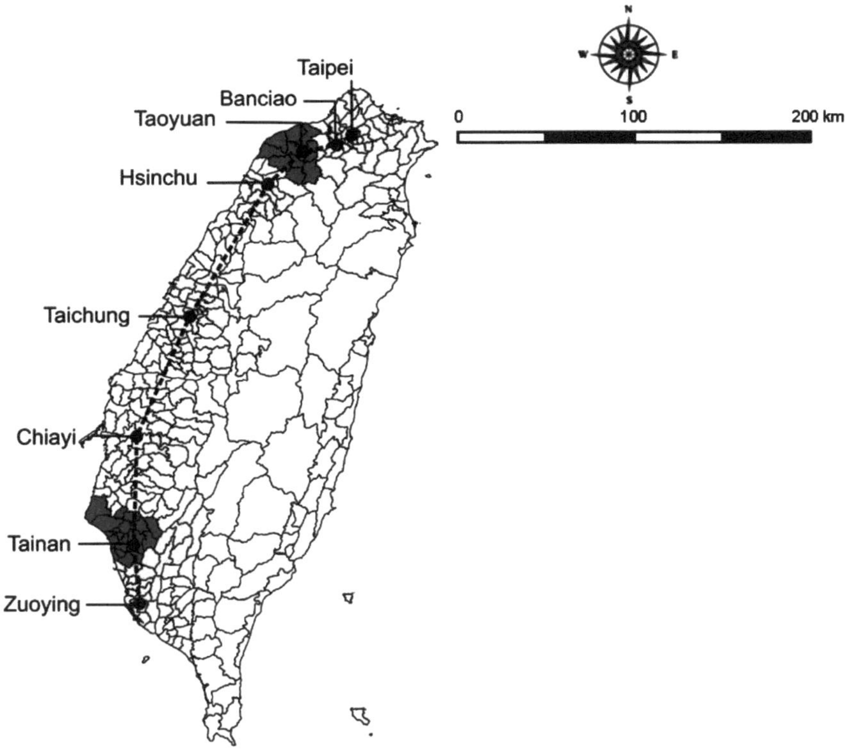

Figure 12.1 Taiwan's high-speed railroad; shaded areas correspond to metropolitan areas as defined in National Statistics, People's Republic of China (2008)

Source: Department of Urban Planning, National Cheng-kung University.

Table 12.2 Metropolitan area populations and access time in minutes from central business districts (CBDs) to HSR stations

HSR station	Metropolitan area population (million)	Access time to CBD (by car)	Access time to CBD (by public transport)
Taipei	6.7	0	0
Banciao	6.7	-	-
Taoyuan	1.9	20	30
Hsinchu	0.8	20	30
Taichung	2.3	25	15
Chiayi	0.3	30	40
Tainan	1.2	30	40
Zuoying (Kaohsiung)	2.7	20	15

Source: National Statistics, Republic of China [Taiwan] (2008).

controls for other correlated factors; this fact makes hedonic price estimation a more appropriate research method than observations of transactions involving undeveloped land.

There are two advantages associated with using real estate prices rather than the commuting flows of the recent past for identifying relevant accessibility considerations. Prices not only tell us something about expectations, they also weigh market actors according to their relative economic impacts. Price measurements take account of the fact that powerful market participants such as property developers or high-income professionals have more "dollar votes" than low-income workers or the unemployed.

In this hedonic study, we estimate the impact of HSR accessibility on residential property prices in the Hsinchu and Tainan metropolitan regions. We interpret HSR accessibility as a proxy for the time distance to the core of the Taipei and Kaohsiung regions, respectively.

2. Methodological Issues – the Use of Hedonic Prices

Hedonic price theory is associated with the introduction of the term in a paper by Sherwin Rosen (1974), using ideas that had already been introduced by a number of economists in the 1960s (see, for example, Lancaster 1966). Rosen uses a utility-maximizing approach to derive implicit attribute prices for multi-attribute goods under conditions of perfect competition, where each attribute has a unique implicit price in equilibrium. Perfect competition, however, rests on assumptions of perfect information, which is not normally approximated in markets for housing or other real estate markets.

Perfect competition is however not a necessary assumption for empirical hedonic price studies. Barzel (1989) approaches multi-attribute goods in a more dynamic way, by building on the insights of property rights theorists such as Demsetz (1967). Webster and Lai (2003) extend Barzel's theory to spatial economics in a way that explicitly takes dynamic processes and imperfect information into account. From such a dynamic standpoint, empirical hedonic price models do not produce stable estimates of equilibrium prices, but rather snapshots of transitional conditions. For example, the discovery of two centers with a metropolitan impact does not necessarily invalidate the common monocentric assumption; it could be a transitional stage where a declining and an emerging center both impact on the willingness to pay of market participants for a finite time period – a reflection of asymmetric and imperfect information among buyers and sellers.

In general, hedonic price models aim at disentangling the attributes of a good from one another for the purpose of estimating implicit prices. In housing models, the purchase price or rent is a function of various attributes, typically divided into structural and location attributes. Location attributes can be further subdivided into general accessibility and localized neighborhood effects.

Regression techniques make it possible to estimate the implicit price for each attribute. Linear models are usually avoided, since the assumption of constant marginal implicit prices is untenable unless there are constant returns to scale in production or costless repackaging of two or more bundles. The most common non-linear models include log-linear, semi-log, and Box-Cox-transformed functions.[1] The log-linear and semi-log functions are pre-specified functions, while Box-Cox functions use an iterative procedure that maximizes the log-likelihood of the function within a pre-specified family of functions. Such maximization ensures a more desirable distribution of the error term than with less flexible estimation techniques.

In this chapter, we report the results of the log-linear and simple both-side Box-Cox functions. The log-linear function yielded higher coefficients of determination and a better distribution of residuals than the semi-log function in both the studied regions, while the simple both-side Box-Cox function yielded log likelihood estimates that were superior to the log likelihood associated with using the simple left-hand side Box-Cox function.

3. Description of the Data

The study is concerned with two medium-sized urban regions in Taiwan: Hsinchu and Tainan. These regions are especially suitable for a comparative study for three reasons. First, the HSR station is in both cases located at a considerable distance from what is usually thought of as the downtown area. Second, both stations are located in suburbs with little prior development. Finally, both cities host government-sponsored science parks, which are often regarded as the high-tech growth engines of Taiwan's economy.

There are also interesting differences, however. Hsinchu has a larger and older science park than Tainan, and an overall economic structure that is much less traditional. Although Hsinchu only ranks as the sixth largest region in terms of population, it has the second-highest per capita income after Taipei. This is in large part due to its role as the location of the Hsinchu Science-based Industrial Park (HSIP), whose 150,000 workers comprised about 1.3 percent of the labor force but accounted for more than three percent of Taiwanese GDP and 8.5 percent of exports in 2004 (Chen 2005).

The HSIP is an important node in the global network of the information technology industry, with especially strong linkages to Silicon Valley and the city of Dongguan in southern China. Two of Taiwan's twelve research-oriented

1 The simple-left-hand-side Box-Cox transformation is: $X_1^\lambda = \beta_1 + \beta_2 X_2 + \ldots + \beta_i X_i + \ldots + \beta_k X_k$.

The simple both-side Box-Cox transformation is: $X_1^\lambda = \beta_1 + \beta_2 X_2^\lambda + \ldots + \beta_i X_i^\lambda + \ldots + \beta_k X_k^\lambda$;

where $X_i^\lambda = (X_i^\lambda - 1) / \lambda$ for $\lambda \neq 0$ and $X_i^\lambda = \ln X_i$ for $\lambda_i = 0$.

universities are also located in Hsinchu, both of which have taken an active part in the development of manufacturing capabilities such as the production of integrated circuits. Figure 12.2 shows the location of the HSIP relative to both the HSR station and the traditional downtown area. Both the HSIP and the HSR station are located to the east of Hsinchu's old center.

Tainan is usually considered Taiwan's fourth largest city, but the population of the metropolitan area actually makes it the fifth largest Taiwanese region. The metropolitan region does however house a population that is about 50 percent greater than Hsinchu's. Although Tainan also hosts one of Taiwan's three science parks, it is more recent, smaller (about 50,000 workers), and has not been as successful in generating exports or revenue as the HSIP. Apart from the science park and its one research university, Tainan has a more traditional economic structure than Hsinchu, with a majority of its population engaged in small-scale manufacturing or retailing activities.

Figure 12.3 is a map of the Tainan metropolitan area, which shows that the HSR station is located in a suburban area to the southeast of the downtown core. The science park (not shown on the map) is located in the middle of the Sinshih Township in the northeast. The HSR station is further away from the science park than from the downtown area.

The observations on transaction prices and structural characteristics were obtained from the Department of Land Administration of the central government, and cover all 846 and 1,550 residential property transactions in 2007 in the

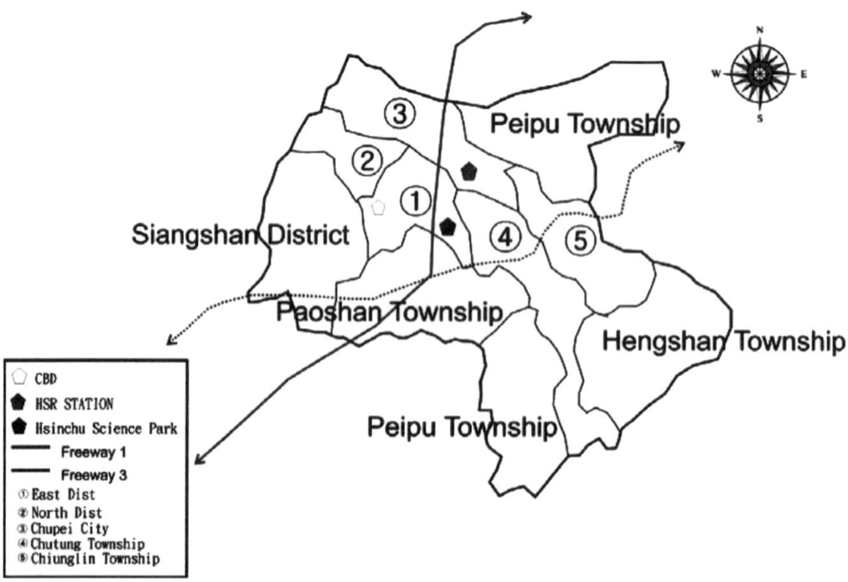

Figure 12.2 Hsinchu Metropolitan Area
Source: Department of Urban Planning, National Cheng-kung University.

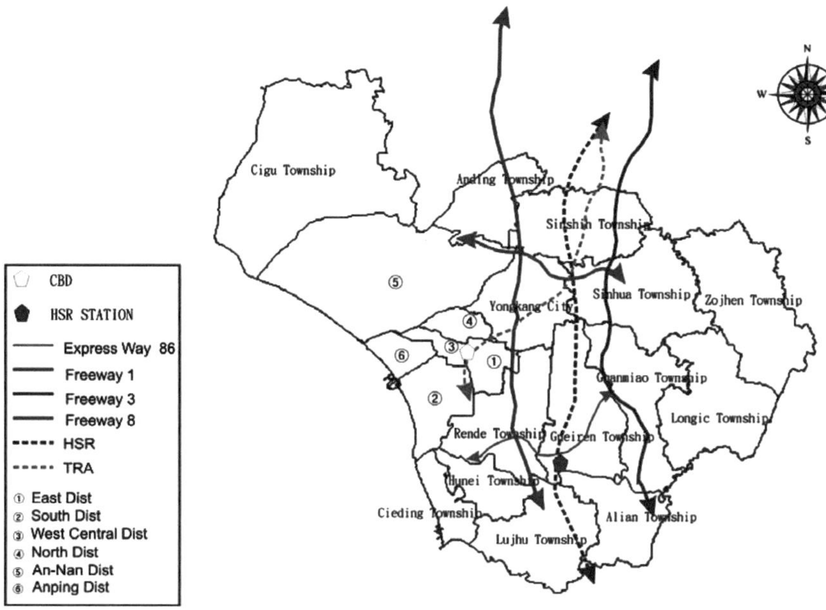

Figure 12.3 Tainan Metropolitan Area

Source: Department of Urban Planning, National Cheng-kung University.

Hsinchu and Tainan metropolitan areas, respectively. The data on socio-economic neighborhood characteristics are for 2004 and were obtained from the Ministry of Finance. The neighborhoods correspond to districts in Hsinchu City and Tainan City and townships in the rest of the metropolitan areas. The distance measurements are proxies for house-specific access to the HSR station, the city center, and the science park, respectively.[2] The distance data correspond to the shortest route for motor vehicles according to a popular geographical information systems (GIS) program that covers the entire road network of Taiwan, known as *PaPaGo R12*.

The hedonic analysis makes use of sales prices rather than rents, since owner-occupied housing accounts for more than 80 percent of Taiwan's housing market. In addition, sales prices reflect expectations of future developments, and should therefore – unlike rents – reflect potential long-term future benefits of new or planned infrastructure investments. Table 12.3 gives descriptive statistics for all variables.

2 We use the distance to the (old) Hsinchu and Tainan railroad stations as our "distance to CBD" measure. The accessibility variables measure distances from the center of the census tract in which the housing unit is located to the facility in question (i.e., city center station, HSR station, science park). Exact locations of property transactions are unavailable since the identity of the transacting parties is confidential.

Table 12.3 Descriptive statistics

Variable	Unit	Mean Hsinchu	Mean Tainan	Standard deviation Hsinchu	Standard deviation Tainan	Expected sign
Sales price	NT$ million	7.0	5.6	4.5	4.0	
Structural						
Floor area	m^2	185.4	177.5	91.3	126.2	+
Lot size	m^2	104.5	95.1	82.2	39.1	+
Age of dwelling	years	15.8	16.8	12.2	12.5	-
Height	stories	3.1	3.2	1.1	1.1	+
Combined shop/ dwelling use	dummy	.03	.1	.2	.4	+
Faces main street	dummy	.3	.3	.5	.5	+
Neighborhood						
Road width	m	14.8	15.6	7.3	7.3	+
Commercial zone	dummy	.03	.1	.2	.3	+
Residential zone	dummy	.7	.9	.5	.3	+
Mean income	NT$ thousand	1091.0	732.9	315.0	116.4	+
Share with at least two years of college	share	.2	.3	.1	.1	+
Accessibility						
Distance to CBD	km	7.3	6.1	6.4	4.4	-
Distance to HSR	km	11.5	16.7	4.1	6.1	-
Distance to science park	km	8.6	17.0	4.5	4.5	-

Sources: Our own calculations, based on official government data (the Bureau of Land Administration and from National Statistics, Republic of China (Taiwan).

The descriptive statistics indicate some of the structural differences between Hsinchu and Tainan. Despite being a supposedly smaller region, housing units in Hsinchu are about 25 percent more expensive than in Tainan, and household incomes – with neighborhoods weighted by property transactions rather than population – are almost 50 percent higher in Hsinchu than in Tainan. In addition, Tainan sprawls more than Hsinchu: the average distance to the HSR station is 45 percent longer in Tainan than in Hsinchu, while the science park is (on average) twice as distant in Tainan.

The tested independent variables are identical in both regions and encompass six structural, five neighborhood and three accessibility attributes. District or township mean income was not included in the hedonic price functions since simple correlation analysis reveals very high positive correlations between neighborhood income and education. Correlations between the socio-economic attributes and center accessibility are negative and relatively high (see Table 12.4). The latter

Table 12.4 Correlations between socio-economic variables and center accessibility in Hsinchu and Tainan

Hsinchu			
	Income	**Education**	**Distance to CBD**
Income	1.00		
Education	.93	1.00	
Distance to CBD	-.73	-.77	1.00
Tainan			
	Income	**Education**	**Distance to CBD**
Income	1.00		
Education	.96	1.00	
Distance to CBD	-.66	-.75	1.00

Source: Our own calculations, based on official government data (the Bureau of Land Administration and from National Statistics, Republic of China (Taiwan).

correlations imply an income elasticity of demand for accessibility that is on average greater than the income elasticity of demand for space in both Hsinchu's and Tainan's housing markets. On the other hand, correlations between different accessibility variables are all quite low.

The neighborhood attributes "commercial zone" and "residential zone" refer to Taiwanese zoning regulations, which are more flexible than in many other jurisdictions. Taiwan's cities have retained a mixed-use character since "residential zones" allow commercial use on the first and second floors of apartment houses and townhouses. "Commercial zones" allow for some residential use on higher floors. For example, downtown residential zones are often used for high-rise apartment blocks with high-value commercial use such as banks and luxury retailing on the first two floors.

4. Results and Analysis

The estimation of hedonic price functions uses two models for each region: the log-linear and the simple both-side Box-Cox model. The height attribute (measured as the total number of stories in a building) was deleted from the Tainan specification because it was highly correlated with the floor area and age attributes, while the mean income of the neighborhood was excluded from both the Hsinchu and Tainan specifications because of its high correlation with the percentage of residents with at least a junior college education.

The results displayed in Table 12.5 show that all remaining structural and neighborhood variables have the expected signs, and all of them (except height in the log-linear Hsinchu model) are highly significant. The log-linear and Box-Cox models are virtually identical in the case of Hsinchu, with a maximum likelihood λ that is very close to zero. The best λ is 0.168 for Tainan's hedonic price function,

Table 12.5 Hedonic price functions, Hsinchu and Tainan metropolitan areas, 2007

Variable	Hsinchu log-linear: estimate (t-value)	Hsinchu BS Box-Cox: estimate (t-value)	Tainan log-linear: estimate (t-value)	Tainan BS Box-Cox: estimate (t-value)
Constant	.76	.76	1.56	2.13
Structure				
Floor area	.53** (19.59)	.53** (14.32)	.55** (26.87)	.65** (21.53)
Lot size	.44** (21.25)	.45** (13.46)	.47** (19.45)	.63** (14.30)
Age	-.04** (-5.69)	-.04** (-5.37)	-.12** (-19.72)	-.18** (-12.78)
Height	.59 (1.40)	.12** (3.47)		
Shop/dwelling use	.13** (2.86)	.14** (2.76)	.14** (6.49)	.20** (6.56)
Street frontage	.11** (6.70)	.11** (6.26)	.19** (11.73)	.25** (10.59)
Neighborhood				
Road width	.05** (2.99)	.05** (2.97)	.10** (6.31)	.12** (6.47)
Commercial zone	.61** (13.51)	.61** (9.40)	.33** (6.49)	.40** (6.11)
Residential zone	.28** (16.33)	.28** (11.68)	.23** (5.75)	.25** (4.91)
Education	.16** (3.87)	.16** (3.83)	.45** (10.42)	.739** (7.66)
Accessibility				
Distance to CBD	-.06** (-4.08)	-.06** (-4.03)	-.11** (-6.97)	-.17** (-6.69)
Distance to HSR	-.18** (-8.99)	-.18** (-6.85)	-.04* (-1.95)	-.05* (-1.93)
Distance to science park	-.09** (-5.47)	-.09** (-5.22)	-.08** (-3.55)	-.06** (-3.03)
Function statistics				
λ		.001		.168
Adjusted R^2	.85		.80	
Log likelihood		-1375.7		-2453.7
N	846	846	1550	1550

*: significant at α=.05; **: significant at α=.01.

which although more distant is still in the general neighborhood of the log-linear function and provides identical qualitative results.

The estimated accessibility effects point to the relative importance of the three nodes in each region. In Hsinchu, the distance to the HSR station has a greater impact on house prices than either distance to the science park or to the old downtown area (CBD). The estimated HSR accessibility effect reflects the economic importance of the Hsinchu-Taipei linkage for the HSIP. All three distance effects are however substantial and statistically significant. The two estimated hedonic price functions lend support to the notion that Hsinchu's downtown and science park nodes have been transformed into outlying sub-centers in an enlarged northern metropolitan region. We may interpret HSR accessibility as a proxy for accessibility to Taipei's central business district. Since the new high-speed rail link has resulted in a substantial reduction of the time distance between Taipei and Hsinchu, it seems that high-speed rail investments may contribute to urban enlargement processes.

In the southern region of Tainan, HSR accessibility has at most a minor effect on residential property prices and the traditional downtown area has retained its position as the predominant accessibility consideration. Estimated HSR accessibility effects in the Tainan region imply relatively low or perhaps even negligible distance elasticity.[3]

The difference between Hsinchu and Tainan regarding HSR accessibility reflects two mutually reinforcing factors in the Tainan region: low intra-regional accessibility of its HSR station and an economic structure where knowledge-intensive services carry much less total and relative weight than in Hsinchu. In Taiwan, only the northern corridor from Taipei to Hsinchu exhibits consistently high land prices and positive population growth. The limited impact of the HSR in the southern part of the island probably reflects the absence of a complementary restructuring of the southern economy. So far, the southern economy has shown no signs of the spontaneous innovative processes that are necessary for a self-generated economic transformation. The southern region is also much less important than northern Taiwan as a center of scientific research and production of other knowledge services.

Another way of looking at the spatial orientation of the two cities is by comparing and ranking estimated price-distance elasticities. Table 12.6 shows that while HSR accessibility is the most important node for generating general accessibility benefits in the Hsinchu region, it is the *least* important node in the Tainan region.

---

3 Additional estimations using semi-logarithmic, left-hand side Box-Cox, and separate both-side Box-Cox functions revealed that while HSR accessibility is highly significant across all functional forms in Hsinchu, this is not the case in Tainan, where only the functional forms reported in this paper yield estimates that are significant at one-tailed $\alpha = .05$.

Table 12.6 Ranking of nodes by estimated price-distance elasticity, Hsinchu and Tainan metropolitan regions, 2007

Node	Region	Estimated elasticity	t-value (OLS)
HSR station	Hsinchu	-.18	-8.99
Downtown area	Tainan	-.11	-6.97
Science park	Hsinchu	-.09	-5.47
Science park	Tainan	-.08	-3.55
Downtown area	Hsinchu	-.06	-4.08
HSR station	Tainan	-.04	-1.95

Source: Our own calculations, based on official government data (the Bureau of Land Administration and from National Statistics, Republic of China (Taiwan)

While HSR or inter-city rail transportation has rarely been included in hedonic price analyzes of urban housing markets, there are at least three exceptions. In two US studies, accessibility to state railroad networks (Massachusetts and Georgia) did not significantly affect house prices (Armstrong and Rodriguez 2006, Bowes and Ihlanfeldt 2001). By contrast, studies of the Dutch national railroad network showed consistent positive rail accessibility effects (Debrezion et al. 2006a; 2006b). These differences are not unexpected. North American metropolitan regions are characterized by more decentralized employment and residential location patterns and lower densities than European or Asian regions. People with mobile jobs – mostly in knowledge services – are also much less likely to live in inner city areas in the United States than in Europe or Asia. There are thus several factors that act in tandem to promote a greater reliance on automobiles among potential long-distance rail commuters in the United States than elsewhere.

The results of this study may however provide a number of guidelines for future development, should voters and policy-makers desire a more energy-efficient and sustainable transportation policy that may also be efficient in terms of raising land values. First, there must be good connectivity between economic nodes – such as science parks – and transportation nodes. Second, it is reasonable to expect that HSR investments have greater economic effects in regions with a more knowledge-intensive occupational structure, since knowledge workers tend to attend extra-regional business meetings when compared with other workers. Third, HSR accessibility becomes especially valuable if it entails access to attractive labor markets at a time cost that seems reasonable to most people. HSR commuting feasibility is therefore enhanced by high-density housing and workplace agglomerations around stations.

5. Concluding Remarks

The attractiveness of HSR commuting is not only a function of relevant time distances, it is also a function of ticket affordability and differences in house prices and wages in various origin-destination pairings. One may expect people to react to long-term, stable differences in local wage rates by commuting or by moving to the higher-wage location. Other relevant factors, such as educational opportunities, service quality and purely subjective factors may of course reinforce or weaken the propensity to move.

The choice to commute is decided by whether the difference in real income – while taking account of the opportunity cost of not living in the destination community – is at least as great as the cost of traveling to and from work. If we assume that high-technology professionals prefer the Taipei to the Hsinchu residential package (for example, due to school quality or cultural amenities), they would need to be offered salaries in Hsinchu that compensate for their total transportation costs, other job attributes being equal. Since certain occupations (for example, electronic engineers) are associated with much higher salaries in the HSIP than elsewhere in Taiwan, it is likely that some Taipei residents will find jobs in Hsinchu with salaries that more than offset the additional transportation costs.

On the other hand, certain occupations (for example in financial services) are concentrated in Taipei's central business district. Some people in financial services and other such activities may be compensated by the additional consumption opportunities that become available due to lower housing costs in Hsinchu, to the extent that the pay differential is greater than the money and time costs associated with commuting.

The much greater land price effect in Hsinchu than in Tainan provides valuable lessons for the external observer. Regular commuting opportunities have much greater aggregate economic impacts than occasional business travel, although environmental reasons may of course still justify long-distance high-speed rail, owing to its role as a substitute for air transportation. Moreover, workers in specialized business services are more likely to have the required purchasing power *and* a favorable workplace location (since well-paid jobs tend to cluster in central business districts or R&D agglomerations). A tentative conclusion is therefore that it makes a great deal of sense to give priority to high-speed links that connect major urban centers and outlying "knowledge nodes" at a distance of 70 to 150 kilometers, rather than to links between large but distant cities.

From a European perspective, the lesson from Taiwan is that a primary aim of connecting large but distant urban centers is likely to be misguided if the objective is to invest in infrastructure with the greatest possible net economic benefits. For example, it seems likely that high-speed links within densely populated knowledge regions such as Randstad, southeast England or western Switzerland are more likely to generate net benefits than more extensive links such as those between Madrid and Seville or Munich and Berlin.

References

Andersson, D.E. and Andersson, A.E. 2008. Requirements for the region's economic development, in *National Atlas of Sweden: The Stockholm-Malaren Region*. Gavle: Kartforlaget.

Armstrong, R.J. and Rodriguez, D.A. 2006. An evaluation of the accessibility benefits of commuter rail in eastern Massachusetts using spatial hedonic price functions. *Transportation*, 33(1), 21–43.

Barzel, Y. 1989. *Economic Analysis of Property Rights*. Cambridge: Cambridge University Press.

Bowes, D.R. and Ihlanfeldt, K.R. 2001. Identifying the impacts of rail transit stations on residential property values. *Journal of Urban Economics*, 50(1), 1–25.

Chen, J.R. 2005. China's way of economic transition. *Transition Studies Review*, 12(2), 315–33.

Debrezion, G., Pels, E. and Rietveld, P. 2006a. The impact of rail transport on real estate prices: an empirical analysis of the Dutch housing market. Tinbergen Institute Discussion Papers, 06–031/3.

Debrezion, G., Pels, E. and Rietveld, P. 2006b. The impact of railway stations on residential and commercial property values: a meta analysis. *Journal of Real Estate and Finance Economics*, 35(2), 161–80.

Demsetz, H. 1967. Towards a theory of property rights. *American Economic Review*, 57(2), 347–59.

Lancaster, K. 1966. A new approach to consumer theory. *Journal of Political Economy*, 74(2), 132–57.

Nakamura, H. and Ueda, T. 1989. "The impacts of the Shinkansen on regional development, in *The Fifth World Conference on Transport Research, Yokohama, 1989, Vol. 3.* Ventura, CA: Western Periodicals.

Rosen, S. 1974. Hedonic prices and implicit markets: product differentiation in pure competition. *Journal of Political Economy*, 82(1), 34–55.

Sands, B.D. 1993. The development effects of high-speed rail stations and implications for California. Working Paper No. 115, University of California Transportation Center, University of California at Berkeley.

Webster, C. and Lai, L.W.-C. 2003. *Property Rights, Planning and Markets: Managing Spontaneous Cities*. Edward Elgar, Cheltenham.

Index

Figures are indicated by **bold** page numbers, tables by *italic* numbers.